English Language Teaching and Linguistic Approach in India

English Language Teaching and Linguistic Approach in India

Prof. Neeharika Rawat
Shri K.O. Shah
College. Dhoraji, Rajkot

Cyber Tech Publications
4264/3, Ansari Road, Darya Ganj
New Delhi-110002 (India)
Phones : 23244078/43559448
E-mail : cybertechpublications@gmail.com

ENGLISH LANGUAGE TEACHING AND LINGUISTIC APPROACH IN INDIA

First Published 2014
ISBN : 978-93-5053-315-4
Price: 1000/-

Page: 264

Published in India by

CYBER TECH PUBLICATIONS
4264/3, Ansari Road, Darya Ganj
New Delhi-110002 (India)
Phones : 23244078/43559448
E-mail : cybertechpublications@gmail.com
Visit us at www.cybertechpublication.com

Printed at : Asian Offset Press Delhi

Preface

English is a language which has great reach and influence; it is taught all over the world under many circumstances. In English-speaking countries, English language teaching has essentially evolved in two broad directions: instruction for people who intend to live there and for those who do not. These divisions have grown firmer as the instructors of these two "industries" have used different terminology, followed distinct training qualifications, formed separate professional associations, and so on. Crucially, these two arms have very different funding structures, public in the former and private in the latter, and to some extent this influences the way schools are established and classes are held. Matters are further complicated by the fact that the United States and the United Kingdom, both major engines of the language, describe these categories in different terms.The other broad grouping is the use of English within the Anglosphere. In what Braj Kachru calls "the inner circle", i.e. countries such as the United Kingdom and the United States, this use of English is generally by refugees, immigrants, and their children. It also includes the use of English in "outer circle" countries, often former British colonies and the Philippines (a former US colony), where English is an official language even if it is not spoken as a mother tongue by a majority of the population.

In the US, Canada, and Australia, this use of English is called *ESL* (English as a second language). This term has been criticized on the grounds that many learners already speak more than one language. A counter-argument says that the word "a" in the phrase "a second language" means there is no presumption that English is *the* second acquired language (see also *Second language*). *TESL* is the teaching of English as a second language. There are also other terms that it may be referred to in the US including; ELL (English Language Learner) and CLD (Culturally and Linguistically Diverse).

In the UK, Ireland, and New Zealand, the term ESL has been replaced by *ESOL* (English for speakers of other languages). In these countries *TESOL* (teaching English to speakers of other languages) is normally used to refer to teaching English only to this group. In the UK and Ireland, people usually use the term *EAL* (English as an additional language), rather than ESOL, when talking about primary and secondary schools, in order to clarify English is not the students' first language, but their second or third.

Other acronyms were created to describe the person rather than the language to be learned. The term LEP (Limited English proficient) was first used in 1975 by the Lau Remedies following a decision of the U.S. Supreme Court. ELL (English Language Learner), used by United States governments and school systems, was created by James Crawford of the Institute for Language and Education Policy in an effort to label learners positively, rather than ascribing a deficiency to them. Recently, some educators have shortened this to EL – English Learner.

—Author

Contents

1

Language Education

Language education is the teaching and learning of a foreign or second language. Language education is a branch of applied linguistics.

NEED FOR LANGUAGE EDUCATION

Increasing globalization has created a large need for people in the workforce who can communicate in multiple languages. The uses of common languages are in areas such as trade, tourism, international relations, technology, media, and science. Many countries such as Korea (Kim Yeong-seo, 2009), Japan (Kubota, 1998) and China (Kirkpatrick & Zhichang, 2002) frame education policies to teach at least one foreign language at the primary and secondary school levels. However, some countries such as India, Singapore, Malaysia, Pakistan, and the Philippines use a second official language in their governments. According to GAO (2010), China has recently been putting enormous importance on foreign language learning, especially the English Language.

HISTORY OF FOREIGN LANGUAGE EDUCATION

Ancient to medieval period

Although the need to learn foreign languages is almost as old as human history itself, the origins of modern language education are in the study and teaching of Latin in the 17th century. Latin had for many centuries been the dominant language of education, commerce, religion, and government in much of the Western world, but it was displaced by French, Italian, and English by the end of the 16th century. John Amos Comenius was one of many people who tried to reverse this trend. He composed a complete course for learning Latin, covering the entire school curriculum, culminating in his *Opera Didactica Omnia*, 1657.

In this work, Comenius also outlined his theory of language acquisition. He is one of the first theorists to write systematically about how languages are learned and about pedagogical methodology for language acquisition. He held that language acquisition must be allied with sensation and experience. Teaching must be oral. The schoolroom should have models of things, and failing that, pictures of them. As a result, he also published the world's first illustrated children's book, *Orbis Sensualium Pictus*. The study of Latin diminished from the study of a living language to be used in the real world to a subject in the school curriculum. Such decline brought about a new justification for its study. It was then claimed that its study developed intellectual abilities, and the study of Latin grammar became an end in and of itself. "Grammar schools" from the 16th to 18th centuries focused on teaching the grammatical aspects of Classical Latin. Advanced students continued grammar study with the addition of rhetoric.

18th century

The study of modern languages did not become part of the curriculum of European schools until the 18th century. Based on the purely academic study of Latin, students of modern languages did much of the same exercises, studying grammatical rules and translating abstract sentences. Oral work was minimal, and students were instead required to memorize grammatical rules and apply these to decode written texts in the target language. This tradition-inspired method became known as the grammar-translation method.

19th–20th century

Innovation in foreign language teaching began in the 19th century and became very rapid in the 20th century. It led to a number of different and sometimes conflicting methods, each trying to be a major improvement over the previous or contemporary methods. The earliest applied linguists included Jean Manesca, Heinrich Gottfried Ollendorff (1803–1865), Henry Sweet (1845–1912), Otto Jespersen (1860–1943), and Harold Palmer (1877–1949). They worked on setting language teaching principles and approaches based on linguistic and psychological theories, but they left many of the specific practical details for others to devise.

Those looking at the history of foreign-language education in the 20th century and the methods of teaching (such as those related below) might be tempted to think that it is a history of failure. Very few students in U.S. universities who have a foreign language as a major manage to reach something called "minimum professional proficiency". Even the "reading knowledge" required for a PhD degree is comparable only to what second-year language students read and only very few researchers who are native English speakers can read and assess information written in languages other than English. Even a number of famous linguists are monolingual.

However, anecdotal evidence for successful second or foreign language learning is easy to find, leading to a discrepancy between these cases and the failure of most language programs, which helps make the research of second language acquisition emotionally charged. Older methods and approaches such as the grammar translation method or the direct method are dismissed and even ridiculed as newer methods and approaches are invented and promoted as the only and complete solution to the problem of the high failure rates of foreign language students.

Most books on language teaching list the various methods that have been used in the past, often ending with the author's new method. These new methods are usually presented as coming only from the author's mind, as the authors generally give no credence to what was done before and do not explain how it relates to the new method. For example, descriptive linguists seem to claim unhesitatingly that there were no scientifically based language teaching methods before their work (which led to the audio-lingual method developed for the U.S. Army in World War II). However, there is significant evidence to the contrary. It is also often inferred or even stated that older methods were completely ineffective or have died out completely when even the oldest methods are still used (e.g. the Berlitz version of the direct method). One reason for this situation is that proponents of new methods have been so sure that their ideas are so new and so correct that they could not conceive that the older ones have enough validity to cause controversy. This was in turn caused by emphasis on new scientific advances, which has tended to blind researchers to precedents in older work.(p. 5)

There have been two major branches in the field of language learning, the empirical and theoretical, and these have almost completely separate histories, with each gaining ground over the other at one point in time or another. Examples of researchers on the empiricist side are Jesperson, Palmer, and Leonard Bloomfield, who promote mimicry and memorization with pattern drills. These methods follow from the basic empiricist position that language acquisition basically results from habits formed by conditioning and drilling. In its most extreme form, language learning is seen as basically the same as any other learning in any other species, human language being essentially the same as communication behaviors seen in other species.

On the theoretical side are, for example, Francois Gouin, M.D. Berlitz, and Elime de Sauzé, whose rationalist theories of language acquisition dovetail with linguistic work done by Noam Chomsky and others. These have led to a wider variety of teaching methods ranging from the grammar-translation method to Gouin's "series method" to the direct methods of Berlitz and de Sauzé. With these methods, students generate original and meaningful sentences to gain a functional knowledge of the rules of grammar. This follows from the rationalist position that man is born to think and that language use is a uniquely human trait impossible in other species. Given that human languages share many common traits, the idea is that humans share a universal grammar which is built into our brain structure. This allows us to create sentences that we have never heard before but that can still be immediately understood by anyone who understands the specific language being spoken. The rivalry of the two camps is intense, with little communication or cooperation between them.

Teaching foreign language in classrooms

Language education may take place as a general school subject or in a specialized language school. There are many methods of teaching languages. Some have fallen into relative obscurity and others are widely used; still others have a small following, but offer useful insights.

While sometimes confused, the terms "approach "method" and "technique" are hierarchical concepts.

An approach is a set of assumptions about the nature of language and language learning, but does not involve procedure or provide any details about how such assumptions should be implemented into the classroom setting. Such can be related to second language acquisition theory.

There are three principal "approaches":

1. The structural view treats language as a system of structurally related elements to code meaning (e.g. grammar).
2. The functional view sees language as a vehicle to express or accomplish a certain function, such as requesting something.
3. The interactive view sees language as a vehicle for the creation and maintenance of social relations, focusing on patterns of moves, acts, negotiation and interaction found in conversational exchanges. This approach has been fairly dominant since the 1980s.

A method is a plan for presenting the language material to be learned, and should be based upon a selected approach. In order for an approach to be translated into a method, an instructional system must be designed considering the objectives of the teaching/learning, how the content is to be selected and organized, the types of tasks to be performed, the roles of students, and the roles of teachers.

1. Examples of structural methods are grammar translation and the audio-lingual method.
2. Examples of functional methods include the oral approach / situational language teaching.
3. Examples of interactive methods include the direct method, the series method, communicative language teaching, language immersion, the Silent Way, Suggestopedia, the Natural Approach, Total Physical Response, Teaching Proficiency through Reading and Storytelling and Dogme language teaching.

A technique (or strategy) is a very specific, concrete stratagem or trick designed to accomplish an immediate objective. Such are derived from the controlling method, and less directly, from the approach.

Online and self-study courses

Hundreds of languages are available for self-study, from scores of publishers, for a range of costs, using a variety of methods. The course itself acts as a teacher and has to choose a methodology, just as classroom teachers do.

Audio recordings and books

Audio recordings use native speakers, and one strength is helping learners improve their accent. Some recordings have pauses for the learner to speak. Others are continuous so the learner speaks along with the recorded voice, similar to learning a song. Audio recordings for self-study use many of the methods used in classroom teaching, and have been produced on records, tapes, CDs, DVDs and websites.

Most audio recordings teach words in the target language by using explanations in the learner's own language. An alternative is to use sound effects to show meaning of words in the target language. The only language in such recordings is the target language, and they are comprehensible regardless of the learner's native language.

Language books have been published for centuries, teaching vocabulary and grammar. The simplest books are phrasebooks to give useful short phrases for travelers, cooks, receptionists, or others who need specific vocabulary. More complete books include more vocabulary, grammar, exercises, translation, and writing practice.

Internet and software

Software can interact with learners in ways that books and audio cannot:

1. Some software records the learner, analyzes the pronunciation, and gives feedback.
2. Software can present additional exercises in areas where a particular learner has difficulty, until the concepts are mastered.
3. Software can pronounce words in the target language and show their meaning by using pictures instead of oral explanations. The only language in such software is the target language. It is comprehensible regardless of the learner's native language.

Websites provide various services geared toward language education. Some sites are designed specifically for learning languages:

1. Some software runs on the web itself, with the advantage of avoiding downloads, and the disadvantage of requiring an internet connection.
2. Some publishers use the web to distribute audio, texts and software, for use offline.
3. Some websites offer learning activities such as quizzes or puzzles to practice language concepts.
4. Language exchange sites connect users with complementary language skills, such as a native Spanish speaker who wants

to learn English with a native English speaker who wants to learn Spanish. Language exchange websites essentially treat *knowledge of a language* as a commodity, and provide a marketlike environment for the commodity to be exchanged. Users typically contact each other via chat, VoIP, or email. Language exchanges have also been viewed as a helpful tool to aid language learning at language schools. Language exchanges tend to benefit oral proficiency, fluency, colloquial vocabulary acquisition, and vernacular usage, rather than formal grammar or writing skills.

Many other websites are helpful for learning languages, even though they are designed, maintained and marketed for other purposes:

1. All countries have websites in their own languages, which learners elsewhere can use as primary material for study: news, fiction, videos, songs, etc. In a study conducted by the Center for Applied Linguistics, it was noted that the use of technology and media has begun to play a heavy role in facilitating language learning in the classroom. With the help of the internet, students are readily exposed to foreign media (music videos, television shows, films) and as a result, teachers are taking heed of the internet's influence and are searching for ways to combine this exposure into their classroom teaching.
2. Translation sites let learners find the meaning of foreign text or create foreign translations of text from their native language.
3. Speech synthesis or text to speech (TTS) sites and software let learners hear pronunciation of arbitrary written text, with pronunciation similar to a native speaker.
4. Course development and learning management systems such as Moodle are used by teachers, including language teachers.
5. Web conferencing tools can bring remote learners together; e.g. Elluminate Live.
6. Players of computer games can practice a target language when interacting in Massively multiplayer online games and

virtual worlds. In 2005, the virtual world Second Life started to be used for foreign language tuition, sometimes with entire businesses being developed. In addition, Spain's language and cultural institute Instituto Cervantes has an "island" on Second Life.

Some Internet content is free, often from government and nonprofit sites such as BBC Online, Book2, Foreign Service Institute, with no or minimal ads. Some is ad-supported, such as newspapers and YouTube. Some requires a payment.

Learning strategies

Language learning strategies have attracted increasing focus as a way of understanding the process of language acquisition.

Listening as a way of learning

Clearly listening is used to learn, but not all language learners employ it consciously. Listening to understand is one level of listening but focused listening is not something that most learners employ as a strategy.

Reading as a way to learn

Many people read to understand but the strategy of reading text to learn grammar and discourse styles can also be employed.

Learning vocabulary

Translation and rote memorization have been the two strategies that have been employed traditionally. There are other strategies that also can be used such as guessing, based on looking for contextual clues. Knowledge about how the brain works can be utilized in creating strategies for how to remember words.

Code switching

Code switching, that is, changing between languages at some point in a sentence or utterance, is a commonly used communication strategy among language learners and bilinguals. While traditional methods of formal instruction often discourage code switching, students, especially those placed in a language immersion situation, often use it. If viewed as a learning strategy, wherein the student uses the target language as much as possible but reverts to their native language for any element of an utterance that they are unable to produce in the target language (as, e.g., in Wolfgang Butzkamm's concept of enlightened monolingualism), then it has the advantages that it encourages fluency development and motivation and a sense of accomplishment by enabling the student to discuss topics of interest to him or her early in the learning process—before requisite vocabulary has been memorized. It is particularly effective for students whose native language is English, due to the high probability of a simple English word or short phrase being understood by the conversational partner.

Teaching strategies

Blended learning

Blended learning combines face-to-face teaching with distance education, frequently electronic, either computer-based or web-based. It has been a major growth point in the ELT (English Language Teaching) industry over the last ten years.

Some people, though, use the phrase 'Blended Learning' to refer to learning taking place while the focus is on other activities. For example, playing a card game that requires calling for cards may allow blended learning of numbers (1 to 10).

Skills teaching

When talking about language skills, the four basic ones are: listening, speaking, reading and writing. However, other, more socially based skills have been identified more recently such as summarizing, describing, narrating etc. In addition, more general learning skills such as study skills and knowing how one learns have been applied to language classrooms.

In the 1970s and 1980s, the four basic skills were generally taught in isolation in a very rigid order, such as listening before speaking. However, since then, it has been recognized that we generally use more than one skill at a time, leading to more integrated exercises. Speaking is a skill that often is underrepresented in the traditional classroom. This is due to the fact that it is considered harder to teach and test. There are numerous texts on teaching and testing writing but relatively few on speaking.

More recent textbooks stress the importance of students working with other students in pairs and groups, sometimes the entire class. Pair and group work give opportunities for more students to participate more actively. However, supervision of pairs and groups is important to make sure everyone participates as equally as possible. Such activities also provide opportunities for peer teaching, where weaker learners can find support from stronger classmates.

Sandwich technique

In foreign language teaching, the sandwich technique is the oral insertion of an idiomatic translation in the mother tongue between an unknown phrase in the learned language and its repetition, in order to convey meaning as rapidly and completely as possible. The mother tongue equivalent can be given almost as an aside, with a slight break in the flow of speech to mark it as an intruder.

When modeling a dialogue sentence for students to repeat, the teacher not only gives an oral mother tongue equivalent for unknown words or phrases, but repeats the foreign language phrase before students imitate it: L2 => L1 => L2. For example, a German teacher of English might engage in the following exchange with the students:

Teacher: "Let me try - lass mich versuchen - let me try."

Students: "Let me try."

Mother tongue mirroring

Mother tongue mirroring is the adaptation of the time-honoured technique of literal translation or word-for word translation for pedagogical purposes. The aim is to make foreign constructions salient and transparent to learners and, in many cases, spare them the technical jargon of grammatical analysis. It differs from literal translation and interlinear text as used in the past since it takes the progress learners have made into account and only focuses upon a specific structure at a time. As a didactic device, it can only be used to the extent that it remains intelligible to the learner, unless it is combined with a normal idiomatic translation. This technique is seldom referred to or used these days.

Back-chaining

Back-chaining is a technique used in teaching oral language skills, especially with polysyllabic or difficult words. The teacher pronounces the last syllable, the student repeats, and then the teacher continues, working backwards from the end of the word to the beginning. For example, to teach the name 'Mussorgsky' a teacher will pronounce the last syllable: *-sky*, and have the student repeat it. Then the teacher will repeat it with *-sorg-* attached before: *-sorg-sky*, and all that remains is the first syllable: *Mus-sorg-sky*.

Language education by region

Practices in language education may vary by region however the underlying understandings which drive it are fundamentally similar. Rote repetition, drilling, memorisation and grammar conjugating are used the world over. Sometimes there are different preferences teaching methods by region. Language immersion is popular in some European countries, but is not used very much in the United States, in Asia or in Australia.

The languages being learned differ; in the United States, Spanish is the most popular language to be learned, whereas the most popular languages to be learned in Australia are Italian and Mandarin Chinese.

Language study holidays

An increasing number of people are now combining holidays with language study in the native country. This enables the student to experience the target culture by meeting local people. Such a holiday often combines formal lessons, cultural excursions, leisure activities, and a homestay, perhaps with time to travel in the country afterwards. Language study holidays are popular across Europe (Malta & UK being the most popular because almost everyone speaks English as a first language) and Asia due to the ease of transportation and variety of nearby countries. These holidays have become increasingly more popular in Central and South America in such countries as Guatemala, Ecuador and Peru. As a consequence of this increasing popularity, several international language education agencies (such as Language International) have flourished in recent years.

With the increasing prevalence of international business transactions, it is now important to have multiple languages at one's disposal. This is also evident in businesses outsourcing their departments to Eastern Europe.

MINORITY LANGUAGE EDUCATION

Minority language education policy

The principle policy arguments in favor of promoting minority language education are the need for multilingual workforces, intellectual and cultural benefits and greater inclusion in global information society. Access to education in a minority language is also seen as a human right as granted by the European Convention on Human Rights and Fundamental Freedoms, the European Charter for Regional or Minority Languages and the UN Human Rights Committee. Bilingual Education has been implemented in many countries including the United States, in order to promote both the use and appreciation of the minority language, as well as the majority language concerned.

Materials and e-learning for minority language education

Suitable resources for teaching and learning minority languages can be difficult to find and access, which has led to calls for the increased development of materials for minority language teaching. The internet offers opportunities to access a wider range of texts, audios and videos. Language learning 2.0 (the use of web 2.0 tools for language education) offers opportunities for material development for lesser-taught languages and to bring together geographically dispersed teachers and learners.

2

Communicative Language Teaching

Communicative language teaching (CLT), or the communicative approach, is an approach to language teaching that emphasizes interaction as both the means and the ultimate goal of study.

BACKGROUND

Societal influences

Communicative language teaching rose to prominence in the 1970s and early 1980s as a result of many disparate developments in both Europe and the United States. First, there was an increased demand for language learning, particularly in Europe. The advent of the European Common Market led to widespread European migration, and consequently there was a large population of people who needed to learn a foreign language for work or for personal reasons. At the same time, children were increasingly able to learn foreign languages in school. The number of secondary schools offering languages rose worldwide in the 1960s and 1970s as part of a general trend of curriculum-broadening and modernization, and foreign-language study ceased to be confined to the elite academies. In

Britain, the introduction of comprehensive schools meant that almost all children had the opportunity to study foreign languages.

This increased demand put pressure on educators to change their teaching methods. Traditional methods such as grammar translation assumed that students were aiming for mastery of the target language, and that students were willing to study for years before expecting to use the language in real life. However, these assumptions were challenged by adult learners who were busy with work, and by schoolchildren who were less academically able. Educators realized that to motivate these students an approach with a more immediate payoff was necessary.

The trend of progressivism in education provided a further pressure for educators to change their methods. Progressivism holds that active learning is more effective than passive learning, and as this idea gained traction in schools there was a general shift towards using techniques where students were more actively involved, such as group work. Foreign-language education was no exception to this trend, and teachers sought to find new methods that could better embody this shift in thinking.

Academic influences

The development of communicative language teaching was also helped by new academic ideas. In Britain, applied linguists began to doubt the efficacy of situational language teaching, the dominant method in that country at the time. This was partly in response to Chomsky's insights into the nature of language. Chomsky had shown that the structural theories of language prevalent at the time could not explain the creativity and variety evident in real communication. In addition, British applied linguists such as Christopher Candlin and Henry Widdowson began to see that a focus on structure was also not helping language students. They saw a need for students to develop communicative skill and functional competence in addition to mastering language structures.

In the United States, the linguist and anthropologist Dell Hymes developed the concept of communicative competence. This was a reaction to Chomsky's concept of the linguistic competence of an ideal native speaker. Communicative competence redefined what it meant to "know" a language; in addition to speakers having mastery over the structural elements of language, according to communicative competence they must also be able to use those structural elements appropriately in different social situations. This is neatly summed up by Hymes's statement, "There are rules of use without which the rules of grammar would be useless." Hymes did not make a concrete formulation of communicative competence, but subsequent authors have tied the concept to language teaching, notably Michael Canale.

Communicative syllabuses

An influential development in the history of communicative language teaching was the work of the Council of Europe in creating new language syllabuses. Education was a high priority for the Council of Europe, and they set out to provide syllabuses that would meet the needs of European immigrants. Among the studies used by the council when designing the course was one by the British linguist, D. A. Wilkins, that defined language using "notions" and "functions", rather than more traditional categories of grammar and vocabulary. Notional categories include concepts such as time, location, frequency, and quantity, and functional categories include communicative acts such as offers, complaints, denials, and requests. These syllabuses were widely used.

Communicative language-learning materials were also developed in Germany. There was a new emphasis on personal freedom in German education at the time, an attitude exemplified in the philosophy of Jürgen Habermas. To fulfill this goal, educators developed materials that allowed learners to choose what they wanted to communicate freely. These materials concentrated on the various different social meanings a given item of grammar could have, and were structured in such a way that learners could choose how to progress through the course themselves. The materials were used in teacher training courses and workshops to encourage teachers to change to using a communicative syllabus. Two similar projects were also undertaken by Candlin at Lancaster University, and by Holec at the University of Nancy.

Meanwhile, at the University of Illinois, there was a study that investigated the effects of the explicit teaching of learning strategies to language learners. The study encouraged learners to take risks while communicating, and to use constructs other than rote memorized patterns. At the study's conclusion, students who were taught communicatively fared no worse on grammatical tests than students that had been taught with traditional methods, but they performed significantly better in tests of communicative ability. This was the case even for beginners. As a result of this study, supplemental communicative activities were created for the French CRÉDIF course Voix et Visages de la France. These materials focused on classroom autonomy, and learners were taught various phrases they could use to negotiate meaning, such as "What's the word for ..." and "I don't understand".

Outline

CLT is usually characterized as a broad *approach* to teaching, rather than as a teaching *method* with a clearly defined set of classroom practices. As such, it is most often defined as a list of general principles or features. One of the most recognized of these lists is David Nunan's (1991) five features of CLT:

1. An emphasis on learning to communicate through interaction in the target language.
2. The introduction of authentic texts into the learning situation.
3. The provision of opportunities for learners to focus, not only on language but also on the learning process itself.
4. An enhancement of the learner's own personal experiences as important contributing elements to classroom learning.

5. An attempt to link classroom language learning with language activities outside the classroom.

These five features are claimed by practitioners of CLT to show that they are very interested in the needs and desires of their learners as well as the connection between the language as it is taught in their class and as it used outside the classroom. Under this broad umbrella definition, any teaching practice that helps students develop their communicative competence in an authentic context is deemed an acceptable and beneficial form of instruction. Thus, in the classroom CLT often takes the form of pair and group work requiring negotiation and cooperation between learners, fluency-based activities that encourage learners to develop their confidence, role-plays in which students practise and develop language functions, as well as judicious use of grammar and pronunciation focused activities.

In the mid 1990s the Dogma 95 manifesto influenced language teaching through the Dogme language teaching movement, who proposed that published materials can stifle the communicative approach. As such the aim of the Dogme approach to language teaching is to focus on real conversations about real subjects so that communication is the engine of learning. This communication may lead to explanation, but that this in turn will lead to further communication.

Classroom activities

Classroom activities used in communicative language teaching include the following:

- Role-play
- Interviews
- information gap
- Games
- Language exchanges
- Surveys
- Pair-work
- Learning by teaching

However, not all courses that utilize the Communicative Language approach will restrict their activities solely to these. Some courses will have the students take occasional grammar quizzes, or prepare at home using non-communicative drills, for instance. William Glasser's "control theory" exemplifies his attempts to empower students and give them voice by focusing on their basic, human needs: Unless students are given power, they may exert what little power they have to thwart learning and achievement through inappropriate behavior and mediocrity. Thus, it is important for teachers to give students voice, especially in the current educational climate, which is dominated by standardization and testing (Simmons and Page, 2010).

Critiques of CLT

One of the most famous attacks on communicative language teaching was offered by Michael Swan in the English Language Teaching Journal in 1985. Henry Widdowson responded in defense of CLT, also in the ELT Journal (1985 39(3):158-161). More recently other writers (e.g. Bax) have critiqued CLT for paying insufficient attention to the context in which teaching and learning take place, though CLT has also been defended against this charge (e.g. Harmer 2003).

Often, the communicative approach is deemed a success if the teacher understands the student. But, if the teacher is from the same region as the student, the teacher will understand errors resulting from an influence from their first language. Native speakers of the target language may still have difficulty understanding them. This observation may call for new thinking on and adaptation of the communicative approach. The adapted communicative approach should be a simulation where the teacher pretends to understand only what any regular speaker of the target language would and reacts accordingly (Hattum 2006).

Probability interpretations

The word probability has been used in a variety of ways since it was first applied to the mathematical study of games of chance. Does probability measure the real, physical tendency of something to occur or is it a measure of how strongly one believes it will occur, or does it draw on both these elements? In answering such questions, we interpret the probability values of probability theory.

There are two broad categories of probability interpretations which can be called "physical" and "evidential" probabilities. Physical probabilities, which are also called objective or frequency probabilities, are associated with random physical systems such as roulette wheels, rolling dice and radioactive atoms. In such systems, a given type of event (such as the dice yielding a six) tends to occur at a persistent rate, or "relative frequency", in a long run of trials. Physical probabilities either explain, or are invoked to explain, these stable frequencies. Thus talking about physical probability makes sense only when dealing with well defined random experiments. The two main kinds of theory of physical probability are frequentist accounts (such as those of Venn, Reichenbach and von Mises) and propensity accounts (such as those of Popper, Miller, Giere and Fetzer).

Evidential probability, also called Bayesian probability (or subjectivist probability), can be assigned to any statement whatsoever, even when no random process is involved, as a way to represent its subjective plausibility, or the degree to which the statement is supported by the available evidence. On most accounts, evidential probabilities are considered to be degrees of belief, defined in terms of dispositions to gamble at certain odds. The four main evidential interpretations are the classical (e.g. Laplace's) interpretation, the subjective interpretation (de Finetti and Savage), the epistemic or inductive interpretation (Ramsey, Cox) and the logical interpretation (Keynes and Carnap).

Some interpretations of probability are associated with approaches to statistical inference, including theories of estimation and hypothesis testing. The physical interpretation, for example, is taken by followers of "frequentist" statistical methods, such as R. A. Fisher, Jerzy Neyman and Egon Pearson.

Statisticians of the opposing Bayesian school typically accept the existence and importance of physical probabilities, but also consider the calculation of evidential probabilities to be both valid and necessary in statistics. This article, however, focuses on the interpretations of probability rather than theories of statistical inference.

The terminology of this topic is rather confusing, in part because probabilities are studied within a variety of academic fields. The word "frequentist" is especially tricky. To philosophers it refers to a particular theory of physical probability, one that has more or less been abandoned. To scientists, on the other hand, "frequentist probability" is just another name for physical (or objective) probability. Those who promote Bayesian inference view "frequentist statistics" as an approach to statistical inference that recognises only physical probabilities. Also the word "objective", as applied to probability, sometimes means exactly what "physical" means here, but is also used of evidential probabilities that are fixed by rational constraints, such as logical and epistemic probabilities.

It is unanimously agreed that statistics depends somehow on probability. But, as to what probability is and how it is connected with statistics, there has seldom been such complete disagreement and breakdown of communication since the Tower of Babel. Doubtless, much of the disagreement is merely terminological and would disappear under sufficiently sharp analysis.

Philosophy

The philosophy of probability presents problems chiefly in matters of epistemology and the uneasy interface between mathematical concepts and ordinary language as it is used by non-mathematicians. Probability theory is an established field of study in mathematics. It has its origins in correspondence discussing the mathematics of games of chance between Blaise Pascal and Pierre de Fermat in the seventeenth century, and was formalized and rendered axiomatic as a distinct branch of mathematics by Andrey Kolmogorov in the twentieth century. In its axiomatic form, mathematical statements about probability theory carry the same sort of epistemological confidence shared by other mathematical statements in the philosophy of mathematics.

The mathematical analysis originated in observations of the behaviour of game equipment such as playing cards and dice, which are designed specifically to introduce random and equalized elements; in mathematical terms, they are subjects of indifference. This is not the only way probabilistic statements are used in ordinary human language: when people say that "*it will probably rain*", they typically do not mean that the outcome of rain versus not-rain is a random factor that the odds currently favor; instead, such statements are perhaps better understood as qualifying their expectation of rain with a degree of confidence. Likewise, when it is written that "the most probable explanation" of the name of Ludlow, Massachusetts "is that it was named after Roger Ludlow", what is meant here is not that Roger Ludlow is favored by a random factor, but rather that this is the most plausible explanation of the evidence, which admits other, less likely explanations.

Thomas Bayes attempted to provide a logic that could handle varying degrees of confidence; as such, Bayesian probability is an attempt to recast the representation of probabilistic statements as an expression of the degree of confidence by which the beliefs they express are held.

Though probability initially had somewhat mundane motivations, its modern influence and use is widespread ranging from Evidence based medicine, through Six sigma, all the way to the Probabilistically checkable proof and the String theory landscape.

Classical definition

The first attempt at mathematical rigour in the field of probability, championed by Pierre-Simon Laplace, is now known as the classical definition. Developed from studies of games of chance (such as rolling dice) it states that probability is shared equally between all the possible outcomes, provided these outcomes can be deemed equally likely.

This can be represented mathematically as follows: If a random experiment can result in N mutually exclusive and equally likely outcomes and if N_A of these outcomes result in the occurrence of the event A, the probability of A is defined by

$$P(A) = \frac{N_A}{N}$$

There are two clear limitations to the classical definition. Firstly, it is applicable only to situations in which there is only a 'finite' number of possible outcomes. But some important random experiments, such as tossing a coin until it rises heads, give rise to an infinite set of outcomes. And secondly, you need to determine in advance that all the possible outcomes are equally likely without relying on the notion of probability to avoid circularity—for instance, by symmetry considerations.

Frequentism

Frequentists posit that the probability of an event is its relative frequency over time, (3.4) i.e., its relative frequency of occurrence after repeating a process a large number of times under similar conditions. This is also known as aleatory probability. The events are assumed to be governed by some random physical phenomena, which are either phenomena that are predictable, in principle, with sufficient information (see Determinism); or phenomena which are essentially unpredictable. Examples of the first kind include tossing dice or spinning a roulette wheel; an example of the second kind is radioactive decay. In the case of tossing a fair coin, frequentists say that the probability of getting a heads is 1/2, not because there are two equally likely outcomes but because repeated series of large numbers of trials demonstrate that the empirical frequency converges to the limit 1/2 as the number of trials goes to infinity.

If we denote by n_a the number of occurrences of an event A in n trials, then if $\lim_{n \to \infty} \frac{n_a}{n} = p$ we say that $P(A) = p$

The frequentist view has its own problems. It is of course impossible to actually perform an infinity of repetitions of a random experiment to determine the probability of an event. But if only a finite number of repetitions of the process are performed, different relative frequencies will appear in different series of trials. If these relative frequencies are to define the probability, the probability will be slightly different every time it is measured. But the real probability should be the same every time. If we acknowledge the fact that we only can measure a probability with some error of measurement attached, we still get into problems as the error of measurement can only be expressed as a probability, the very concept we are trying to define. This renders even the frequency definition circular.

LOGICAL, EPISTEMIC, AND INDUCTIVE PROBABILITY

It is widely recognised that the term "probability" is sometimes used in contexts where it has nothing to do with physical randomness. Consider, for example, the claim that the extinction of the dinosaurs was probably caused by a large meteorite hitting the earth. Statements such as "Hypothesis H is probably true" have been interpreted to mean that the (presently available) empirical evidence (E, say) supports H to a high degree. This degree of support of H by E has been called the logical probability of H given E, or the epistemic probability of H given E, or the inductive probability of H given E.

The differences between these interpretations are rather small, and may seem inconsequential. One of the main points of disagreement lies in the relation between probability and belief. Logical probabilities are conceived (for example in Keynes' Treatise on Probability) to be objective, logical relations between propositions (or sentences), and hence not to depend in any way upon belief. They are degrees of (partial) entailment, or degrees of logical consequence, not degrees of belief. (They do, nevertheless, dictate proper degrees of belief, as is discussed below.) Frank P. Ramsey, on the other hand, was skeptical about the existence of such objective logical relations and argued that (evidential) probability is "the logic of partial belief". (p 157) In other words, Ramsey held that epistemic probabilities simply *are* degrees of rational belief, rather than being logical relations that merely *constrain* degrees of rational belief.

Another point of disagreement concerns the *uniqueness* of evidential probability, relative to a given state of knowledge. Rudolf Carnap held, for example, that logical principles always determine a unique logical probability for any statement, relative to any body of evidence. Ramsey, by contrast, thought that while degrees of belief are subject to some rational constraints (such as, but not limited to, the axioms of probability) these constraints usually do not determine a unique value. Rational people, in other words, may differ somewhat in their degrees of belief, even if they all have the same information.

Propensity

Propensity theorists think of probability as a physical propensity, or disposition, or tendency of a given type of physical situation to yield an outcome of a certain kind or to yield a long run relative frequency of such an outcome. This kind of objective probability is sometimes called 'chance'.

Propensities, or chances, are not relative frequencies, but purported causes of the observed stable relative frequencies. Propensities are invoked to explain why repeating a certain kind of experiment will generate given outcome types at persistent rates, which are known as propensities or chances. Frequentists are unable to take this approach, since relative frequencies do not exist for single tosses of a coin, but only for large ensembles or collectives. In contrast, a propensitist is able to use the law of large numbers to explain the behaviour of long-run frequencies. This law, which is a consequence of the axioms of probability, says that if (for example) a coin is tossed repeatedly many times, in such a way that its probability of landing heads is the same on each toss, and the outcomes are probabilistically independent, then the relative frequency of heads will be close to the probability of heads on each single toss. This law allows that stable long-run frequencies are a manifestation of invariant *single-case* probabilities. In addition to explaining the emergence of stable relative frequencies, the idea of propensity is motivated by the desire to make sense of single-case probability attributions in quantum mechanics, such as the probability of decay of a particular atom at a particular time.

The main challenge facing propensity theories is to say exactly what propensity means. (And then, of course, to show that propensity thus defined has the required properties.) At present, unfortunately, none of the well-recognised accounts of propensity comes close to meeting this challenge.

A propensity theory of probability was given by Charles Sanders Peirce. A later propensity theory was proposed by philosopher Karl Popper, who had only slight acquaintance with the writings of C. S. Peirce, however. Popper noted that the outcome of a physical experiment is produced by a certain set of "generating conditions". When we repeat an experiment, as the saying goes, we really perform another experiment with a (more or less) similar set of generating conditions. To say that a set of generating conditions has propensity p of producing the outcome E means that those exact conditions, if repeated indefinitely, would produce an outcome sequence in which E occurred with limiting relative frequency p. For Popper then, a deterministic experiment would have propensity 0 or 1 for each outcome, since those generating conditions would have same outcome on each trial. In other words, non-trivial propensities (those that differ from 0 and 1) only exist for genuinely indeterministic experiments.

A number of other philosophers, including David Miller and Donald A. Gillies, have proposed propensity theories somewhat similar to Popper's.

Other propensity theorists (e.g. Ronald Giere) do not explicitly define propensities at all, but rather see propensity as defined by the theoretical role it plays in science. They argue, for example, that physical magnitudes such as electrical charge cannot be explicitly defined either, in terms of more basic things, but only in terms of what they do (such as attracting and repelling other electrical charges). In a similar way, propensity is whatever fills the various roles that physical probability plays in science.

What roles does physical probability play in science? What are its properties? One central property of chance is that, when known, it constrains rational belief to take the same numerical value. David Lewis called this the *Principal Principle,* (3.3 & 3.5) a term that philosophers have mostly adopted. For example, suppose you are certain that a particular biased coin has propensity 0.32 to land heads every time it is tossed. What is then the correct price for a gamble that pays $1 if the coin lands heads, and nothing otherwise? According to the Principal Principle, the fair price is 32 cents.

Subjectivism

Subjectivists, also known as Bayesians or followers of epistemic probability, give the notion of probability a subjective status by regarding it as a measure of the 'degree of belief' of the individual assessing the uncertainty of a particular situation. Epistemic or subjective probability is sometimes called credence, as opposed to the term chance for a propensity probability.

Some examples of epistemic probability are to assign a probability to the proposition that a proposed law of physics is true, and to determine how probable it is that a suspect committed a crime, based on the evidence presented.

Gambling odds don't reflect the bookies' belief in a likely winner, so much as the other bettors' belief, because the bettors are actually betting against one another. The odds are set based on how many people have bet on a possible winner, so that even if the high odds players always win, the bookies will always make their percentages anyway.

The use of Bayesian probability raises the philosophical debate as to whether it can contribute valid justifications of belief. Bayesians point to the work of Ramsey (p 182) and de Finetti (p 103) as proving that subjective beliefs must follow the laws of probability if they are to be coherent. Evidence casts doubt on human coherence.

The use of Bayesian probability involves specifying a prior probability. This may be obtained from consideration of whether the required prior probability is greater or lesser than a reference probability associated with an urn model or a thought experiment. The issue is that for a given problem, multiple thought experiments could apply, and choosing one is a matter of judgement: different people may assign different prior probabilities, known as the reference class problem. The "sunrise problem" provides an example.

Prediction

An alternative account of probability emphasizes the role of *prediction* – predicting future observations on the basis of past observations, not on unobservable parameters. In its modern form, it is mainly in the Bayesian vein. This was the main function of probability before the 20th century, but fell out of favor compared to the parametric approach, which modeled phenomena as a physical system that was observed with error, such as in celestial mechanics. The modern predictive approach was pioneered by Bruno de Finetti, with the central idea of exchangeability – that future observations should behave like past observations. This view came to the attention of the Anglophone world with the 1974 translation of de Finetti's book, and has since been propounded by such statisticians as Seymour Geisser.

Axiomatic probability

The mathematics of probability can be developed on an entirely axiomatic basis that is independent of any interpretation: see the articles on probability theory and probability axioms for a detailed treatment.

3

Teaching English as a Foreign Language

Teaching English as a foreign language (TEFL) refers to teaching English to students whose first language is not English. TEFL usually occurs in the student's own country, either within the state school system, or privately, e.g., in an after-hours language school or with a tutor. TEFL teachers may be native or non-native speakers of English.

TEACHING TECHNIQUES

Language education may take place as a general school subject, in a specialized language school, or out of school with a rich selection of proprietary methods online and in books, CDs and DVDs. There are many methods of teaching languages. Some have fallen into relative obscurity and others are widely used; still others have a small following, but offer useful insights.

There are three principal views

1. The structural view treats language as a system of structurally related elements to code meaning (e.g. grammar).

2. The functional view sees language as a vehicle to express or accomplish a certain function, such as requesting something.
3. The interactive view sees language as a vehicle for the creation and maintenance of social relations, focusing on patterns of moves, acts, negotiation and interaction found in conversational exchanges. This view has been fairly dominant since the 1980s.

Methodology

In the late 1800s and most of the 1900s, language teaching was usually conceived in terms of *method*. In seeking to improve teaching practices, teachers and researchers would typically try to find out which method was the most effective. However, *method* is an ambiguous concept in language teaching, and has been used in many different ways. According to Bell, this variety in use "offers a challenge for anyone wishing to enter into the analysis or deconstruction of methods".

Approach, method and technique

In 1963, Anthony formulated a framework to describe various language teaching methods, which consisted three levels: *approach, method*, and *technique*. According to Anthony, "The arrangement is hierarchical. The organizational key is that techniques carry out a method which is consistent with an approach." His concept of *approach* was of a set of principles or ideas about the nature of language learning which would be consistent over time; "an approach is axiomatic". His *method* was more procedural; "an overall plan for the orderly presentation of language material, no part of which contradicts, and all of which is based upon, the selected approach." Finally, his concept of *technique* referred to the actual implementation in the language classroom; "a particular trick, stratagem, or contrivance used to accomplish an immediate objective." He saw techniques as being consistent with a given method and by extension, with a given approach.

A method is a plan for presenting the language material to be learned and should be based upon a selected approach. In order for an approach to be translated into a method, an instructional system must be designed considering the objectives of the teaching/learning, how the content is to be selected and organized, the types of tasks to be performed, the roles of students and the roles of teachers. A technique is a very specific, concrete stratagem or trick designed to accomplish an immediate objective. Such are derived from the controlling method, and less-directly, with the approach.

Anthony's framework was welcomed by the language teaching community when it was introduced, and it was seen as a useful way of classifying different teaching practices. However, it did not clearly define the difference between *approach, method,* and *technique,* and Kumaravadivelu reports that due to this ambiguity there was "widespread dissatisfaction" with it. Anthony himself recognized the limitations of his framework, and was open to the idea of improvements being made to it.

Approach, design and procedure

Richards and Rogers' 1982 approach expanded on Anthony's three-level framework; however, instead of *approach, method* and *technique,* they chose the terms *approach, design,* and *procedure.* Their concept of *approach* was similar to Anthony's, but their *design* and *procedure* were of broader scope than Anthony's *method* and *technique.* Their *design* referred to all major practical implications in the classroom, such as syllabus design, types of activities to be used in the classroom, and student and teacher roles; *procedure* referred to different behaviors, practices and techniques observed in the classroom. These new terms were intended to address limitations in Anthony's framework, and also gave them specific criteria by which they could evaluate different "methods". This evaluation process was a key way that their formulation differed from Anthony's, as Anthony's framework was intended as purely descriptive.

Despite Richards and Rogers' efforts to clearly define *approach, design,* and *procedure,* their framework has been criticized by Kumaravadivelu for having "an element of artificiality in its conception and an element of subjectivity in its operation". Kumaravadivelu also points to similar objections raised by Pennyworth and by the *Routledge Encyclopedia of Language Teaching and Learning*. Brown also questions the suitability of Richards and Rogers' term *design*; he points out that in English teaching *design* is usually used to refer specifically to curriculum design, rather than the broad definition Richards and Rogers used. Most current teacher training manuals favor the terms *approach, method,* and *technique*.

Structural methods

Grammar-translation method

The grammar translation method instructs students in grammar, and provides vocabulary with direct translations to memorize. It was the predominant method in Europe in the 19th century. Most instructors now acknowledge that this method is ineffective by itself. It is now most commonly used in the traditional instruction of the classical languages, however it remains the most commonly practiced method of English teaching in Japan.

At school, the teaching of grammar consists of a process of training in the rules of a language which must make it possible to all the students to correctly express their opinion, to understand the remarks which are addressed to them and to analyze the texts which they read. The objective is that by the time they leave college, the pupil controls the tools of the language which are the vocabulary, grammar and the orthography, to be able to read, understand and write texts in various contexts. The teaching of grammar examines texts, and develops awareness that language constitutes a system which can be analyzed. This knowledge is acquired gradually, by traversing the facts of language and the syntactic mechanisms, going from simplest to the most complex. The exercises according to the program of the course must untiringly be practiced to allow the assimilation of the rules stated in the course. That supposes that the teacher corrects the exercises.

The pupil can follow his progress in practicing the language by comparing his results. Thus can he adapt the grammatical rules and control little by little the internal logic of the syntactic system. The grammatical analysis of sentences constitutes the objective of the teaching of grammar at the school. Its practice makes it possible to recognize a text as a coherent whole and conditions the training of a foreign language. Grammatical terminology serves this objective. Grammar makes it possible for each one to understand how the mother tongue functions, in order to give him the capacity to communicate its thought.

Audio-lingual method

The audio-lingual method was developed in the USA around World War II when governments realized that they needed more people who could conduct conversations fluently in a variety of languages, work as interpreters, code-room assistants, and translators. However, since foreign language instruction in that country was heavily focused on reading instruction, no textbooks, other materials or courses existed at the time, so new methods and materials had to be devised. For example, the U.S. Army Specialized Training Program created intensive programs based on the techniques Leonard Bloomfield and other linguists devised for Native American languages, where students interacted intensively with native speakers and a linguist in guided conversations designed to decode its basic grammar and learn the vocabulary. This "informant method" had great success with its small class sizes and motivated learners.

The U.S. Army Specialized Training Program only lasted a few years, but it gained a lot of attention from the popular press and the academic community. Charles Fries set up the first English Language Institute at the University of Michigan, to train English as a second or foreign language teachers. Similar programs were created later at Georgetown University, University of Texas among others based on the methods and techniques used by the military. The developing method had much in common with the British oral approach although the two developed independently. The main difference was the developing audio-lingual methods allegiance to structural linguistics, focusing on grammar and contrastive analysis to find differences between the student's native language and the target language in order to prepare specific materials to address potential problems. These materials strongly emphasized drill as a way to avoid or eliminate these problems.

This first version of the method was originally called the oral method, the aural-oral method or the structural approach. The audio-lingual method truly began to take shape near the end of the 1950s, this time due government pressure resulting from the space race. Courses and techniques were redesigned to add insights from behaviorist psychology to the structural linguistics and constructive analysis already being used. Under this method, students listen to or view recordings of language models acting in situations. Students practice with a variety of drills, and the instructor emphasizes the use of the target language at all times. The idea is that by reinforcing 'correct' behaviors, students will make them into habits.

The typical structure of a chapter employing the Audio-Lingual-Method (ALM—and there was even a text book entitled ALM [1963]) was usually standardized as follows: 1. First item was a dialog in the foreign language (FL) to be memorized by the student. The teacher would go over it the day before. 2. There were then questions in the FL about the dialog to be answered by the student(s) in the target language. 3. Often a brief introduction to the grammar of the chapter was next, including the verb(s) and conjugations. 4. The mainstay of the chapter was "pattern practice," which were drills expecting "automatic" responses from the student(s) as a noun, verb conjugation, or agreeing adjective was to be inserted in the blank in the text (or during the teacher's pause).

The teacher could have the student use the book or not use it, relative to how homework was assigned. Depending on time, the class could respond as a chorus, or the teacher could pick individuals to respond. It was really a sort of "mimicry-memorization." And it was "Julian Dakin in 'The Language

Laboratory and Language Learning' (Longman 1973) who coined the phrase 'meaningless drills' to describe pattern practice of the kind inspired by the above ideas." 5. There was a vocabulary list, sometimes with translations to the mother tongue. 6. The chapter usually ended with a short reading exercise.

Due to weaknesses in performance, and more importantly because of Noam Chomsky's theoretical attack on language learning as a set of habits, audio-lingual methods are rarely the primary method of instruction today. However, elements of the method still survive in many textbooks.

Functional methods

The oral approach and situational language teaching

The oral approach was developed from the 1930s to the 1960s by British applied linguists such as Harold Palmer and A.S. Hornsby. They were familiar with the direct method as well as the work of 19th-century applied linguists such as Otto Jesperson and Daniel Jones but attempted to formally develop a more scientifically founded approach to teaching English than was evidenced by the direct method.

A number of large-scale investigations about language learning and the increased emphasis on reading skills in the 1920s led to the notion of "vocabulary control". It was discovered that languages have a core basic vocabulary of about 2,000 words that occur frequently in written texts, and it was assumed that mastery of these would greatly aid reading comprehension. Parallel to this was the notion of "grammar control", emphasizing the sentence patterns most-commonly found in spoken conversation. Such patterns were incorporated into dictionaries and handbooks for students. The principal difference between the oral approach and the direct method was that methods devised under this approach would have theoretical principles guiding the selection of content, gradation of difficulty of exercises and the presentation of such material and exercises.

The main proposed benefit was that such theoretically based organization of content would result in a less-confusing sequence of learning events with better contextualization of the vocabulary and grammatical patterns presented. Last but not least, all language points were to be presented in "situations". Emphasis on this point led to the approach's second name. Proponents claim that this approach leads to students' acquiring good habits to be repeated in their corresponding situations. Teaching methods stress PPP (presentation (introduction of new material in context), practice (a controlled practice phase) and production (activities designed for less-controlled practice)).

Although this approach is all but unknown among language teachers today, elements of it have had long-lasting effects on language teaching, being the basis of many widely used English as a Second/Foreign Language textbooks as late as the 1980s and elements of it still appear in current texts. Many of the structural elements of this approach were called into question in the 1960s, causing modifications of this method that led to communicative language teaching. However, its emphasis on oral practice, grammar and sentence patterns still finds widespread support among language teachers and remains popular in countries where foreign language syllabuses are still heavily based on grammar.

Directed practice

Directed practice has students repeat phrases. This method is used by U.S. diplomatic courses. It can quickly provide a phrasebook-type knowledge of the language. Within these limits, the student's usage is accurate and precise. However the student's choice of what to say is not flexible.

Interactive methods

Direct method

The direct method, sometimes also called *natural method,* is a method that refrains from using the learners' native language and just uses the target language. It was established in Germany and France around 1900 and is best represented by the methods devised by Berlitz and de Sauzé, although neither claims originality and it has been re-invented under other names. The direct method operates on the idea that second language learning must be an imitation of first language learning, as this is the natural way humans learn any language: a child never relies on another language to learn its first language, and thus the mother tongue is not necessary to learn a foreign language. This method places great stress on correct pronunciation and the target language from outset. It advocates teaching of oral skills at the expense of every traditional aim of language teaching. Such methods rely on directly representing an experience into a linguistic construct rather than relying on abstractions like mimicry, translation and memorizing grammar rules and vocabulary.

According to this method, printed language and text must be kept away from second language learners for as long as possible, just as a first language learner does not use printed words until he has good grasp of speech. Learning of writing and spelling should be delayed until after the printed word has been introduced, and grammar and translation should also be avoided because this would involve the application of the learner's first language. All above items must be avoided because they hinder the acquisition of a good oral proficiency.

The method relies on a step-by-step progression based on question-and-answer sessions which begin with naming common objects such as doors, pencils, floors, etc. It provides a motivating start as the learner begins using a foreign language almost immediately. Lessons progress to verb forms and other grammatical structures with the goal of learning about thirty new words per lesson.

The series method

In the 19th century, Francois Gouin went to Hamburg to learn German. Based on his experience as a Latin teacher, he thought the best way to do this would be memorize a German grammar book and a table of its 248 irregular verbs. However, when he went to the academy to test his new language skills, he was disappointed to find out that he could not understand anything. Trying again, he similarly memorized the 800 root words of the language as well as re-memorizing the grammar and verb forms. However, the results were the same. During this time, he had isolated himself from people around him, so he tried to learn by listening, imitating and conversing with the Germans around him, but found that his carefully constructed sentences often caused native German speakers to laugh. Again he tried a more classical approach, translation, and even memorizing the entire dictionary but had no better luck.

When he returned home, he found that his three-year-old nephew had learned to speak French. He noticed the boy was very curious and upon his first visit to a mill, he wanted to see everything and be told the name of everything. After digesting the experience silently, he then reenacted his experiences in play, talking about what he learned to whoever would listen or to himself. Gouin decided that language learning was a matter of transforming perceptions into conceptions, using language to represent what one experiences. Language is not an arbitrary set of conventions but a way of thinking and representing the world to oneself. It is not a conditioning process, but one in which the learner actively organizes his perceptions into linguistics concepts.

The series method is a variety of the direct method in that experiences are directly connected to the target language. Gouin felt that such direct "translation" of experience into words, makes for a "living language". (p59) Gouin also noticed that children organize concepts in succession of time, relating a sequence of concepts in the same order. Gouin suggested that students learn a language more quickly and retain it better if it is presented through a chronological sequence of events. Students learn sentences based on an action such as leaving a house in the order in which such would be performed. Gouin found that if the series of sentences are shuffled, their memorization becomes nearly impossible. For this, Gouin preceded psycholinguistic theory of the 20th century. He found that people will memorize events in a logical sequence, even if they are not presented in that order.

He also discovered a second insight into memory called "incubation". Linguistic concepts take time to settle in the memory. The learner must use the new concepts frequently after presentation, either by thinking or by speaking, in order to master them. His last crucial observation was that language was learned in sentences with the verb as the most crucial component. Gouin would write a series in two columns: one with the complete sentences and the other with only the verb. With only the verb elements visible, he would have students recite the sequence of actions in full sentences of no more than twenty-five sentences. Another exercise involved having the teacher solicit a sequence of sentences by basically ask him/her what s/he would do next. While Gouin believed that language was rule-governed, he did not believe it should be explicitly taught.

His course was organized on elements of human society and the natural world. He estimated that a language could be learned with 800 to 900 hours of instruction over a series of 4000 exercises and no homework. The idea was that each of the exercises would force the student to think about the vocabulary in terms of its relationship with the natural world. While there is evidence that the method can work extremely well, it has some serious flaws. One of which is the teaching of subjective language, where the students must make judgments about what is experienced in the world (e.g. "bad" and "good") as such do not relate easily to one single common experience. However, the real weakness is that the method is entirely based on one experience of a three-year-old. Gouin did not observe the child's earlier language development such as naming (where only nouns are learned) or the role that stories have in human language development. What distinguishes the series method from the direct method is that vocabulary must be learned by translation from the native language, at least in the beginning.

Communicative language teaching

Communicative language teaching(CLT), also known as *the Communicative Approach*, emphasizes interaction as both the means and the ultimate goal of learning a language. Despite a number of criticisms it continues to be popular, particularly in Europe, where constructivist views on language learning and education in general dominate academic discourse. Although the 'Communicative Language Teaching' is not so much a method on its own as it is an approach.

In recent years, task-based language learning (TBLL), also known as task-based language teaching (TBLT) or task-based instruction (TBI), has grown steadily in popularity. TBLL is a further refinement of the CLT approach, emphasizing the successful completion of tasks as both the organizing feature and the basis for assessment of language instruction. Dogme language teaching shares a philosophy with TBL, although differs in approach. Dogme is a communicative approach, and encourages teaching without published textbooks and instead focusing on conversational communication among the learners and the teacher.

Language immersion

Language immersion in school contexts delivers academic content through the medium of a foreign language, providing support for L2 learning and first language maintenance. There are three main types of immersion education programs in the United States: foreign language immersion, dual immersion, and indigenous immersion.

Foreign language immersion programs in the U.S. are designed for students whose home language is English. In the early immersion model, for all or part of the school day elementary school children receive their content (academic) instruction through the medium of another language: Spanish, French, German, Chinese, Japanese, etc. In early total immersion models, children receive all the regular kindergarten and first grade content through the medium of the immersion language; English reading is introduced later, often in the second grade. Most content (math, science, social studies, art, music) continues to be taught through the immersion language. In early partial immersion models, part of the school day (usually 50%) delivers content through the immersion language, and part delivers it through English.

French-language immersion programs are common in Canada in the provincial school systems, as part of the drive towards bilingualism and are increasing in number in the United States in public school systems (Curtain & Dahlbert, 2004). Branaman & Rhodes (1998) report that between 1987 and 1997 the percentage of elementary programs offering foreign language education in the U.S. through immersion grew from 2% to 8% and Curtain & Dahlberg (2004) report 278 foreign language immersion programs in 29 states. Research by Swain and others (Genesee 1987) demonstrate much higher levels of proficiency achieved by children in foreign language immersion programs than in traditional foreign language education elementary school models.

Dual immersion programs in the U.S. are designed for students whose home language is English as well as for students whose home language is the immersion language (usually Spanish). The goal is bilingual students with mastery of both English and the immersion language. As in partial foreign language immersion academic content is delivered through the medium of the immersion language for part of the school day, and through English the rest of the school day.

Indigenous immersion programs in the U.S. are designed for American Indian communities desiring to maintain the use of the native language by delivering elementary school content through the medium of that language. Hawaiian Immersion programs are the largest and most successful in this category.

Reading

TEFL that uses literature aimed at children and teenagers is rising in popularity. Youth-oriented literature offers simpler material ("simplified readers" are produced by major publishers), and often provides a more conversational style than literature for adults. Children's literature in particular sometimes provides subtle cues to pronunciation, through rhyming and other word play. One method for using these books is the *multiple-pass technique*. The instructor reads the book, pausing often to explain certain words and concepts. On the second pass, the instructor reads the book completely through without stopping.

COMMUNICATIVE LANGUAGE TEACHING

Communicative language teaching (CLT) emphasizes interaction as both the means and the ultimate goal of learning a language. Despite a number of criticisms, it continues to be popular, particularly in Japan, Taiwan, and Europe.

The task-based language learning (TBLL) approach to CLT has gained ground in recent years. Proponents believe CLT is important for developing and improving speaking, writing, listening, and reading skills, and that it prevents students' merely listening passively to the teacher without interaction. Dogme is a similar communicative approach that encourages teaching without published textbooks, instead focusing on conversational communication among the learners and the teacher.

Blended learning

Blended learning is a combination of face-to-face teaching and online interactions (also known as CALL or computer-assisted language learning), achieved through a virtual learning environment (VLE).

VLEs have been a major growth point in the ELT industry over the last five years. There are two types:

- Externally hosted platforms that a school or institution exports content to (e.g., the proprietary Web Course Tools, or the open source Moodle)
- Content-supplied, course-managed learning platforms (e.g. the *Macmillan English Campus*)

The former provides pre-designed structures and tools, while the latter supports course-building by the language school—teachers can blend existing courses with games, activities, listening exercises, and grammar reference units contained online. This supports classroom, self-study or remote practice (for example in an internet café).

Online classroom

Advances in technology made it possible to get a TEFL qualification online. Students can enroll into online classes that are accredited by organizations such as Accreditat. It should be noted that there is no single overarching accreditation body for TEFL. Study materials are divided into modules. Students take one or multiple tests per study module. Support is handled by tutors, who can be reached via email. After successfully finishing the last module the student is granted a certificate. It comes in digital form or can be shipped to the student's address. Getting such a certificate can be beneficial in many ways. The student can get a bigger paycheck or teach English in foreign countries.

Qualifications for TEFL teachers

Qualification requirements vary considerably from country to country and among employers within the same country. In many institutions it is possible to teach without a degree or teaching certificate. Some institutions will consider it necessary to be a native speaker with an MA TESOL. A university degree in English language and literature can also be of value, as indeed can any specialist degree. Other institutions consider a proof of English proficiency, a University degree and a basic teaching qualification to be more than sufficient. However, the level of academic qualification need not be the most important qualification, as many schools will be more interested in your interpersonal skills. For trainers wishing to enter the academic field, publications can be as important as qualifications, especially if they relate to English use in your field. Where there is a high demand for teachers and no statutory requirements, employers may accept otherwise unqualified candidates. Each country is different, and acceptance depends on demand for English teachers and the teacher's previous teaching and life experiences.

As a general rule schools will tend to prefer qualifications that involve a significant amount of assessed teaching: it is often said that "Learning to teach without classroom practice is like learning to drive without ever encountering traffic". Shorter courses and online courses often lack assessed teaching practice. Course makers have recognized this and have begun introducing combined TEFL courses which have an element of assessed teaching.

Some educational facilities are now offering two or three well-defined certificates instead of one general certificate. For example, ILT (Introduction to Language Teaching) - 40 hours, PLT (Practice of Language Training) - 30 hours, and Literacy - 30 hours.

Private language schools are likely to require at least a certificate based on successful completion of a course consisting of a minimum of 100 hours. Major programs like EPIK will offer a higher salary to teachers who have completed any TEFL Course, online or otherwise, so long as the program meets the minimum 100 hour requirement. Internet-based TEFL courses are generally accepted worldwide, and particularly in Asia, where the largest jobs markets exist in China, Korea, Taiwan and Japan.

Age/gender requirements might also be encountered. In some countries outside Europe and America, for example the Middle East, schools might hire men over women or vice versa. And they might hire only teachers in a certain age range; usually between 20 and 40 years of age. Anyone under 19 may be able to teach TEFL, but usually only in a volunteer situation, such as a refugee camp.

Pay and conditions worldwide

As in most fields, the pay depends greatly on education, training, experience, seniority, and expertise. As with much expatriate work, employment conditions vary among countries, depending on the level of economic development and how much people want to live there. In relatively poor countries, even a low wage may equate to a comfortable middle class lifestyle. EFL Teachers who wish to earn money often target countries in East Asia such as China, South Korea and Japan where demand is high. The Middle East is also often named as one of the best paying areas, although usually better qualifications are needed: at least a CELTA and one or two years' experience.

There is a danger of exploitation by employers. Spain in particular has encountered widespread criticism given the overwhelming number of small to medium businesses (including TEFL schools) which routinely dodge the teachers' social security contributions as a means of maximising profits. The result is that most teachers are entitled to less unemployment or sick pay than they would be entitled to if their salaries and contributions were declared in accordance with the law. Similar situations increase in countries with labor laws that may not apply to foreign employees, or which may be unenforced. An employer might ignore contract provisions, especially regarding working hours, working days, and end-of-contract payments. Difficulties faced by foreign teachers regarding language, culture, or simply limited time can make it difficult to demand pay and conditions that their contracts stipulate. Some disputes arise from cross-cultural misunderstandings. Teachers who can't adapt to living and working in a foreign country often leave after a few months.

TEFL REGION AND COUNTRY LOCATIONS

Europe

Major European cities have established language schools on-site or operated as agencies sending teachers to various locations. September is the peak recruiting month, and many annual contracts last from October until June. Employers prefer graduates with experience in teaching Business English or in teaching young learners.

Instructors from the United Kingdom and Ireland, countries within the European Union, do not need any visas to work within the EU, which reduces demand for non-EU teachers. Immigration laws require that non-EU job applicants submit documents from their home countries in person after the European employer files an officially documented job offer. If the worker has travelled to Europe to find the job, this means they must return home and wait for some time. Following the process correctly does not guarantee getting a visa. Many private-sector employers do not subsidise them at all, because they are able to hire the staff easily from the EU countries.

International schools hire some experienced and well-qualified non-EU teachers. Education ministries, i.e. those of France and Spain, offer opportunities for assistant language instructors in public schools. Part-time employment is usually allowed under an education visa, but this visa also requires proper attendance at an accredited EU college or university, institute, or other educational program. Other teachers work illegally under tourist visas, since the "don't ask, don't tell" method is the only viable solution to avoiding impossible bureaucracy and eventual job rejection.

Despite claims from websites that sell courses, state schools often do not accept brief TEFL courses as a substitute for a university degree in English education.

Demand for TEFL tends to be stronger in countries which joined the European Union recently. They also tend to have lower costs of living. Non-EU teachers usually find legal work there with less difficulty. The Balkan former Yugoslav countries have seen recent growth in TEFL—private schools have recruited Anglophone teachers there for several years.

Very few foreign instructors work in Scandinavia, where stricter immigration laws and a policy of relying on bilingual local teachers apply.

ASIA

Cambodia

Demand for English teachers in Cambodia has grown over the past decade, though the country has a small population and is dependent on foreign aid for much of its economic development, limiting growth.

China

Many opportunities exist within the People's Republic of China, including preschool, university, private schools and institutes, companies, and tutoring. NGOs, such as Teach For China, are an opportunity as well. The provinces and the Ministry of Education in Beijing tightly govern public schools, while private schools have more freedom to set work schedules, pay, and requirements.

English teaching salaries in China are dependent on multiple factors including; Teaching hours specified in contract, location, inclusions/bonuses, and public vs private sector. It is important to note that due to high demand, salaries have increased significantly over recent years. A standard contract within the public school system generally entails less than 20 hours of teaching time, weekends off, included accommodations, flight stipend/reimbursement for 1 year contracts, paid public holidays, medical insurance and Z visa (working permit) sponsorship. These positions offer an average base salary of 6,000 - 7,000 RMB per month in smaller cities and rural areas. In Beijing, Shanghai, Shenzhen, and Guangzhou these positions now offer 10,000 RMB plus per month due to higher living costs. The private sector is less uniform with salaries going as high as 20,000 RMB per month for DOS's in major cities. Private positions tend to demand higher hours, may include teaching in multiple locations, and often require weekend and evening working schedules. They also are more flexible with housing options, often offering teachers a choice between provided accommodations, or a stipend towards rental costs.

By law, all non-Chinese English teachers should hold a minimum bachelors degree in any discipline, be at least 25 years old, have at least 2 years of working experience (unrelated is fine). Due to demand, these rules are often overlooked, and schools often are able to obtain work permits for teachers who do not meet the minimums, although this is tightening up in the major cities.

Public schools usually pay during vacations, but not for summer break unless the teacher renews the contract, while many private schools have shortened vacation schedules and may pay for whatever short number of days is allowed for vacation.

Company jobs vary, depending on the number of employees they want to train. They may employ a teacher for one or two classes, or a complete set of 14 to 16 hours a week. Tutoring also varies, as in some cases a whole family of students or just one family member.

Some teachers work successfully on an independent basis with several contracts for tutoring, individual college classes, and some company work. The majority of teachers accept contracts with schools. Public school contracts are fairly standard, while private schools set their own requirements. Schools try to hire teachers from Anglophone countries, but because of demand, others with good English language skills can find positions.

Hong Kong

Hong Kong was once a British Crown colony, and English-language education is taken seriously there, as demonstrated by government-funded research.[11] Hong Kong was handed back to the People's Republic of China in 1997 and became known as Hong Kong Special Administrative Region (HKSAR).

Teaching English in Hong Kong has become quite a business. Many English teaching institutions have since opened. Big private names include Headstart Group Limited and English for Asia. Native English speakers may quickly find a job teaching English, although foreigners should be aware of shady companies who often pull tricks on their employees. A qualification in Teaching English as a Foreign Language (TEFL) has become a pre-requisite to enter the Native English-speaking Teacher Scheme (NET scheme), which is funded by the HKSAR government and provides the ultimate career destination for an English teacher. On top of attractive salary, housing is provided with all the other fringe benefits including full holiday pay, provident fund and health insurance. Housing or rental support is the biggest incentive to foreign teachers as housing cost in HK is ranked one of the highest in the world.

Once a teacher is on the NET scheme, he can move from school to school after completion of a normally two-year contract. Therefore, a teacher has a lot of opportunities to land himself an ideal position at an ideal school, provided he has strong track record. While many foreigners think coming to HK with a short online TEFL qualification is sufficient, both public and private schools are looking for TEFL qualifications listed with the Hong Kong Council for Accreditation of Vocational and Academic Qualifications and Hong Kong Education Bureau There are less than a handful of them. Acquiring one of those qualifications gives a foreigner a definite advantage to securing a preferred teaching position at a formal school, whether private or public, kindergarten, primary or secondary. When selecting NET, schools will not normally consider learning centre experience due to the differences in class size, continuity of student group, level of classroom management skills and sophistication in teaching pedagogy required between schools and centres.

Japan

In Japan, the JET Programme employs assistant language teachers and teaching assistants to work in Japanese high schools and elementary schools. Other teachers work in *eikaiwa* (private language schools). The largest of these chains are Aeon and ECC. The sector is not well regulated. Nova, one of the largest chains with over 900 branches, collapsed in October 2007, leaving thousands of foreign teachers without income or, for some, a place to live. Other teachers work in universities. Agencies are increasingly used to send English speakers into kindergartens, primary schools, and private companies whose employees need to improve their Business English. Agencies, known in Japan as *haken*, or dispatch companies, have recently been competing among themselves to get contracts from various Boards of Education for Elementary, Junior and Senior High Schools, and wages have decreased steadily. JALT (the Japan Association for Language Teaching) is the largest NPO for language teachers (mainly native English speakers), with nearly 3,000 members.

Laos

English language has been increasingly important in education, international trade and cooperation in Laos since the 1990s. The government started to promote foreign direct investment, and the introduction of Laos as an observer at ASEAN in 1992 also increased the necessity of English. Laos was considered as a full member of ASEAN in 1997. From 1992-97, the government had to improve its fluency in English.

More recently, high-ranking officials, business people, and shareholders have started to work at their English. This trend looks set to increase as English is due to be included and taught in the field of education too.

Middle East

Saudi Arabia and the United Arab Emirates are the main locations for instructors to work in this region. Many positions here offer higher salaries, ample vacation time, and paid airfare to and from the instructor's home country, but also tend to require more qualifications and experience. Private academies and university programs are the main venues of instruction. Some public primary and secondary schools, such as those in Abu Dhabi, have begun to recruit foreign English instructors.

Mongolia

The Peace Corps has 136 volunteers in Mongolia, many of whom are English teachers mostly teaching in the vast rural areas, where the population density is low. In Ulaanbaatar, a modest number of professional NETs teach at private institutes and some schools. In addition to foreign instructors from the major English-speaking countries, there are Filipinos teaching in Mongolian schools, institutes and large industrial or mining companies.

South Korea

There is great demand for native English speakers willing to teach in South Korea, though it is dropping. In 2013, the number of native English speakers teaching in public schools dropped 7.7% in one year to 7,011. Most of the nation's provinces are removing foreign English teachers from their middle and high schools. As with Japan, Korea is also nurturing a government-run program for teacher placement called English Program in Korea (EPIK). EPIK reported that it recruited 6,831 foreign teachers to work in Korean public schools. There are a number of associations for English teachers in Korea, the largest one with a significant number of native speakers is KOTESOL.

Institutions commonly provide round-trip airfare and a rent-free apartment for a one-year contract. Note that since March 15, 2008, visa rules have changed. Prospective teachers must now undergo a medical examination and a criminal background check, produce an original degree certificate, and provide sealed transcripts. On arriving in South Korea, teachers must undergo a further medical check before they receive an ARC (Alien Registration Card) card.

Korean labor law provides all workers with a severance pay equivalent to one month's salary is paid at the end of a contract. Most job contracts are for 1 year and include entrance and exit plane tickets. Citizens of the USA, Canada and Australia also receive back their pension contributions and their employers' part of the pension contributions on leaving the country. The average starting pay for those with no previous teaching experience and no degree in the English language is usually between USD $1,800 to USD $2,200.

There are four main places to work in South Korea: universities, private schools, public schools (EPIK), and private language academies (known in South Korea as *hagwons*). Private language academies (in 2005 there were over thirty thousand such academies teaching English), the most common teaching location in Korea, can be for classes of school children, housewives, university students (often at the university itself), or businesspeople. There are numerous, usually small independent *hagwons* but also numerous large chains.

Taiwan

In Taiwan, most teachers work in cram schools, known locally as *bushibans* or buxibans. Some are part of chains, like Hess and Kojen. Others operate independently. Such schools pay around US$2,000 per month. End-of-contract bonuses equivalent to an extra month's pay are not mandated by law as in South Korea, and are uncommon in Taiwan. Also, under current law it is illegal for foreigners to teach English in pre-schools or kindergartens, though it is almost always overlooked by both the schools and the government, thereby making the practice common and accepted. To teach English and live in Taiwan, you must be a holder of an Alien Resident Card (ARC) which is supplied to passport holders of native English speaking countries, by hiring schools ARC candidates must hold a Bachelor degree from a four-year university, or an accredited.

Thailand

Thailand has a great demand for native English speakers, and has a ready-made workforce in the form of travelers and expatriates attracted by the local lifestyle despite relatively low salaries. Teachers can expect to earn a starting salary of around 25,000 Baht. Because Thailand prohibits foreigners from most non-skilled and skilled occupations, a high percentage of foreign residents teach English for a living, and are able to stay in the country. There is also a growing demand for Filipino English teachers, as they are often hired for about half the salary of a native speaker. Qualifications for EFL teachers in Thailand have become stricter in the last couple of years, with most schools now requiring a Bachelor's degree plus a 120-hour TEFL course . It is possible to find work without a degree in Thailand. However, as a degree makes getting a work permit far easier, to work without a degree is often to work illegally, opening teachers up to exploitation by employers.

Americas

There has been significant growth in TEFL within the wealthier non-Anglophone countries of North, Central, and South America as well as the Caribbean. In particular, many teachers work in Mexico, Costa Rica, Argentina, Brazil, and Chile. Chile has even made it a national goal to become a bilingual nation within the coming years. As proof of its commitment to this goal the Chilean Ministry of Education sponsors English Opens Doors, a program that recruits English speakers to work in Chilean Public High Schools.

Costa Rica

Costa Rica is a popular choice among EFL teachers in light of the high market demand for English instructors, the stable economic and political atmosphere, and the vibrant culture. Teaching positions are available through public and private schools, language schools, universities and colleges, and through private tutoring. Language schools typically hire all year round, and teachers of Business English are also in high demand. There are quality Costa Rica TEFL training courses that offer certification as well as job placement assistance following completion of a course.

Africa

TEFL in Africa has historically been linked to aid programs such as the US Peace Corps or the multinational Voluntary Service Overseas organization, as well as other aid programs. Most African countries employ bilingual local teachers. Poverty and instability in some African countries has made it difficult to attract foreign teachers. There has been increasing government investment in education and a growing private sector.

ENGLISH AS A SECOND OR FOREIGN LANGUAGE

English as a second language (ESL) is the use or study of English by speakers with different native languages.

English is a language which has great reach and influence; it is taught all over the world under many circumstances. In English-speaking countries, English language teaching has essentially evolved in two broad directions: instruction for people who intend to live there and for those who do not. These divisions have grown firmer as the instructors of these two "industries" have used different terminology, followed distinct training qualifications, formed separate professional associations, and so on. Crucially, these two arms have very different funding structures, public in the former and private in the latter, and to some extent this influences the way schools are established and classes are held. Matters are further complicated by the fact that the United States and the United Kingdom, both major engines of the language, describe these categories in different terms.

Terminology and types

The many acronyms and abbreviations used in the field of English teaching and learning may be confusing and the following technical definitions may have their currency contested upon various grounds.

English as a Second Language is also known as English for speakers of other languages (ESOL), English as an additional language (EAL) and as English as a foreign language (EFL). The precise usage, including the different use of the terms ESL and ESOL in different countries, is described below. These terms are most commonly used in relation to teaching and learning English as a second language, but they may also be used in relation to demographic information.

English language teaching (ELT) is a widely used teacher-centered term, as in the English language teaching divisions of large publishing houses, ELT training, etc. Teaching English as a second language (TESL), teaching English to speakers of other languages (TESOL), and teaching English as a foreign language (TEFL) are also used.

Other terms used in this field include English as an international language (EIL), English as a lingua franca (ELF), English for special purposes and English for specific purposes (ESP), and English for academic purposes (EAP). Those who are learning English are often referred to as English language learners (ELL).

English outside English-speaking countries

EFL, English as a foreign language, indicates the teaching of English in a non–English-speaking region. Study can occur either in the student's home country, as part of the normal school curriculum or otherwise, or, for the more privileged minority, in an anglophone country that they visit as a sort of educational tourist, particularly immediately before or after graduating from university. *TEFL* is the teaching of English as a foreign language; note that this sort of instruction can take place in any country, English-speaking or not. Typically, EFL is learned either to pass exams as a necessary part of one's education, or for career progression while one works for an organization or business with an international focus. EFL may be part of the state school curriculum in countries where English has no special status (what linguistic theorist Braj Kachru calls the "expanding circle countries"); it may also be supplemented by lessons paid for privately. Teachers of EFL generally assume that students are literate in their mother tongue. The *Chinese EFL Journal* and *Iranian EFL Journal* are examples of international journals dedicated to specifics of English language learning within countries where English is used as a foreign language.

English within English-speaking countries

The other broad grouping is the use of English within the Anglosphere. In what Braj Kachru calls "the inner circle", i.e. countries such as the United Kingdom and the United States, this use of English is generally by refugees, immigrants, and their children. It also includes the use of English in "outer circle" countries, often former British colonies and the Philippines (a former US colony), where English is an official language even if it is not spoken as a mother tongue by a majority of the population.

In the US, Canada, and Australia, this use of English is called *ESL* (English as a second language). This term has been criticized on the grounds that many learners already speak more than one language. A counter-argument says that the word "a" in the phrase "a second language" means there is no presumption that English is *the* second acquired language (see also *Second language*). *TESL* is the teaching of English as a second language. There are also other terms that it may be referred to in the US including; ELL (English Language Learner) and CLD (Culturally and Linguistically Diverse).

In the UK, Ireland, and New Zealand, the term ESL has been replaced by *ESOL* (English for speakers of other languages). In these countries *TESOL* (teaching English to speakers of other languages) is normally used to refer to teaching English only to this group. In the UK and Ireland, people usually use the term *EAL* (English as an additional language), rather than ESOL, when talking about primary and secondary schools, in order to clarify English is not the students' first language, but their second or third.

Other acronyms were created to describe the person rather than the language to be learned. The term LEP (Limited English proficient) was first used in 1975 by the Lau Remedies following a decision of the U.S. Supreme Court. ELL (English Language Learner), used by United States governments and school systems, was created by James Crawford of the Institute for Language and Education Policy in an effort to label learners positively, rather than ascribing a deficiency to them. Recently, some educators have shortened this to EL – English Learner.

Typically, a student learns this sort of English to function in the new host country, e.g. within the school system (if a child), to find and hold down a job (if an adult), or to perform the necessities of daily life (cooking, taking a cab/public transportation, or eating in a restaurant, etc.) The teaching of it does not presuppose literacy in the mother tongue. It is usually paid for by the host government to help newcomers settle into their adopted country, sometimes as part of an explicit citizenship program. It is technically possible for ESL to be taught not in the host country, but in, for example, a refugee camp, as part of a pre-departure program sponsored by the government soon to receive new potential citizens. In practice, however, this is extremely rare.

Particularly in Canada and Australia, the term *ESD* (English as a second dialect) is used alongside ESL, usually in reference to programs for aboriginal Canadians or Australians. The term refers to the use of standard English by speakers of a creole or non-standard variety. It is often grouped with ESL as *ESL/ESD*.

Umbrella terms

All these ways of denoting the teaching of English can be bundled together into an umbrella term. Unfortunately, not all of the English teachers in the world can agree on just one term. The term *TESOL* (teaching English to speakers of other languages) is used in American English to include both TEFL and TESL. This is also the case in Canada. British English uses *ELT* (English language teaching), because TESOL has a different, more specific meaning; see above.

Systems of simplified English

Several models of "simplified English" have been suggested or developed for international communication, among them:

- Basic English, developed by Charles Kay Ogden (and later also I. A. Richards) in the 1930s; a recent revival has been initiated by Bill Templer
- Threshold Level English, developed by van Ek and Alexander
- Globish, developed by Jean-Paul Nerrière
- Basic Global English, developed by Joachim Grzega
- Nuclear English, proposed by Randolph Quirk and Gabriele Stein but never fully developed

Difficulties for learners

Language teaching practice often assumes that most of the difficulties that learners face in the study of English are a consequence of the degree to which their native language differs from English (a contrastive analysis approach). A native speaker of Chinese, for example, may face many more difficulties than a native speaker of German, because German is more closely related to English than Chinese is. This may be true for anyone of any mother tongue (also called first language, normally abbreviated L1) setting out to learn any other language (called a target language, second language or L2). See also second language acquisition (SLA) for mixed evidence from linguistic research.

Language learners often produce errors of syntax, vocabulary, and pronunciation thought to result from the influence of their L1, such as mapping its grammatical patterns inappropriately onto the L2, pronouncing certain sounds incorrectly or with difficulty, and confusing items of vocabulary known as false friends. This is known as L1 transfer or "language interference". However, these transfer effects are typically stronger for beginners' language production, and SLA research has highlighted many errors which cannot be attributed to the L1, as they are attested in learners of many language backgrounds (for example, failure to apply 3rd person present singular -s to verbs, as in 'he make' not 'he makes').

Some students may have very different cultural perceptions in the classroom as far as learning a second language is concerned. Cultural differences in communication styles and preferences are also significant. For example, a study looked at Chinese ESL students and British teachers and found that the Chinese learners did not see classroom discussion and interaction as important but placed a heavy emphasis on teacher-directed lectures.

Pronunciation

English contains a number of sounds and sound distinctions not present in some other languages. Speakers of languages without these sounds may have problems both with hearing and with pronouncing them. For example:

- The interdentals, /è/ and /ð/ (both written as *th*) are relatively rare in other languages.
- Phonemic contrast of /i/ with /j/ (*beat* vs *bit* vowels), of /u/ with /Š/ (*fool* vs *full* vowels), and of /[/ with /æ/ (*bet* vs *bat* vowels) is rare outside northwestern Europe, so

unusual mergers or exotic pronunciations such as [bet] for *bit* may arise. Note that [bjt] is a pronunciation often used in England and Wales for *bet*, and also in some dialects of American English. See Northern cities vowel shift, and Pin-pen merger.

- Native speakers of Japanese, Korean, and most Chinese dialects have difficulty distinguishing /r/ and /l/, also present for speakers of some Caribbean Spanish dialects (only at the end of syllables), what is known as lallation.
- Native speakers of Brazilian Portuguese, Spanish or Galician, and Ukrainian may pronounce [h]-like sounds where a /r/, /s/, or /a/, respectively, would be expected, as those sounds often or almost always follow this process in their native languages, what is known as debuccalization.
- Native speakers of Arabic, Tagalog, Japanese, Korean, and important dialects of all current Iberian Romance languages (including about all of Spanish) have difficulty at distinguishing [b] and [v], what is known as betacism.
- Native speakers of almost all of Brazilian Portuguese, of some African Portuguese registers, of Portuguese-derived creole languages, some dialects of Swiss German, and several pontual processes in several Slavic languages, such as Bulgarian and Ukrainian, and many dialects of other languages, have instances of /l/ or /k/ always becoming [w] at the end of a syllable in a given context, so that *milk* may be variously pronounced as [mju/k], [mjŠ/k], or [mjo/k]. This is present in some English registers—known as l-vocalization—but may be shunned as substandard or bring confusion in others.
- Native speakers of many widely spoken languages (including Dutch and all the Romance ones) distinguish voiceless stop pairs /p/, /t/, /k/ from their voiced counterparts /b/, /d/, /a/ merely by their sound (and in Iberian Romance languages, the latter trio does not even need to be stopped, so its native speakers unconsciously pronounce them as [â], [ð], and [c ~ p] – voiced fricatives or approximants in the very same mouth positions – instead much or most of the time, that native English speakers may

erroneously interpret as the /v/ or /w/, /ð/ and /h/, /w/, or /r/ of their language). In English, German, Danish, and some other languages, though, the main distinguishing feature in the case of initial or stressed stopped voiceless consonants from their voiced counterparts is that they are aspirated [p° t° k°] (unless if immediately preceded or followed by /s/), while the voiced ones are not. As a result, much of the non-English /p/, /t/ and /k/ will sound to native English ears as /b/, /d/ and /a/ instead (i.e. *parking* may sound more like *barking*).

Languages may also differ in syllable structure; English allows for a cluster of up to three consonants before the vowel and five after it (e.g. *strengths, straw, desks, glimpsed, sixths*). Japanese and Brazilian Portuguese, for example, broadly alternate consonant and vowel sounds so learners from Japan and Brazil often force vowels between the consonants (e.g. *desks* becomes [desukusu] or [d[skis], and *milk shake* becomes [mi}ukuUeÐku] or [miwki Uejki], respectively). Similarly, in most Iberian dialects, a word can begin with [s], and [s] can be followed by a consonant, but a word can never begin with [s] immediately followed by a consonant, so learners whose mother tongue is in this language family often have a vowel in front of the word (e.g. *school* becomes [eskul], [iskuk ~ iskuw], [oskuk] or [Yskuk] for native speakers of Spanish, Brazilian and European Portuguese, and Catalan, respectively).

Grammar

- Tense, aspect, and mood – English has a relatively large number of tense–aspect–mood forms with some quite subtle differences, such as the difference between the simple past "I ate" and the present perfect "I have eaten." Progressive and perfect progressive forms add complexity. (See English verbs.)
- Functions of auxiliaries – Learners of English tend to find it difficult to manipulate the various ways in which English uses auxiliary verbs. These include negation (e.g. *He hasn't been drinking.*), inversion with the subject to form a question (e.g. *Has he been drinking?*), short answers (e.g. *Yes, he has.*)

and tag questions (*has he?*). A further complication is that the dummy auxiliary verb *do /does /did* is added to fulfil these functions in the simple present and simple past, but not to replace the verb *to be* (*He drinks too much./Does he?* but *He is an addict/Is he?*)

- Modal verbs – English has several modal auxiliary verbs, which each have a number of uses. These verbs convey a special sense or mood such as obligation, necessity, ability, probability, permission, possibility, prohibition, intention etc. These include "must", "can", "have to", "has to", "need to", "will", "shall", "ought to", "will have to", "may", and "might".

For example, the opposite of "You must be here at 8" (obligation) is usually "You don't have to be here at 8" (lack of obligation, choice). "Must" in "You must not drink the water" (prohibition) has a different meaning from "must" in "You must have eaten the chocolate" (deduction). This complexity takes considerable work for most English language learners to master.

All these modal verbs or "modals" take the first form of the verb after them. These modals do not have past or future inflection, i.e. they do not have past or future tense.

- Idiomatic usage – English is reputed to have a relatively high degree of idiomatic usage. For example, the use of different main verb forms in such apparently parallel constructions as "try to learn", "help learn", and "avoid learning" pose difficulty for learners. Another example is the idiomatic distinction between "make" and "do": "make a mistake", not "do a mistake"; and "do a favor", not "make a favor".
- Articles – English has two forms of article: *the* (the definite article) and *a* and *an* (the indefinite article). In addition, at times English nouns can or indeed must be used without an article; this is called the zero article. Some of the differences between definite, indefinite and zero article are fairly easy to learn, but others are not, particularly since a learner's native language may lack articles, have only one form, or use them differently from English. Although the

information conveyed by articles is rarely essential for communication, English uses them frequently (several times in the average sentence) so that they require some effort from the learner.

Vocabulary

- Phrasal verbs – Phrasal verbs (also known as multiple-word verbs) in English can cause difficulties for many learners because of their syntactic pattern and because they often have several meanings. There are also a number of phrasal verb differences between American and British English.
- Prepositions – As with many other languages, the correct use of prepositions in the English language is difficult to learn, and it can turn out to be quite a frustrating learning experience for ESL/EFL learners. For example, the prepositions "on" (rely on, fall on), "of" (think of, because of, in the vicinity of),and "at" (turn at, meet at, start at) are used in so many different ways and contexts, it is very difficult to remember the exact meaning for each one. Furthermore the same words are often used as adverbs (come in, press on, listen in, step in) as part of a compound verb (make up, give up, get up, give in, turn in, put on), or in more than one way with different functions and meanings (look up, look on, give in) (*He looked up her skirt/He looked up the spelling; He gave in his homework/First he refused but then he gave in; He got up at 6 o'clock/He got up the hill/He got up a nativity play*). When translating back to the ESL learners' respective L1, a particular preposition's translation may be correct in one instance, but when using the preposition in another sense, the meaning is sometimes quite different. "One of my friends" translates to (transliterated) *wahed min isdiqa'i* in Arabic. *Min* is the Arabic word for "from" .... so one "from" my friends. "I am on page 5" translates to *ich bin auf Seite 5* in German just fine, but in Arabic it is *Ana fee safha raqm 5* .... I am "in" page 5.
- Word formation – Word formation in English requires a lot of rote learning. For example, an adjective can be negated by using the prefixes *un-* (e.g. *unable*), *in-* (e.g. *inappropriate*),

dis- (e.g. *dishonest*), *non-* (non-standard) or *a-* (e.g. *amoral*), as well as several rarer prefixes.

- Size of lexicon – The history of English has resulted in a very large vocabulary, including one stream from Old English and one from the Norman infusion of Latin-derived terms. (Schmitt & Marsden claim that English has one of the largest vocabularies of any known language.) This requires more work for a learner to master the language.
- Collocations – Collocation in English refers to the tendency for words to occur together with others. For example, nouns and verbs that go together (ride a bike/drive a car). Native speakers tend to use chunks of collocations and ESL learners make mistakes with collocations.
- Slang and Colloquialisms In most native English speaking countries, large numbers of slang and colloquial terms are used in everyday speech. Many learners may find that classroom based English is significantly different from how English is usually spoken in practice. This can often be difficult and confusing for learners with little experience of using English in Anglophone countries. Also, slang terms differ greatly between different regions and can change quickly in response to popular culture. Some phrases can become unintentionally rude if misused.

First-language literacy

Learners who have had less than eight years of formal education in their first language are sometimes called *adult ESL literacy learners*. Usually these learners have had their first-language education interrupted. Many of these learners require a different level of support, teaching approaches and strategies, and a different curriculum from mainstream adult ESL learners. For example, these learners may lack study skills and transferable language skills, and these learners may avoid reading or writing. Often these learners do not start classroom tasks immediately, do not ask for help, and often assume the novice role when working with peers. Generally these learners may lack self-confidence. For some, prior schooling is equated with status, cultured, civilized, high class, and they may experience shame among peers in their new ESL classes.

Differences between spoken and written English

As with most languages, written language tends to use a more formal register than spoken language.

- *Spelling and pronunciation*: probably the biggest difficulty for non-native speakers, since the relation between English spelling and pronunciation does not follow the alphabetic principle consistently. Because of the many changes in pronunciation which have occurred since a written standard developed, the retention of many historical idiosyncrasies in spelling, and the large influx of foreign words (mainly from Norman French, Classical Latin and Greek) with different and overlapping spelling patterns, English spelling and pronunciation are difficult even for native speakers to master. This difficulty is shown in such activities as spelling bees. The generalizations that exist are quite complex and there are many exceptions, leading to a considerable amount of rote learning. The spelling and pronunciation system causes problems in both directions: a learner may know a word by sound but be unable to write it correctly (or indeed find it in a dictionary) or they may see a word written but not know how to pronounce it or mislearn the pronunciation. However, despite the variety of spelling patterns in English, there are dozens of rules that are 75% or more reliable.

There is also debate about "meaning-focused" learning and "correction-focused" learning. Supporters for the former think that using speech as the way to explain meaning is more important. However, supporters of the latter do not agree with that and instead think that grammar and correct habit is more important.

Technology

Language has a very significant role in our lives. It symbolizes the cultures in our societies where individuals interact and use it to communicate between each other. The development of transportation has influenced the global relations to be more practical where people need to interact and share common interests. However, communication is the key power to facilitate interactions among individuals which would provide them with stronger relationships. In places like America where immigration plays a role in social, economic and cultural aspects, there is an increase in the number of new immigrants yearly. "The number of non-native English speaking children in U.S. public schools continues to rise dramatically.

Even though America is one of the most diverse countries in the world, there are few languages that are commonly used such as English and Spanish. English is an international language that the majority of the people use to communicate in America and especially when it comes to an international interrelationships.

Although many non-English speakers tend to practice English classes in their countries before they migrate to any anglophone country to make it easier for them to interact with the people, many of them still struggle when they experience the reality of communicating with a real anglophone. Therefore, society forces them to improve their communication skills as soon as possible. Immigrants cannot afford to waste time learning to speak English especially for those who come with certain financial issues. The most common choice people make to build up their communication skills is to take some ESL classes. There are many steps that need to be followed in order to be successful in this aspect. However, the use of the new technology makes the learning process more convenient, reliable and productive.

Computers have made an entry into education in the past decades and have brought significant benefits to teachers and students alike. The use of Computers is a tool one can use to improve his/her learning skills. Computers help learners to be more responsible for their own learning abilities. Studies have shown that one of the best ways of improving one's learning ability is to use a computer where all the information one might need can be found. In today's developed world, a computer is one of a number of systems which help learners to improve their language. Computer Assisted Language Learning (CALL) is a system which aids learners to improve and practice language skills. It provides a stress-free environment for learners and makes them more responsible.

Computers can provide help to the ESL learners in many different ways such as teaching students to learn a new language. The computer can be used to test students about the language they already learn. It can assist them to practice certain tasks. The computer permits students to communicate easily with other from different places.

The learning ability of language learners can be more reliable with the influence of the a dictionary. Learners tend to carry or are required to have a dictionary which allows them to learn independently and become more responsible for their own work. In these modern days, education has upgraded its methods of teaching and learning with dictionaries where digital materials are being applied as tools. Electronic dictionaries are increasingly a more common choice for ESL students. Most of them contain native-language equivalents and explanations, as well as definitions and example sentences in English. They can speak the English word to the learner, and they are easy to carry around. However, they are expensive and easy to lose, so students are often instructed to put their names on them.

Varieties of English

- The English language in England (and other parts of the United Kingdom) exhibits significant differences by region and class, noticeable both in accent (pronunciation) and in dialect (vocabulary and grammar).
- The numerous communities of English native speakers in countries all over the world also have some noticeable differences. See Irish English, Australian English, Canadian English, Newfoundland English, etc.
- English has no organization that controls a prestige dialect of the language – unlike the French *Academie de la langue française*, Spain's *Real Academia Española*, Brazil's *Academia Brasileira de Letras*, or Esperanto's *Akademio*.

Teaching English therefore involves not only helping the student to use the form of English most suitable for their purposes, but also exposure to regional forms and cultural styles so that the student will be able to discern meaning even when the words, grammar, or pronunciation are different from the form of English they are being taught to speak. Some professionals in the field have recommended incorporating information about non-standard forms of English in ESL programs. For example, in advocating for classroom-based instruction in African-American English (also known as Ebonics), linguist Richard McDorman has argued, "Simply put, the ESL syllabus must break free of the longstanding intellectual imperiousness of the standard to embrace instruction that encompasses the many "Englishes" that learners will encounter and thereby achieve the culturally responsive pedagogy so often advocated by leaders in the field."

SOCIAL CHALLENGES AND BENEFITS

Class placement

ESL students often suffer from the effects of tracking and ability grouping. Students are often placed into low ability groups based on scores on standardized tests in English and Math. There is also low mobility among these students from low to high performing groups, which can prevent them from achieving the same academic progress as native speakers. Similar tests are also used to place ESL students in college level courses. Students have voiced frustration that only non-native students have to prove their language skills, when being a native speaker in no way guarantees college level academic literacy. Studies have shown that these tests can cause different passing rates among linguistic groups regardless of high school preparation.

Dropout rates

Dropout rates for ESL students in multiple countries are much higher than dropout rates for native speakers. The

National Center for Education Statistics (NCES) in the United States reported that the percentage of dropouts in the non-native born Hispanic youth population between the ages of 16 and 24 years old is 43.4%. A study in Canada found that the high school dropout rate for all ESL students was 74%. High dropout rates are thought to be due to difficulties ESL students have in keeping up in mainstream classes, the increasing number of ESL students who enter middle or high school with interrupted prior formal education, and accountability systems. The accountability system in the US is due to the No Child Left Behind Act. Schools that risk losing funding, closing, or having their principals fired if test scores are not high enough begin to view students that do not perform well on standardized tests as liabilities. Because dropouts actually increase a school's performance, critics claim that administrators let poor performing students slip through the cracks. A study of Texas schools operating under No Child Left Behind found that 80% of ESL students did not graduate from high school in five years.

Access to higher education

ESL students face several barriers to higher education. Most colleges and universities require four years of English in high school. In addition, most colleges and universities only accept one year of ESL English. It is difficult for ESL students that arrive in the United States relatively late to finish this requirement because they must spend a longer time in ESL English classes in high school, or they might not arrive early enough to complete four years of English in high school. This results in many ESL students not having the correct credits to apply for college, or enrolling in summer school to finish the required courses.

ESL students can also face additional financial barriers to higher education because of their language skills. Those that don't place high enough on college placement exams often have to enroll in ESL courses at their universities. These courses can cost up to $1,000 extra, and can be offered without credit towards graduation. This adds additional financial stress on ESL students that often come from families of lower socioeconomic status. The latest statistics show that the median household income for school-age ESL students is $36,691 while that of non-ESL students is $60,280. College tuition has risen sharply in the last decade, while family income has fallen. In addition, while many ESL students receive a Pell Grant, the maximum grant for the year 2011–2012 covered only about a third of the cost of college.

Interaction with native speakers

ESL students often have difficulty interacting with native speakers in school. Some ESL students avoid interactions with native speakers because of their frustration or embarrassment at their poor English. Immigrant students often also lack knowledge of popular culture, which limits their conversations with native speakers to academic topics. In classroom group activities with native speakers, ESL students often do not participate, again because of embarrassment about their English, but also because of cultural differences: their native cultures may value silence and individual work at school in preference to social interaction and talking in class. These interactions have been found to extend to teacher–student interactions as well. In most mainstream classrooms, teacher-led discussion is the most common form of lesson. In this setting, some ESL students will fail to participate, and often have difficulty understanding teachers because they talk too fast, do not use visual aids, or use native colloquialisms. ESL students also have trouble getting involved with extracurricular activities with native speakers for similar reasons. Students fail to join extra-curricular activities because of the language barrier, cultural emphasis of academics over other activities, or failure to understand traditional pastimes in their new country.

Social benefits

Supporters of ESL programs claim they play an important role in the formation of peer networks and adjustment to school and society in their new homes. Having class among other students learning English as a second language relieves the pressure of making mistakes when speaking in class or to peers. ESL programs also allow students to be among others who appreciate their native language and culture, the expression of which is often not supported or encouraged in mainstream settings. ESL programs also allow students to meet and form friendships with other non-native speakers from different cultures, promoting racial tolerance and multiculturalism.

Exams for learners

Learners of English are often eager to get accreditation and a number of exams are known internationally:

- TOEFL (Test of English as a Foreign Language), an Educational Testing Service product, developed and used primarily for academic institutions in the USA, and now widely accepted in tertiary institutions in Canada, New Zealand, Australia, the UK, South Korea, and Ireland. The current test is an Internet-based test, and is thus known as the TOEFL iBT. Used as a proxy for English for Academic Purposes.
- iTEP (International Test of English Proficiency), developed by former ELS Language Centers President Perry Akins' Boston Educational Services, and used by colleges and universities such as the California State University system. iTEP Business is used by companies, organizations and governments, and iTEP SLATE (Secondary Level Assessment Test of English) is designed for middle and high school-age students.
- PTE Academic (Pearson Test of English Academic), a Pearson product, measures reading, writing, speaking and listening as well as grammar, oral fluency, pronunciation, spelling, vocabular and written discourse. The test is computer-based and is designed to reflect international English for academic admission into any university requiring English proficiency.
- TOEIC (Test of English for International Communication), an Educational Testing Service product for Business English used by 10,000 organizations in 120 countries. Includes a listening and reading test as well as a speaking and writing test introduced in selected countries beginning in 2006.

- Trinity College London ESOL offers the Integrated Skills in English (ISE) series of 5 exams which assesses reading, writing, speaking and listening and is accepted by academic institutions in the UK. They also offer Graded Examinations in Spoken English (GESE), a series of 12 exams, which assesses speaking and listening, and ESOL Skills for Life and ESOL for Work exams in the UK only.
- Cambridge English Language Assessment offers a suite of eighteen globally available examinations including General English: Key English Test (KET), Preliminary English Test (PET), First Certificate in English (FCE), Certificate in Advanced English (CAE) and Certificate of Proficiency in English (CPE).
- London Tests of English from Pearson Language Tests, a series of six exams each mapped to a level from the Common European Framework (CEFR) – see below.
- Secondary Level English Proficiency test
- MTELP (Michigan Test of English Language Proficiency), is a language certificate measuring a students English ability as a second or foreign language. Its primary purpose is to assess a learner's English language ability at an academic or advanced business level.

Many countries also have their own exams. ESOL learners in England, Wales and Northern Ireland usually take the national Skills for Life qualifications, which are offered by several exam boards. EFL learners in China may take the College English Test. In Greece English students may take the PALSO (PanHellenic Association of Language School Owners) exams.

The Common European Framework

Between 1998 and 2000, the Council of Europe's language policy division developed its Common European Framework of Reference for Languages. The aim of this framework was to have a common system for foreign language testing and certification, to cover all European languages and countries.

The Common European Framework (CEF) divides language learners into three levels:

- A. Basic User
- B. Independent User
- C. Proficient User

Each of these levels is divided into two sections, resulting in a total of six levels for testing (A1, A2, B1, etc.).

This table compares ELT exams according to the CEF levels:

Qualifications for teachers

Non-native speakers

Most people who teach English are in fact not native speakers. They are state school teachers in countries around the world, and as such they hold the relevant teaching qualification of their country, usually with a specialization in teaching English. For example, teachers in Hong Kong hold the Language Proficiency Assessment for Teachers. Those who work in private language schools may, from commercial pressures, have the same qualifications as native speakers (see below). Widespread problems exist of minimal qualifications and poor quality providers of training, and as the industry becomes more professional, it is trying to self-regulate to eliminate these.

Canadian qualifications

Teachers teaching adult ESL in Canada in the federally funded Language Instruction to Newcomers (LINC) program must be TESL certified. Most employers in Ontario encourage certification by TESL Ontario. Often this requires completing an eight month graduate certificate program at an accredited university or college. See the TESL Ontario or TESL Canada websites for more information.

United States qualifications

Most U.S. instructors at community colleges private language schools and universities qualify to teach English to adult non-native speakers by completing a Master of Arts (MA) in TESOL. Other degrees may be a Master in Adult Education and Training or Applied Linguistics. This degree also qualifies them to teach in most EFL contexts. There are also a growing number of online programs offering TESOL degrees. In fact, "the growth of Online Language Teacher Education (OLTE) programs from the mid-1990s to 2009 was from 20 to more than 120".

In many areas of the United States, a growing number of K-12 public school teachers are involved in teaching ELLs (English Language Learners, that is, children who come to school speaking a home language other than English.) The qualifications for these classroom teachers vary from state to state but always include a state-issued teaching certificate for public instruction. This state licensing requires substantial practical experience as well as course work. In some states, an additional specialization in ESL/ELL is required. This may be called an "endorsement". Endorsement programs may be part of a graduate program or may be completed independently to add the endorsement to the initial teaching certificate.

An MA in TESOL may or may not meet individual state requirements for K-12 public school teachers. It is important to determine if a graduate program is designed to prepare teachers for adult education or K-12 education.

The MA in TESOL typically includes second language acquisition theory, linguistics, pedagogy, and an internship. A program will also likely have specific classes on skills such as reading, writing, pronunciation, and grammar. Admission requirements vary and may or may not require a background in education and/or language. Many graduate students also participate in teaching practica or clinicals, which provide the opportunity to gain experience in classrooms.

In addition to traditional classroom teaching methods, speech pathologists, linguists, actors, and voice professionals are actively involved in teaching pronunciation of American English—called accent improvement, accent modification, and accent reduction—and serve as resources for other aspects of spoken English, such as word choice.

It is important to note that the issuance of a teaching certificate or license for K-12 teachers is not automatic following completion of degree requirements. All teachers must complete a battery of exams (typically the Praxis test or a specific state test subject and method exams or similar, state-sponsored exams) as well as supervised instruction as student teachers. Often, ESL certification can be obtained through extra college coursework. ESL certifications are usually only valid when paired with an already existing teaching certificate. Certification requirements for ESL teachers vary greatly from state to state; out-of-state teaching certificates are recognized if the two states have a reciprocity agreement.

British qualifications

Common, respected qualifications for teachers within the United Kingdom's sphere of influence include certificates and diplomas issued by Trinity College London ESOL and Cambridge English Language Assessment (henceforth Trinity and Cambridge).

A certificate course is usually undertaken before starting to teach. This is sufficient for most EFL jobs (see TEFL for an extended discussion of travel-teaching) and for some ESOL ones. CertTESOL (Certificate in Teaching English to Speakers of Other Languages), issued by Trinity, and CELTA (Certificate in English Language Teaching to Adults), issued by Cambridge, are the most widely taken and accepted qualifications for new teacher trainees. Courses are offered in the UK and in many countries around the world. It is usually taught full-time over a one-month period or part-time over a period up to a year.

Teachers with two or more years of teaching experience who want to stay in the profession and advance their career prospects (including school management and teacher training) can take a diploma course. Trinity offers the Trinity Licentiate Diploma in Teaching English to Speakers of Other Languages (DipTESOL) and Cambridge offers the Diploma in English Language Teaching to Adults (DELTA). These diplomas are considered to be equivalent and are both accredited at level 7 of the revised National Qualifications Framework. Some teachers who stay in the profession go on to do an MA in a relevant discipline such as applied linguistics or ELT. Many UK master's degrees require considerable experience in the field before a candidate is accepted onto the course.

The above qualifications are well-respected within the UK EFL sector, including private language schools and higher education language provision. However, in England and Wales, in order to meet the government's criteria for being a qualified teacher of ESOL in the Learning and Skills Sector (i.e. post-compulsory or further education), teachers need to have the Certificate in Further Education Teaching Stage 3 at level 5 (of the revised NQF) and the Certificate for ESOL Subject Specialists at level 4. Recognised qualifications which confer one or both of these include a Postgraduate Certificate in Education (PGCE) in ESOL, the CELTA module 2 and City & Guilds 9488. Teachers of any subject within the British state sector are normally expected to hold a PGCE, and may choose to specialise in ELT.

Chile qualifications

Native speakers will often be able to find work as an English teacher in Chile without an ESL teaching certificate. However, many private institutes give preference to teachers with a TEFL, CELTA or TESOL certificate. The Chilean Ministry of Education also sponsors the English Opens Doors program, which recruits native English speakers to come work as teaching assistants in Chilean public schools. English Opens Doors requires only a Bachelors degree in order to be considered for acceptance.

Professional associations and unions

- Teachers of English to Speakers of Other Languages (TESOL Inc.) is a professional organization based in the United States. In addition, there are many large state-wide and regional affiliates, see below.
- The International Association of Teachers of English as a Foreign Language (IATEFL) is a professional organization based in the United Kingdom.
- Professional organizations for teachers of English exist at national levels. Many contain phrases in their title such as

the Japan Association for Language Teaching (JALT), TESOL Greece in Greece, or the Society of Pakistan English Language Teachers (SPELT). Some of these organizations may be bigger in structure (supra-national, such as TESOL Arabia in the Gulf states), or smaller (limited to one city, state, or province, such as CATESOL in California). Some are affiliated to TESOL or IATEFL.

- The National Association for Teaching English and other Community Languages to Adults (NATECLA) which focuses on teaching ESOL in the United Kingdom.
- National Union of General Workers is a Japanese union which includes English teachers.
- University and College Union is a British trade union which includes lecturers of ELT.

4

Non-native Pronunciations of English

Non-native pronunciations of English result from the common linguistic phenomenon in which non-native users of any language tend to carry the intonation, phonological processes and pronunciation rules from their mother tongue into their English speech. They may also create innovative pronunciations for English sounds not found in the speaker's first language.

OVERVIEW

The speech of non-native English speakers may exhibit pronunciation characteristics that result from such speakers imperfectly learning the pronunciation of English, either by transferring the phonological rules from their mother tongue into their English speech ("interference") or through implementing strategies similar to those used in primary language acquisition. They may also create innovative pronunciations for English sounds not found in the speaker's first language.

The age at which speakers begin to immerse themselves into a language (such as English) is linked to the degree in which native speakers are able to detect a non-native accent; the exact nature of the link is disputed amongst scholars and may be affected by "neurological plasticity, cognitive development, motivation, psychosocial states, formal instruction, language learning aptitude", and the usage of their first (L1) and second (L2) languages.

English is unusual in that speakers rarely produce an audible release between consonant clusters and often overlap constriction times. Speaking English with a timing pattern that is dramatically different may lead to speech that is difficult to understand.

More transparently, differing phonological distinctions between a speaker's first language and English create a tendency to neutralize such distinctions in English, and differences in the inventory or distribution of sounds may cause substitutions of native sounds in the place of difficult English sounds and/or simple deletion. This is more common when the distinction is subtle between English sounds or between a sound of English and of a speaker's primary language. While there is no evidence to suggest that a simple absence of a sound or sequence in one language's phonological inventory makes it difficult to learn, several theoretical models have presumed that non-native speech perceptions reflect both the abstract phonological properties and phonetic details of the native language.

Such characteristics may be transmitted to the children of bilinguals, who will then exhibit a number of the same characteristics even if they are monolingual.

Examples

Arabic

- Speakers tend to speak with a rhotic accent and pronounce /r/ as [yÚ] or [r].
- Speakers tend to have difficulty pronouncing /p/.

Brazilian Portuguese

Various pronunciation mistakes are bound to happen among Brazilian L2 speakers of English, among which:

Pronunciation of vowels

- Confusion of /j i(Ð)/, usually realized as [i], and of /Š u(Ð)/ , usually realized as [u]
- Especially in a British context, confusion of /YŠ/ and / R/. The Brazilian /T/ is equivalent to RP English /R/, and often English orthography makes no clear demarcation between the phonemes, thus *cold* (ideally [Èk\Š/kd]) might be homophone with *called* /ÈkRld/. / YŠ/ might be within a range more difficult to be perceived than North American /oŠ/, that is close to the Portuguese diphthong [ow], given the nonexistence of an exact schwa concept in Portuguese (different from a mid-central pronunciation of /a ~ P/), and its proximity with the English /Œ/ range.
- In a British context, the diphthong /YŠ/ might also be pronounced as the Portuguese diphthong *eu*, [ew].
- Persistent preference for /æ/ over /QÐ/ (even if the target pronunciation is England's prestige accent), and use of / æ/ within the IPA [[] space (Portuguese /[/ is often [æ], what makes it even more due to confusion in production and perception), so that *can't*, even in RP, might sound like an American pronunciation of *Kent* or an Australian one of *can't*. Some might even go as far as having [lest] instead of /læst ~ lQÐst/ for *last*.
- Brazilian Portuguese is more syllable-timed than English, but, in some dialects in particular, its articulation of unstressed vowels might impair communication, as they might be breathy-voiced, voiceless or reduced to secondary articulation of consonants, being effectively "nullified" to many untrained ears.

Pronunciation of consonants and related

- Difficulty with dental fricatives /è ð/, that might be instead fronted [f v], stopped [t* d*] or hissed [s; z;]
- In the start of a word, guttural ar pronunciations (aside the archaic Spanish-like trill) are the only valid in Portuguese. Once in English, these sounds might be interpreted as /h/

, and often are indeed homophonous with it. As such, there might be confusion between *ray* and *hay*, *red* and *head*, *height* and *right*, etc.

- Neutralization of coda /m n K/, giving preference to a multitude of nasal vowels (often forming random diphthongs with [jÞ wÞ pÞ], or also randomly losing them, so that *sent* and *saint*, and *song* and *sown*, are homophonous) originating from their deletion. Vowels are also often strongly nasalized when stressed and succeeded by a nasal consonant, even if said consonant starts a full syllable after it.
- Fluctuation of the levels of aspiration of voiceless stops /p t k/, that might sound like /b d g/. Portuguese, alike Japanese, is more aspirated than Spanish, but less so than English, and its aspirated stops might be in post-stressed syllables, highly unusual for English.
- Loss of contrast between coronal stops /t d/ and post-alveolar affricates /tʃ d'/ due to palatalization of the earlier, before vowels such as /iÐ/, /j/, /juÐ/, and /h/.
- Pervasive or all-encompassing use of epenthetic /j ~ iÐ/ (equivalents to Portuguese /i/) before consonant clusters (including those involving /tʃ d'/), between coronal stops /t d/ and /s z/, at the end of consonant-ending words, among others. Brazilian Portuguese phonotactics is a lot like the Japanese one at being intolerant to most instances of consonant codas.
- Palatalization due to epenthetic /j ~ iÐ/, so that *night* sounds slightly like *nightch* ([ÈnajtU ~ ÈnajtUi%] rather than /Ènajt/) and *light* sounds like *lightchie* ([ÈlajtUi] rather than /lajt/).
- Loss of unstressed, syllable-final [i ~ j ~ h] to palatalization, so that *city* sounds slightly like *sitch* ([ÈsitU ~ sitUi%] rather than /Èsjti/). (This might be less common in an isolating environment than e.g. pronouncing "New York City" in the middle of a sentence, due to how using the English pronunciation in the original Portuguese rather than using

it as if it was not a loan – what Brazilians would be used to due to common use – would be regarded as affected by many.)

- Post-alveolar affricates /tʃ d'/ are easily confused with their fricative counterparts /ʃ '/, often turning *chip* and *ship*, *cheap* and *sheep*, and *pledger* and *pleasure* homophones.
- Absence of contrast of voice for coda fricatives. *He's*, *hiss* and *his* are easily homophonous. Spelling pronunciations, with all words with historical schwas left in the orthography being pronounced /z/ even when the usual would be /s/ , are also possible.
- English is less prone to perfect liaison-style sandhi than Portuguese, Spanish and French might be. Often, two identical or very similar consonants follow each other within a row, each in a different word, and both should be pronounced. Brazilians might either perform epenthesis or delete one of them. As such, *this stop* is produced either [Èdis i%sÈtRpi% ~ Èdiz isÈtRpi%] or [Èdi sÈtRpi%], instead of expected /ðjs ÈstRp/
- In Portuguese, the consonants [j] and [w], known natively as *semivogais*, are often – and controversially – regarded to be, unlike in English, not phonemic in nature, being instead allophones of the vowels /i/ and /u/, generally observed in pairs [j.j] [w.w] when separating vowels in different syllables (*maior* might be pronounced both as [majÈTʊ] and [majÈjTʊ]). As such, lenition of these approximant consonants to their corresponding vowels might be expected in some positions (e.g. [Èaj ÈlPviÐ ĚuÐ] for *I love you*); they might as well be epenthetically inserted between vowels of very dissimilar qualities.
- To the exception of /s ~ z/ (here represented with a loss of contrast at the end of a word) and /r/, consonants tend to not elide corresponding to or assimilate to the next word's phoneme, even in connected speech. This means, for example, occasional epenthesis even if the following word starts in a vowel, as in their native language (*not*[Ui] *really*).

Cantonese

Catalan

- Devoicing of final consonants: /b d a v z d' '/ to [p t k f s t*f* *f*].

  E.g. *phaze* can be pronounced like *face* (even though Catalan has both /s/ and /z/ phonemes).
- Vowel length confusions.
- Confusion of /æ/ /Q(Ð)/ /Œ/, usually realized as [a]
- Confusion of /j/ /i(Ð)/, usually realized as [i].
- Confusion of /Š/ /u(Ð)/, usually realized as [u].
- Confusion of /T(Ð)/ /R/, usually realized as [T] or [o].
- Confusion of /b/ /v/, usually realized as [b~â] (/b/ /v/ are only distinguished in Valencian and Balearic).
- Rhotic pronunciation, with /r/ pronounced as a trill [r] or a flap [~].
- Difficulties with words beginning with /s/ plus consonant, where an epenthetic *e* is usually added.

  E.g. *stop* being pronounced *estop*.
- Simplification of some word consonant clusters.

  E.g. *instant* being pronounced *instan*
- Narrower pitch range, with emphasis marked with extra length instead of extra pitch variation.
- Problems with variable stress.

  E.g. *the blackbird*. vs. *the black bird*.
- Problems with contrastive stress.

E.g. *with sugar or without sugar?* (the second *sugar* is more heavily stressed)

Chinese

French

- Because of the phonetic differences between English and French rhotics, speakers may perceive English /r/, allophonically labialized to /y·/, as /w/-like and have trouble distinguishing between /r/ and /w/.

- French speakers have difficulty with /h/ and systematically delete it, as most French dialects do not have this sound.
- /è/, /ð/ are often pronounced as /s/, /z/ (th-alveolarization) or fronted to /f/, /v/
  - o Quebecers pronounce generally /è/, /ð/ as /t/, /d/ (see th-stopping).
  - /æ/, /QĐ/ and sometimes /ŒÚ/ become /a/;
- /\r/ might become /œ/ or /ø/;
- /j/ and /iĐ/ become /i/;
- /da'/ can become /'/;
- /oŠ/ becomes /o/;
- /TĐ/ becomes /o/ or /Q/ (Quebec);
- /R/ becomes /T/;
- /Œ/ becomes /œ/, /a/, or /T/ (Quebec)

German

- Speakers may not velarize /l/ in coda positions as most native speakers do.
- They have a smaller pitch range, less consonant cluster reduction and less vowel reduction.
- Speakers are likely to insert ["Ú] before words that begin with vowels.
- German speakers often use [v] instead of [w], due to the lack of /w/ in most German varieties. Also, some speakers might pronounce [w] or [‹Ú] where native speakers would pronounce [v], in an example of hypercorrection.
- The /æ/ vowel is usually realised as [[Ú].
- Most native speakers pronounce the high vowels /i/ and / u/ with an offglide (approximately [ij] and [uw], respectively). Most German speakers will use their native [i] and [u] instead.
- Some German speakers will devoice obstruents word-finally, as is common in German. Also, word-initial

obstruents are also often devoiced by German speakers. (German /b/ and /p/ are pronounced [b%] and [p°Ú] respectively at the beginning of a word.)

Hebrew

- The lack of discrimination in Hebrew between tense and lax vowels makes correctly pronouncing English words such as *hit/heat* and *cook/kook* difficult.
- The dental fricatives /ð/ (as in "the") and /è/ (as in "think") are often mispronounced.
- Hebrew speakers may confuse /w/ and /v/
- In Hebrew, word stress is usually on the last (ultimate) or penultimate syllable of a word; speakers may carry their stress system into English, which has a much more varied stress system. Hebrew speakers may also use Hebrew intonation patterns which mark them as foreign speakers of English.

Hungarian

- The dental fricatives /è/ and /ð/ may be replaced by [s;] and [d*] respectively.
- Since Hungarian lacks the phoneme /w/, many Hungarian speakers substitute /v/ for /w/ when speaking in English. A less frequent practice is hypercorrection: substituting / w/ for /v/ in instances where the latter is actually correct.
- Consonants may be geminated when they are written in double (examples: lock, better, tick, patton). Gemination does not exist in standard English.
- /K/ may be shifted to /KaÚ/
- /æ/ may be shifted to /a/ or /[Ú/
- /\Úr/ and /YÚ/ may be shifted to /øÐÚ/ and /ø/
- /TÐ/ and /ŒÚ/ may be shifted to /oÐÚ/ and /o/
- Consonant clusters involving /j/ may assimilate to palatal positions: [_Ú] for /dj/, [c] for /tj/, [rÚ] for /nj/, [ŽÚ] for /lj/.
- As in most European languages, Hungarian dialects are always "rhotic" (the phoneme /r/ is present in coda). It

might sound more marked, through the use of [r] instead of [yÚ ~ {Ú], approximants familiar to native English speakers, or rhotic vowels when in coda

- Tendency to replace the English high lax vowels /j/ and /Š/ with [i] and [u] (ex: "fill" and "feel" are homophones, as are "cook" and "kook"), since Hungarian does not have these vowels.

Italian

A study on Italian children's pronunciation of English revealed the following characteristics:

- Tendency to replace the English high lax vowels /j/ and /Š/ with [i] and [u] (ex: "fill" and "feel" are homophones, as are "cook" and "kook"), since Italian does not have these vowels.
- Tendency to replace /K/ with [Ka] ("singer" rhymes with "finger") or as [n] because Italian [K] is an allophone of /n/ before velar stops.
- Tendency to replace word-initial /sm/ with [zm], e.g. *small* [zmTl]. This voicing also applies to /sl/ and /sn/.
- Tendency to add /h/ to some vowel-initial words, due to hypercorrection.
- Tendency to replace /Œ/ with [a] so that *mother* is pronounced [Èmad*[r], since Italian does not have Œ.
- Italian does not have dental fricatives:
    - o Voiceless /è/ may be replaced with [t*] or with [f].
    - o Voiced /ð/ may become [d*].
- Since /t/ and /d/ are typically pronounced as dental stops anyway, words like *there* and *dare* can become homophones.
- /æ/ is replaced with [[˜], so that *bag* sounds like *beg* [b[a].
- Tendency to pronounce /p, t, k/ as unaspirated stops.
- Schwa [Y˜] does not exist in Italian; speakers tend to give the written vowel its full pronunciation, e.g. *lemon* [È˜l[˜mT˜n], *television* [Ì˜t[˜leÈ˜vi'Tn], *parrot* [È˜p[˜rT˜t], *intelligent* [inÈ˜t[˜lid'[nt], *water* [È˜wT˜t[˜r], *sugar* [È*f*ua˜ar].

- Italian speakers may pronounce consonant-final English words with a strong vocalic offset, especially in isolated words, e.g. *dog* [dTaJ"]. This has led to the stereotype of Italians adding [Y˜] to the ends of English words.
- Tendency to pronounce /r/ as [r]; a trill rather than the native approximant [y˜ ~ {˜].

In addition, Italians learning English have a tendency to pronounce words as they are spelled, so that *walk* is [wT˜lk], *guide* is [a˜wid], and *boiled* is [È˜bT˜il[˜d]. This is also true for loanwords borrowed from English as *water*, which is pronounced [vat[˜r] instead of [È˜wTÐtY˜]. Related to this is the fact that many Italians produce /r/ wherever it is spelled (e.g. *star* [star]), resulting in a rhotic accent, even when the dialect of English they are learning is nonrhotic. Consonants written double may be pronounced as geminates, e.g. Italians pronounce *apple* as [æppel].

Japanese

- Speakers tend to confuse /l/ and /r/ both in perception and production, since the Japanese language does not distinguish any consonants by laterality. The closest Japanese phoneme to either of these is /zÚ/, though speakers may hear English /r/ as similar to the Japanese /w/.

Korean

Malaysian

Russian

- There is no /w/ in Russian; speakers typically substitute [v] or [u].
- Native Russian speakers tend to produce an audible release for final consonants and in consonant clusters and are likely to transfer this to English speech, creating inappropriate releases of final bursts that sound overly careful and stilted and even causing native listeners to perceive extra unstressed syllables.

- There are no dental fricatives (/è/ and /ð/) in Russian, and native Russian speakers may pronounce them as [s] and [z].
- Difficulty with English vowels. Russian speakers may have difficulty distinguishing /iÐÚ/ and /jÚ/, /æ/ and /[Ú/, and /uÐÚ/ and /ŠÚ/; similarly, speakers' pronunciation of long vowels may sound more like their close counterpart (e.g. /QÐ/ may sound closer to /æ/)
- There is no [yÚ] in Russian; speakers typically use Russian /r/ for English /r/.
- Likewise, /h/ may be pronounced like its closest Russian equivalent, [x].

Spanish

- Vowel length confusions.
- Confusion of /æ/ /Q(Ð)/ /Œ/, usually realized as /a/
- Confusion of /j/ /i(Ð)/, usually realized as /i/.
- Confusion of /Š/ /u(Ð)/, usually realized as /u/.
- Confusion of /T(Ð)/ /R/, usually realized as /o/.
- Since Spanish does not make voicing contrasts between its fricatives (and its one affricate), speakers may neutralize contrasts between /s/ and /z/; likewise, fricatives may assimilate the voicing of a following consonant.
- Rhotic pronunciation, with /r/ pronounced as a trill [r] or a flap [~].
- Cuban and other Central American speakers tend to merge /tʃ/ with /ʃ/, and /d','/ with /j/.
- /j/ and /w/ often have a fluctuating degree of closure.
- For the most part (especially in colloquial speech), Spanish allows only five (or six) word-final consonants: /è/, /s/, /n/, /r/ and /l/; speakers may omit word-final consonants other than these, or alter them (for example, by turning /m/ to /n/ or /K/).
- In Spanish, /s/ must immediately precede or follow a vowel; often a word beginning with [s] + consonant will

obtain an epenthetic vowel (typically [e]) to make *stomp* pronounced [esÈÚtomp] rather than [stRÚmp].

- In Spanish, the /è/ phoneme exists only in Spain; where this sound appears in English, speakers of other Spanish dialects substitute /t/, /s/ or /f/.
- Speakers tend to merge /ð/ and /d/, pronouncing both as a plosive unless they occur in intervocalic position, in which case they are pronounced as a fricative. A similar process occurs with /v/ and /b/.
- The three nasal phonemes of Spanish neutralize in coda-position; speakers may invariably pronounce nasal consonants as homorganic to a following consonant; if word-final (as in *welcome*) common realizations include [n], deletion with nasalization of the preceding vowel, or [K].
- Devoicing of final consonants.
- Narrower pitch range, with emphasis marked with extra length instead of extra pitch variation.
- Problems with variable stress.

  E.g. *the blackbird.* vs. *the black bird.*
- Problems with contrastive stress.

  E.g. *with sugar or without sugar?*

  (the second *sugar* is more heavily stressed)

Vietnamese

Note: There are three main dialects in Vietnamese, a northern one centered around Hanoi, a central one whose prestige accent is centered around Hu¿, and a southern one centered around Ho Chi Minh City.

- Speakers may not produce final consonants since there are fewer final consonants in Vietnamese and those that do exist differ in their phonetic quality:
  - o Final /b/ is likely to be confused with /p/.
  - o Final /d/ is likely to be confused with /t/.
  - o Final /f/ is likely to be confused with /p/.
  - o Final /v/ is likely to be confused with /p/.

- o Final /s/ is likely to be omitted.
- o Final /ƒÚ/ is likely to be omitted.
- o Final /z/ is likely to be omitted.
- o Final /tƒÚ/ is likely to be omitted.
- o Final /l/ is likely to be confused with /n/, but some Vietnamese pronounce the word *bell* as [S[u/]
- o Final /t/ is likely to be confused with /k/ by southern Vietnamese.
- o Final /n/ is likely to be omitted when it is before the diphthong /ajÚ/, /aŠÚ/ and /Tj/.
- o Final /p/, /t/ and /k/ is likely unreleased ([p, t, k]).

- Speakers also have difficulty with English consonant clusters, with segments being omitted or epenthetic vowels being inserted.
- Speakers may not aspirate initial /p/, /t/, /k/ and /tƒÚ/ , native English-speakers think that they pronounce as /d/ and /aÚ/. For example, when Vietnamese people pronounced the word *tie,* native English-speakers think that they say the word *die* or *dye*. respectively.
- Speakers often have difficulty with the following phonemes, which may depend in some cases upon where in Vietnam they are originally from:
  - o /è/, which is confused with /t/, /s/ or /f/.
  - o /ð/, which is confused with /d/, /z/ or /v/.
  - o /p/, which is confused with /b/ (especially in southern dialects).
  - o /d'/, which is confused with /z/, /j/ or /'/.
  - o /'/, which is confused with /z/ /j/ or /d'/.
  - o /s/, which is confused with /ƒ/ by northern Vietnamese.
  - o /tr/, which is confused with /d'/, /tƒ/, /dr/ or /t/ by northern Vietnamese.
  - o /j/, which is confused with /iÐ/.
  - o /Š/, which is confused with /uÐ/.

- o /æ/, which is confused with /QĐ/.
- o /R˜/, which is confused with /TĐ/.

- Due to the use of the QuÑc ngï alphabet, speakers may try to replace the affricate /t*f*˜/ and the cluster /tr/, which have orthographic forms *ch* and *tr*, by /c/ and /t,˜/, respectively.
- Vietnamese is a tonal language and speakers may try to use the Vietnamese tonal system or use a mid tone with English words, but they pronounce with a high tone when the closed syllable is followed by /p, t, k/. They may also associate tones onto the intonational pattern of a sentence and become confused with such inflectional changes.

This is one of a series of articles about the differences between British English and American English, which, *for the purposes of these articles*, are defined as follows:

- British English (BrE) is the form of English used in the United Kingdom. It includes all English dialects used in the United Kingdom.
- American English (AmE) is the form of English used in the United States. It includes all English dialects used in the United States.

Written forms of British and American English as found in newspapers and textbooks vary little in their essential features, with only occasional noticeable differences in comparable media (comparing American newspapers with British newspapers, for example). This kind of formal English, particularly written English, is often called "standard English".

The spoken forms of British English vary considerably, reflecting a long history of dialect development amid isolated populations. In the United Kingdom, dialects, word use and accents vary not only between England, Northern Ireland, Scotland and Wales, but also within them. *Received Pronunciation* (RP) refers to a way of pronouncing standard English that is actually used by about two percent of the UK population. It remains the accent upon which dictionary pronunciation guides are based, and for teaching English as a foreign language. It is referred to colloquially as "the Queen's English", "Oxford English" and "BBC English", although by no means do all graduates of the university speak with such an accent and the BBC no longer requires it or uses it exclusively.

An unofficial standard for *spoken* American English has also developed, as a result of mass media and geographic and social mobility, and broadly describes the English typically heard from network newscasters, commonly referred to as non-regional diction, although local newscasters tend toward more parochial forms of speech. Despite this unofficial standard, regional variations of American English have not only persisted but have actually intensified, according to linguist William Labov.

Regional dialects in the United States typically reflect some elements of the language of the main immigrant groups in any particular region of the country, especially in terms of pronunciation and vernacular vocabulary. Scholars have mapped at least four major regional variations of spoken American English: Northern, Southern, Midland, and Western. After the American Civil War, the settlement of the western territories by migrants from the east led to dialect mixing and levelling, so that regional dialects are most strongly differentiated in the eastern parts of the country that were settled earlier. Localized dialects also exist with quite distinct variations, such as in Southern Appalachia and New York.

British and American English are the reference norms for English as spoken, written, and taught in the rest of the world, excluding countries where English is spoken natively such as Australia, Canada, Ireland and New Zealand. In many former British Empire countries where English is not spoken natively, British English forms are closely followed, alongside numerous AmE usages which have become widespread throughout the Anglosphere. Conversely, in many countries historically influenced by the United States where English is not spoken natively, American English forms are closely followed. Many of these countries, while retaining strong BrE or AmE influences, have developed their own unique dialects, which include Indian English and Philippine English.

Chief among other native English dialects are Canadian English and Australian English, which rank third and fourth in the number of native speakers. For the most part, Canadian English, while featuring numerous British forms alongside indigenous Canadianisms, shares vocabulary, phonology and syntax with American English, leading many to recognize *North American English* as an organic grouping of dialects. Australian English likewise shares many American and British English usages alongside plentiful features unique to Australia, and retains a significantly higher degree of distinctiveness from both the larger varieties than does Canadian English. South African English, New Zealand English and the Hiberno-English of Ireland are also distinctive and rank fifth, sixth and seventh in the number of native speakers.

HISTORICAL BACKGROUND

The English language was first introduced to the Americas by British colonization, beginning in 1607 in Jamestown, Virginia. Similarly, the language spread to numerous other parts of the world as a result of British trade and colonization elsewhere and the spread of the former British Empire, which, by 1921, held sway over a population of 470–570 million people, approximately a quarter of the world's population at that time.

Over the past 400 years the form of the language used in the Americas—especially in the United States—and that used in the United Kingdom have diverged in a few minor ways, leading to the versions now occasionally referred to as American English and British English. Differences between the two include pronunciation, grammar, vocabulary (lexis), spelling, punctuation, idioms, and formatting of dates and numbers, although the differences in written and most spoken grammar structure tend to be much less than those of other aspects of the language in terms of mutual intelligibility. A small number of words have completely different meanings in the two versions or are even unknown or not used in one of the versions. One particular contribution towards formalizing these differences came from Noah Webster, who wrote the first American dictionary (published 1828) with the intention of showing that people in the United States spoke a different dialect from Britain, much like a regional accent.

This divergence between American English and British English has provided opportunities for humorous comment, e.g. George Bernard Shaw has a character say that the United States and United Kingdom are "two countries divided by a common language";, and Oscar Wilde that "We have really everything in common with America nowadays, except, of course, the language" (*The Canterville Ghost*, 1888). Henry Sweet incorrectly predicted in 1877 that within a century American English, Australian English and British English would be mutually unintelligible. It may be the case that increased worldwide communication through radio, television, the Internet and globalization has reduced the tendency towards regional variation. This can result either in some variations becoming extinct (for instance, *the wireless*, being progressively superseded by *the radio*) or in the acceptance of wide variations as "perfectly good English" everywhere.

Although spoken American and British English are generally mutually intelligible, there are occasional differences which might cause embarrassment—for example, in American English a *rubber* is usually interpreted as a *condom* rather than an *eraser*; and a British *fanny* refers to the female pubic area, while the American *fanny* refers to an *ass* (US) or an *arse* (UK).

Grammar

Nouns

Formal and notional agreement

In British English (BrE), collective nouns can take either singular (*formal agreement*) or plural (*notional agreement*) verb forms, according to whether the emphasis is on the body as a whole or on the individual members respectively; compare *a committee was appointed* with *the committee were unable to agree*. The term *the Government* always takes a plural verb in British civil service convention, perhaps to emphasise the principle of cabinet collective responsibility. Compare also the following lines of Elvis Costello's song "Oliver's Army": *Oliver's Army is here to stay / Oliver's Army are on their way* . Some of these nouns, for example *staff*, actually combine with plural verbs most of the time.

In American English (AmE), collective nouns are almost always singular in construction: *the committee was unable to agree*. However, when a speaker wishes to emphasize that the individuals are acting separately, a plural pronoun may be employed with a singular or plural verb: *the team takes their seats*, rather than *the team takes its seats*. However, such a sentence would most likely be recast as *the team members take their seats*. Despite exceptions such as usage in *The New York Times*, the names of sports teams are usually treated as plurals even if the form of the name is singular.

The difference occurs for all nouns of multitude, both general terms such as *team* and *company* and proper nouns (for example where a place name is used to refer to a sports team). For instance, BrE: *SuperHeavy is a band that shouldn't work* or *First Aid Kit are a band full of contradictions;* AmE: *The Clash is a well-known band*.

BrE: *Spain are the champions*; AmE: *Spain is the champion*.

Proper nouns that are plural in form take a plural verb in both AmE and BrE; for example, *The Beatles are a well-known band; The Seahawks are the champions*, with one major exception: largely for historical reasons, in American English, the *United States is* is almost universal. This is due to the growth in federal control over state governments following the American Civil War (*cf.* the inclusion of the term "indivisible" in the Pledge of Allegiance to the United States flag); before this, the construction "*the United States are*" was more common.

Verbs

Verb morphology

- The past tense and past participle of the verbs *learn, spoil, spell, burn, dream, smell, spill, leap*, and others, can be either irregular (*learnt, spoilt,* etc.) or regular (*learned, spoiled,* etc.). In BrE, both irregular and regular forms are current, but for some words (such as *smelt* and *leapt*) there is a strong tendency towards the irregular forms, especially by users of Received Pronunciation. For other words (such as *dreamed, leaned,* and *learned*) the regular forms are somewhat more common. In most accents of AmE, the irregular forms are never or rarely used (except for *burnt, leapt* and *dreamt*).

The *t* endings may be encountered frequently in older American texts. Usage may vary when the past participles are used as adjectives, as in *burnt toast*. (The two-syllable form *learnèd* /È˜l\˜rnj˜d/, usually written without the accent, is used as an adjective to mean "educated" or to refer to academic institutions in both BrE and AmE.) Finally, the past tense and past participle of *dwell* and *kneel* are more commonly *dwelt* and *knelt* in both standards, with *dwelled* and *kneeled* as common variants in the US but not in the UK.

- *Lit* as the past tense of *light* is more common than *lighted* in the UK; American English uses *lit* to mean "set afire" / "kindled" / "made to emit light" but *lighted* to mean "cast light upon" (*e.g.*, "The stagehand *lighted* the set and then *lit* a cigarette."). Conversely, British English favours *fitted* as the past tense of *fit* generally, whereas the preference of American English is more complex: AmE prefers *fitted* for the metaphorical sense of having made an object [adjective-]"fit" (*i.e.*, suited) for a purpose; in spatial transitive contexts, AmE uses *fitted* for the sense of having made an object conform to an unchanged object that it surrounds (*e.g.*, "*fitted* X around Y") but *fit* for the sense of having made an object conform to an unchanged object that surrounds it (*e.g.*, "*fit*[-past] X into Y"); and for the spatial senses (both intransitive and transitive) of having been matching with respect to contour, with no alteration of either object implied, AmE prefers *fit* ("The clothes [past-]*fit*."; "The clothes [past-]*fit* me well.").

- The past tense of *spit* "expectorate" is *spat* in BrE, *spit* or *spat* in AmE. AmE typically has *spat* in figurative contexts, for example, "He spat out the name with a sneer", or in the context of expectoration of an object that is not saliva, for example, "He spat out the foul-tasting fish" but *spit* for "expectorated" when it refers only to the expulsion of phlegm or saliva.

- The past participle of *saw* is normally *sawn* in BrE and *sawed* in AmE (as in *sawn-off/sawed-off shotgun*).
- The past participle *gotten* is never used in modern BrE (apart from in the dialects of North-Eastern and Western England), which generally uses *got*, except in old expressions such as *ill-gotten gains*. According to the Compact Oxford English Dictionary, "The form *gotten* is not used in British English but is very common in North American English." The American dictionary Merriam-Webster, however, lists "gotten" as a standard past participle of "get." In AmE *gotten* emphasizes the action of acquiring and *got* tends to indicate simple possession (for example, *Have you gotten it?* versus *Have you got it?*). *Gotten* is also typically used in AmE as the past participle for phrasal verbs using *get*, such as *get off, get on, get into, get up,* and *get around*: *If you hadn't gotten up so late, you might not have gotten into this mess.* AmE, but not BrE, has *forgot* as a less common alternative to *forgotten* for the past participle of *forget*.
- In BrE, the past participle *proved* is strongly preferred to *proven*; in AmE, *proven* is now about as common as *proved*. (Both dialects use *proven* as an adjective, and in formulas such as *not proven*).
- AmE further allows other irregular verbs, such as *dive* (*dove*) or *sneak* (*snuck*), and often mixes the preterite and past participle forms (*spring–sprang*, US also *spring–sprung*), sometimes forcing verbs such as *shrink* (*shrank–shrunk*) to have a further form, thus *shrunk–shrunken*. These uses are often considered nonstandard; the AP Stylebook in AmE treats some irregular verbs as colloquialisms, insisting on the regular forms for the past tense of *dive, plead* and *sneak*. *Dove* and *snuck* are usually considered nonstandard in Britain, although *dove* exists in some British dialects and *snuck* is occasionally found in British speech.
- By extension of the irregular verb pattern, verbs with irregular preterits in some variants of colloquial AmE also

have a separate past participle, for example, "to buy": past tense *bought* spawns *boughten*. Such formations are highly irregular from speaker to speaker, or even within idiolects. This phenomenon is found chiefly in the northern US and other areas where immigrants of German descent are predominant and may have developed as a result of German influence. Even in areas where the feature predominates, however, it has not gained widespread acceptance as standard usage.

Use of tenses

- Traditionally, BrE uses the present perfect to talk about an event in the recent past and with the words *already*, *just* and *yet*. In American usage these meanings can be expressed with the present perfect (to express a fact) or the simple past (to imply an expectation). This American style has become widespread only in the past 20 to 30 years; the British style is still in common use as well. Recently the American use of *just* with simple past has made inroads into BrE, most visibly in advertising slogans and headlines such as "Cable broadband just got faster".
  - o BrE: "I have just arrived home" or "I've just arrived home." AmE: "I just arrived home."
  - o BrE: "I have already eaten" or "I've already eaten." AmE: "I already ate."
- Similarly AmE occasionally replaces the past perfect with the simple past.
- In BrE, *have got* or *have* can be used for possession and *have got to* and *have to* can be used for the modal of necessity. The forms that include *got* are usually used in informal contexts and the forms without *got* in contexts that are more formal. In American speech the form without *got* is used more than in the UK, although the form with *got* is often used for emphasis. Colloquial AmE informally uses *got* as a verb for these meanings—for example, *I got two cars, I got to go.*
- In conditional sentences, US spoken usage often substitutes *would* and *would have* (usually shortened to *[I]'d* and

would've) for the simple past and for the pluperfect (*If you'd leave now, you'd be on time. / If I would have [would've] cooked the pie we could have [could've] had it for lunch*). This tends to be avoided in writing because it is often still considered non-standard although such use of *would* is widespread in spoken US English in all sectors of society. Some reliable sources now label this usage as acceptable US English and no longer label it as colloquial. (There are situations where *would* is used in British English too in seemingly counterfactual conditions, but these can usually be interpreted as a modal use of *would*: *If you would listen to me once in a while, you might learn something*.) In cases in which the action in the *if* clause takes place after that in the main clause, use of *would* in counterfactual conditions is, however, considered standard and correct usage in even formal UK and US usage: *If it would make Bill happy, I'd [I would] give him the money.*

- The subjunctive mood (morphologically identical with the bare infinitive) is regularly used in AmE in mandative clauses (as in *They suggested that he apply for the job*). In BrE, this usage declined in the 20th century in favour of constructions such as *They suggested that he should apply for the job* (or even, more ambiguously, *They suggested that he applied for the job*). However, the mandative subjunctive has always been used in BrE.

Verbal auxiliaries

- *Shall* (as opposed to *will*) is more commonly used by the British than by Americans. *Shan't* is almost never used in AmE; rather, it is almost invariably replaced by *won't* or *am/are/is not going to*. American grammar also tends to ignore some traditional distinctions between *should* and *would*; however, expressions like *I should be happy* are rather formal even in BrE.
- The periphrastic future "*be going to*" is about twice as frequent in AmE as in BrE.
- Pro-predicate "do"

- Use of "do" as a pro-predicate is almost exclusively British usage.
- example:"Did Frank love nature or fair play?" — "Why, he must have done."

where the AmE response would be "Why, he must have." omitting the form of "do". The BrE usage is commonly found with all forms of "do", for example:

I have done.

I haven't done.

I will do.

I might have done.

I could do.

I could have done.

I should do.

I should have done.

Transitivity

The following verbs show differences in transitivity between BrE and AmE:

- *agree*: Transitive or intransitive in BrE, usually intransitive in AmE (*agree a contract/agree to* or *on a contract*). However, in formal AmE legal writing one often sees constructions such as *as may be agreed between the parties* (rather than *as may be agreed* upon *between the parties*).
- *appeal* (as a decision): Usually intransitive in BrE (used with *against*) and transitive in AmE (*appeal against the decision to the Court/appeal the decision to the Court*).
- *catch up* ("to reach and overtake"): Transitive or intransitive in BrE, strictly intransitive in AmE (*to catch somebody up/to catch up with somebody*). A transitive form exists in AmE, with a different meaning: *to catch somebody up* means that the subject will help the object catch up, rather the opposite of the BrE transitive meaning.

- *cater* ("to provide food and service"): Intransitive in BrE, transitive or intransitive in AmE (*to cater for a banquet/to cater a banquet*).
- *claim*: Sometimes intransitive in BrE (used with *for*), strictly transitive in AmE.
- *meet*: AmE uses intransitively *meet* followed by *with* to mean "to have a meeting with", as for business purposes (*Yesterday we met with the CEO*), and reserves transitive *meet* for the meanings "to be introduced to" (*I want you to meet the CEO; she is such a fine lady*), "to come together with (someone, somewhere)" (*Meet the CEO at the train station*), and "to have a casual encounter with". BrE uses transitive *meet* also to mean "to have a meeting with"; the construction *meet with*, which actually dates back to Middle English, appears to be coming back into use in Britain, despite some commentators who preferred to avoid confusion with *meet with* meaning "receive, undergo" (*the proposal was met with disapproval*). The construction *meet up with* (as in *to meet up with someone*), which originated in the US, has long been standard in both dialects.
- *protest*: In sense "oppose", intransitive in BrE, transitive in AmE (*The workers protested against the decision/The workers protested the decision*). The intransitive *protest against* in AmE means "to hold or participate in a demonstration against". The older sense "proclaim" is always transitive (*protest one's innocence*).
- *write*: In BrE, the indirect object of this verb usually requires the preposition *to*, for example, *I'll write* to *my MP* or *I'll write* to *her* (although it is not required in some situations, for example when an indirect object pronoun comes before a direct object noun, for example, *I'll write* her *a letter*). In AmE, *write* can be used monotransitively (*I'll write my congressman; I'll write him*).

Complementation

- The verbs *prevent* and *stop* can be found in two different constructions: "prevent/stop someone *from* doing something" and "prevent/stop someone doing something". The latter is well established in BrE, but not in AmE.

- Some verbs can take either a to+infinitive construction or a gerund construction (for example, *to start to do something / to start doing something*). For example, the gerund is more common:
  - o In AmE than BrE, with *start, begin, omit, enjoy;*
  - o In BrE than AmE, with *love, like, intend.*

Presence or absence of syntactic elements

- Where a statement of intention involves two separate activities, it is acceptable for speakers of AmE to use *to go* plus bare infinitive. Speakers of BrE would instead use *to go and* plus bare infinitive. Thus, where a speaker of AmE may say *I'll go take a bath,* BrE speakers would say *I'll go* and *have a bath.* (Both can also use the form *to go to* instead to suggest that the action may fail, as in *He went to take/have a bath, but the tub was full of children.*) Similarly, *to come* plus bare infinitive is acceptable to speakers of AmE, where speakers of BrE would instead use *to come and* plus bare infinitive. Thus, where a speaker of AmE may say *come see what I bought,* BrE speakers would say *come and see what I've bought* (notice the present perfect: a common British preference). The contraction 'n' for and is often used in AmE such as "come 'n' get it" and "wait 'n' see".
- Use of prepositions before days denoted by a single word. Where British people would say *She resigned on Thursday,* Americans often say *She resigned Thursday,* but both forms are common in American usage. Occasionally the preposition is also absent when referring to months: *I'll be here December* (although this usage is generally limited to colloquial speech).
- In the UK, *from* is used with single dates and times more often than in the United States. Where British speakers and writers may say *the new museum will be open from Tuesday,* Americans most likely say *the new museum will be open starting* or *on Tuesday.* (This difference does not apply to

phrases of the pattern *from A to B*, which are used in both BrE and AmE.) A variation or alternative of this is the mostly American *the play opens Tuesday* and the mostly British *the play opens on Tuesday*.

- American legislators and lawyers always use the preposition *of* between the name of a legislative act and the year it was passed; their British counterparts do not. Compare *Americans with Disabilities Act of 1990* to the *Disability Discrimination Act 1995*.

The definite article

- A few 'institutional' nouns take no definite article when a certain role is implied: for example, *at sea* (as a sailor), *in prison* (as a convict), and *at/in college* (for students). Among this group, BrE has *in hospital* (as a patient) and *at university* (as a student), where AmE requires *in the hospital* and *at the university* (though AmE does allow *in college* and *in school*). When the implied roles of patient or student do not apply, the definite article is used in both dialects. However, both variations drop the definite article with *rush hour*: *at rush hour* (BrE)/*in rush hour* (AmE).
- BrE distinguishes *in future* ("from now on") from *in the future* ("at some future time"); AmE uses *in the future* for both senses.
- AmE omits, and BrE requires, the definite article in a few expressions such as *tell (the) time, play (the) piano*.
- In BrE, numbered highways usually take the definite article (for example "the M25", "the A14"); in America they usually do not ("I-495", "Route 66"). Upstate New York, Southern California English and Arizona are exceptions, where "the 33", "the 5" or "the 10" are the standard. A similar pattern is followed for named roads (for example, Strand in London is almost always referred to as *the* Strand), but in America, there are local variations and older American highways tend to follow the British pattern ("the Boston Post Road").
- AmE distinguishes *in back of* [behind] from *in the back of*; the former is unknown in the UK and liable to misinterpretation

as the latter. Both, however, distinguish *in front of* from *in the front of*.

- Dates usually include a definite article in UK spoken English, such as "the eleventh of July", or "July the eleventh"; American speakers most commonly say "July eleventh" and the form "July eleven" is now occasionally used by American speakers.

Prepositions and adverbs

- In the United States, the word *through* can mean "up to and including" as in *Monday through Friday*. In the UK (and for many Americans) *Monday to Friday*, or *Monday to Friday inclusive* is used instead; *Monday through to Friday* is also sometimes used. (In some parts of Northern England, mainly parts of Lancashire and Yorkshire, the term *while* can be used in the same way, as in *Monday while Friday*, whereas in Ireland and other parts of northern England *Monday till Friday* would be more natural.)
- British sportsmen play *in a team*; American athletes play *on a team*. (Both may play *for* a particular team.)
- In AmE, the use of the function word *out* as a preposition in *out the door* and *out the window* is standard to mean "out through". For example, in AmE, one jumps "out of a boat" by jumping "out the porthole," and it would be incorrect in standard AmE to "jump out the boat" or climb "out of the porthole." (Although "out of the porthole" is used in certain Northeastern American dialects) In BrE, *out of* is preferred in writing for both meanings, but *out* is common in some speech dialects. Several other uses of *out of* are peculiarly British (*out of all recognition, out of the team*; cf. above);
- In the New York City area, "on line" (two words) refers to the state of waiting in a line or queue; for example, standing on a sidewalk waiting for a table at a restaurant. Elsewhere in AmE, one waits "in line". Throughout AmE, going "online" (one word) refers to using the Internet. Usage of "queue" among Americans has increased in the last twenty

years. In BrE, *queue* is the universal term and no variants of *line* are used in relation to waiting in turn. In BrE, people talk of standing in a queue, queuing up, joining the queue, sitting in a queue (for example, when driving) and simply queuing; Britons may be confused by the expression "in line", thinking that a row rather than a column of people is meant.

- To refer to an animal's sexually receptive time, the phrase *on heat* is heard in the UK (Regional Variation) but *in heat* in the US.
- The intransitive verb *affiliate* can take either *with* or *to* in BrE, but only *with*, or, in the case that "affiliate" is used as a noun, "of" (as in the phrase "Microsoft is an affiliate of my company") in AmE.
- The verb *enrol(l)* usually takes *on* in BrE and *in* in AmE (as in "to enrol(l) on/in a course") and the *on/in* difference is used when *enrolled* is dropped (as in "I am (enrolled) on the course that studies....").
- In AmE, one always speaks of the street *on* which an address is located, whereas in BrE *in* can also be used in some contexts. *In* suggests an address on a city street, so a service station (or a tourist attraction or indeed a village) would always be *on* a major road, but a department store might be *in* Oxford Street. Moreover if a particular place on the street is specified then the preposition used is whichever is idiomatic to the place, thus "*at* the end of Churchill Road."
- BrE favours the preposition *at* with *weekend* ("at (the) weekend(s)"); the constructions *on, over* and *during (the) weekend(s)* are found in both varieties but are all more common in AmE than BrE. See also *Word derivation and compounds*.
- Adding *at* to the end of a question requesting a location is common in the southern states of the U.S, for example, "where are you *at*?", but is not considered correct in standard American English and would be considered superfluous in standard BrE (though not in some dialects).

However, some south-western British dialects use *to* in the same context; for example "where are you *to*?", to mean "where are you".

- After *talk* or *chat* American can also use the preposition *with* but British always uses *to* (that is, *I'll talk with Dave / I'll talk to Dave*). The former form is sometimes seen as more politically correct in British organizations, inducing the ideal of discussing (with) as opposed to lecturing (to). This is unless talk is being used as a noun; for example: "I'll have a talk with him" in which case this is acceptable in both BrE and AmE.
- In both dialects, *from* is the preposition prescribed for use after the word *different*: *American English is different from British English in several respects.* However, *different than* is also commonly heard in the US, and is often considered standard when followed by a clause (*American English is different than it used to be*), whereas *different to* is a common alternative in BrE.
- It is common in BrE to say *opposite to* as an alternative to *opposite of* when used as a noun, the only form normally found in AmE. The use of *opposite* as a preposition (*opposite the post office*) has long been established in both dialects but appears to be more common in British usage.
- The noun *opportunity* can be followed by a verb in two different ways: *opportunity* plus *to*-infinitive ("the opportunity to do something") or *opportunity* plus *of* plus gerund ("the opportunity of doing something"). The first construction is the most common in both dialects but the second has almost disappeared in AmE and is often regarded as a Briticism.
- Both British and Americans may say (for example) that a river is named *after* a state, but "named *for* a state" would rightly be regarded as an Americanism.
- BrE sometimes uses *to* with *near* (*we live near to the university*); AmE avoids the preposition in most usages dealing with literal, physical proximity (*we live near the university*), although the *to* reappears in AmE when *near* takes the

comparative or superlative form, as in *she lives nearer/nearest to the deranged axe murderer's house.*

- In BrE, one rings someone *on* his or her telephone number; in AmE, one calls someone *at* his or her telephone number.
- When referring to the constituency of an American legislator, the preposition "from" is usually used: "Senator from New York," whereas British MPs are "for" their constituency: "MP for East Cleveland."
- In AmE, the phrases *aside from* and *apart from* are used about equally; in BrE, *apart from* is far more common.
- In AmE, the compound "off of" may be used where BrE almost always uses "off", and "off of" is considered slang. Compare AmE "He jumped off of the box" and BrE "He jumped off the box".
- In AmE *absent* is sometimes used as a preposition to introduce a prepositional phrase (*Absent any objections, the proposal was approved.*). The equivalent in BrE would be *In the absence of any objections, the proposal was approved;* this form is also common in AmE.

Phrasal verbs

- Influenced by the German "ausfüllen", in the US forms are usually but not invariably *filled out* but in Britain they are usually *filled in.* However, in reference to individual parts of a form Americans may also use *in* (*fill in the blanks*). In AmE the direction *fill it all in* (referring to the form as a collection of blanks, perhaps) is as common as *fill it all out.*
- Britons facing extortionate prices may have no option but to *fork out,* whereas Americans are more likely to *fork (it) over* or sometimes *up*; however, the *out* usage is found in both dialects.
- In both countries, thugs will *beat up* their victim; AmE also allows *beat on* (as both would for an inanimate object, such as a drum) or *beat up on,* which are often considered slang.
- When an outdoor event is postponed or interrupted by rain, it is *rained off* in the UK and *rained out* in the US.

Miscellaneous grammatical differences

- In names of American rivers the word *river* usually comes after the name (for example, *Colorado River*) whereas for British rivers it comes before (as in *the River Thames*). Exceptions in BrE include the *Fleet River*, which is rarely called the *River Fleet* by Londoners outside official documentation, and also where the river name is an adjective (*the Yellow River*). Exceptions in the US are the *River Rouge* and the *River Raisin*, both in Michigan and named by the French. The American convention is used in Australia, while convention is mixed in some Commonwealth nations, where both arrangements are often seen.
- In BrE speech, some descriptions of offices do not become titles (*Margaret Thatcher, the Prime Minister* and *Mr Jones, the team's coach*), while they do in AmE (*Prime Minister Thatcher* and *Coach Jones*).
- In BrE the word *sat* is often colloquially used to cover *sat, sitting*, and *seated*: *I've been sat here waiting for half an hour. The bride's family will be sat on the right-hand side of the church.* This construction is not often heard outside the UK. In the 1960s, its use would mark a speaker as coming from the north of England but by the turn of the 21st century this form had spread to the south. Its use often conveys lighthearted informality, when many speakers intentionally use a dialect or colloquial construction they would probably not use in formal written English. This colloquial usage is widely understood by British speakers. Similarly *stood* can be used instead of *standing*. To an American and still to many Britons these usages are passive and may imply that the subject had been involuntarily forced to sit or stand or directed to hold that location.
- In a few areas of the Upper Midwest of the United States, the word *with* is also used as an adverb: *I'll come with* instead of *I'll come along*, although it is rarely used in writing. *Come with* is used as an abbreviation of *come with me*, as in *I'm going to the office – come with* by speakers in Minnesota and parts of the adjoining states. These parts of the United States

have high concentrations of both Scandinavian and German American populations (German *mitkommen*). It is similar to South African English, where the expression comes from Dutch, and is used by Afrikaans speakers when speaking English. These contractions are rarely used by native BrE speakers.

- The word *also* is used at the end of a sentence in AmE (just as *as well* and *too* are in both dialects) but not so commonly in BrE, although it is encountered in Northern Ireland. Additionally, the sentence-ending *as well* is more formal in AmE than in BrE.
- Before some words beginning with a pronounced (not silent) *h* in an unstressed first syllable, such as *hallucination, hilarious, historic(al), horrendous* and *horrific,* some (especially older) British writers prefer to use *an* over *a* (*an historical event,* etc.). *An* is also preferred before *hotel* by some writers of BrE (probably reflecting the relatively recent adoption of the word from French, where the *h* is not pronounced). The use of "an" before words beginning with an unstressed "h" is more common generally in BrE than American. Such usage would now be seen as affected or incorrect in AmE. American writers normally use *a* in all these cases, although there are occasional uses of *an historic(al)* in AmE. According to the New Oxford Dictionary of English, such use is increasingly rare in BrE too. Unlike BrE, AmE typically uses *an* before *herb,* since the *h* in this word is silent for most Americans.

Word derivation and compounds

- Directional suffix *-ward(s)*: British *forwards, towards, rightwards,* etc.; American *forward, toward, rightward.* In both dialects distribution varies somewhat: *afterwards, towards,* and *backwards* are not unusual in America; while in Britain *forward* is common, and standard in phrasal verbs such as *look forward to*. The forms with *-s* may be used as adverbs (or preposition *towards*) but rarely as adjectives: in Britain as in America, one says "an upward motion". The Oxford

English Dictionary in 1897 suggested a semantic distinction for adverbs, with *-wards* having a more definite directional sense than *-ward;* subsequent authorities such as Fowler have disputed this contention.

- AmE freely adds the suffix *-s* to *day, night, evening, weekend, Monday,* etc. to form adverbs denoting repeated or customary action: *I used to stay out evenings; the library is closed Saturdays.* This usage has its roots in Old English but many of these constructions are now regarded as American (for example, the OED labels *nights* "now chiefly N. Amer. colloq." in constructions such as *to sleep nights,* but *to work nights* is standard in BrE).
- In BrE, the agentive *-er* suffix is commonly attached to *football* (also *cricket;* often *netball;* occasionally *basketball*). AmE usually uses *football player.* Where the sport's name is usable as a verb, the suffixation is standard in both dialects: for example, *golfer, bowler* (in Ten-pin bowling and in Lawn Bowls), and *shooter.* AmE appears sometimes to use the BrE form in *baller* as slang for a basketball player, as in the video game *NBA Ballers.* However, this is derived from slang use of *to ball* as a verb meaning to play basketball.
- English writers everywhere occasionally (and from time immemorial) make new compound words from common phrases; for example, *health care* is now being replaced by *healthcare* on both sides of the Atlantic. However, AmE has made certain words in this fashion that are still treated as phrases in BrE.
- In compound nouns of the form <verb><noun>, sometimes AmE favours the bare infinitive where BrE favours the gerund. Examples include (AmE first): *jump rope / skipping rope; racecar / racing car; rowboat / rowing boat; sailboat / sailing boat; file cabinet / filing cabinet; dial tone / dialling tone; drainboard / draining board.*
- Generally AmE has a tendency to drop inflectional suffixes, thus favouring clipped forms: compare *cookbook* v. *cookery book; Smith, age 40* v. *Smith, aged 40; skim milk* v. *skimmed milk; dollhouse* v. *dolls' house; barbershop* v. *barber's shop.* This has recently been extended to appear on professionally

printed commercial signage and some boxes themselves (not mere greengrocers' chalkboards): *can vegetables* and *mash potatoes* appear in the US.

- Singular attributives in one country may be plural in the other, and *vice versa*. For example the UK has a *drugs problem*, while the United States has a *drug problem* (although the singular usage is also commonly heard in the UK); Americans read the *sports* section of a newspaper; the British are more likely to read the *sport* section. However, BrE *maths* is singular, just as AmE *math* is: both are abbreviations of *mathematics*.

Vocabulary

Most of the differences in lexis or vocabulary between British and American English are in connection with concepts originating from the 19th century to the mid 20th century, when new words were coined independently. Almost the entire vocabularies of the car/automobile and railway/railroad industries (see Rail terminology) are different between the UK and US, for example. Other sources of difference are slang or vulgar terms (where frequent new coinage occurs) and idiomatic phrases, including phrasal verbs. The differences most likely to create confusion are those where the same word or phrase is used for two different concepts. Regional variations, even within the US or the UK, can create the same problems. From the mid-20th century, movies and television have spread new words in both countries, usually from the US to the UK.

It is not a straightforward matter to classify differences of vocabulary. David Crystal identifies some of the problems of classification on the facing page to his list of American English/British English lexical variation and states "this should be enough to suggest caution when working through an apparently simple list of equivalents".

Overview of lexical differences

Note: A lexicon is not made up of different words but different "units of meaning" (lexical units or lexical items e.g. "fly ball" in baseball), including idioms and figures of speech. This makes it easier to compare the dialects.

Though the influence of cross-culture media has done much to familiarize BrE and AmE speakers with each other's regional words and terms, many words are still recognized as part of a single form of English. Though the use of a British word would be acceptable in AmE (and vice versa), most listeners would recognize the word as coming from the other form of English and treat it much the same as a word borrowed from any other language. For instance a British speaker using the word *chap* or *mate* to refer to a friend would be heard in much the same way as an American using the Spanish word *amigo*.

Words and phrases that have their origins in BrE

Most speakers of AmE are aware of some BrE terms, although they may not generally use them or may be confused as to whether someone intends the American or British meaning (such as for *biscuit*). It is generally very easy to guess what some words, such as "driving licence", mean. However, use of many other British words such as *naff* (slang but commonly used to mean "not very good") are unheard of in American English.

Words and phrases that have their origins in AmE

Speakers of BrE are likely to understand most common AmE terms, examples such as "sidewalk", "gas (gasoline/petrol)", "counterclockwise" or "elevator (lift)", without any problem, thanks in part to considerable exposure to American popular culture and literature. Certain terms that are heard less frequently, especially those likely to be absent or rare in American popular culture, e.g. "copacetic (satisfactory)", are unlikely to be understood by most BrE speakers.

Divergence

Words and phrases with different meanings

Words such as *bill* and *biscuit* are used regularly in both AmE and BrE but mean different things in each form. In AmE a bill is usually paper money (as in "dollar bill") though it can mean the same as in BrE, an invoice (as in "the repair bill was £250"). In AmE a biscuit is what in BrE is called a scone. In BrE a biscuit is what AmE calls a cookie. As chronicled by Winston Churchill, the opposite meanings of the verb *to table* created a misunderstanding during a meeting of the Allied forces; in BrE to table an item on an agenda means to *open it up* for discussion whereas in AmE, it means to *remove* it from discussion, or at times, to suspend or delay discussion.

The word "football" in BrE refers to Association football, also once known as soccer. In AmE, "football" means American football. However, the standard AmE term "soccer", a contraction of "association (football)", is also of British origin, derived from the formalization of different codes of football in the 19th century, and was a fairly unremarkable usage (possibly marked for class) in BrE until relatively recently; it has lately become perceived incorrectly as an Americanism.

Similarly, the word "hockey" in BrE refers to field hockey and in AmE, "hockey" means ice hockey.

Other ambiguity (complex cases)

Words with completely different meanings are relatively few; most of the time there are either (1) words with one or more shared meanings and one or more meanings unique to one variety (for example, bathroom and toilet) or (2) words the meanings of which are actually common to both BrE and AmE but that show differences in frequency, connotation or denotation (for example, *smart, clever, mad*).

Some differences in usage and/or meaning can cause confusion or embarrassment. For example the word *fanny* is a slang word for vulva in BrE but means buttocks in AmE—the AmE phrase *fanny pack* is *bum bag* in BrE. In AmE the word *fag* (short for *faggot*) is a highly offensive term for a homosexual male but in BrE it is a normal and well-used term for a cigarette, for hard work, or for a chore, while a faggot itself is a sort of meatball. In AmE the word *pissed* means being annoyed whereas in BrE it is a coarse word for being d unk (in both varieties, *pissed off* means irritated). Similarly, in AmE the word *pants* is the common word for the BrE *trousers,* while the majority of BrE speakers would understand *pants* to mean *underwear.* Many dialects in the North of England agree with the AmE usage and use *pants* to refer to *trousers;* this is often incorrectly considered an Americanism by people from elsewhere in Britain. The word *pants* is a shortening of the archaic *pantaloons,* which shares the same source as the French for trousers, *pantalon.*

Sometimes the confusion is more subtle. In AmE the word *quite* used as a qualifier is generally a reinforcement: for example, "I'm quite hungry" means "I'm very hungry". In BrE *quite* (which is much more common in conversation) may have this meaning, as in "quite right" or "quite mad", but it more commonly means "somewhat", so that in BrE "I'm quite hungry" can mean "I'm somewhat hungry". This divergence of use can lead to misunderstanding.

Frequency

- In the UK the word *whilst* is historically acceptable as a conjunction (as an alternative to *while,* especially prevalent in some dialects). In AmE only *while* is used in both contexts.
- In the UK generally the term *fall* meaning "autumn" is obsolete. Although found often from Elizabethan literature to Victorian literature, continued understanding of the word is usually ascribed to its continued use in America.
- In the UK the term *period* for a full stop is not used; in AmE the term *full stop* is rarely, if ever, used for the punctuation mark. For example, Tony Blair said, "Terrorism is wrong, full stop", whereas in AmE, "Terrorism is wrong, period." The use of the interjection: *period* to mean *"and nothing else; end of discussion"* is beginning to be used in colloquial British English.

SOCIAL AND CULTURAL DIFFERENCES

Lexical items that reflect separate social and cultural development.

Education

School

In the US, 5th grade is typically a part of elementary school while 8th grade is often the third and final year of junior high. The US does not have a uniform nationwide system of schooling and even within individual states there can be different systems depending on the school district or town/city.

In the UK the US equivalent of a *high school* is often referred to as a *secondary school* regardless of whether it is state funded or private. Secondary education in the United States also includes *middle school* or *junior high school*, a two- or three-year transitional school between elementary school and high school. "Middle school" is sometimes used in the UK as a synonym for the younger *junior school*, covering the second half of the primary curriculum—current years 4 to 6 in some areas. But in Dorset (South England) it is used to describe the second school in the three-tier system, which is normally from year 5 to year 8, In other regions such as a town called Evesham and the surrounding area in Worcestershire the second tier goes from year 6 to year 8, and both starting secondary school in year 9. In Kirklees, West Yorkshire in the villages of the Dearne Valley there is a 3 tier system: First Schools year Reception to year 5, Middle School (Scissett/Kirkburton Middle School) year 6 to year 8 and High School ()years 9 to year 13.

A *public school* has opposite meanings in the two countries. In the US this is a government-owned institution supported by taxpayers. In England and Wales the term strictly refers to an ill-defined group of prestigious private independent schools funded by students' fees, although it is often more loosely used to refer to any independent school. Independent schools are also known as *private schools*, and the latter is the correct term in Scotland and Northern Ireland for all such fee-funded schools. Strictly, the term *public school* is not used in Scotland and Northern Ireland in the same sense as in England, but nevertheless Gordonstoun, the Scottish private school which Charles, Prince of Wales attended, is sometimes referred to as a *public school,* as are some other Scottish private schools. Government-funded schools in Scotland and Northern Ireland are properly referred to as *state schools*—but are sometimes confusingly referred to as *public schools* (with the same meaning as in the US); whereas in the US, where most public schools are administered by local governments, a *state school* is typically a college or university run by one of the states. The UK use of the term "public" school is in contrast with "private" education, i.e. to be educated privately with a tutor.

Speakers in both the United States and the United Kingdom use several additional terms for specific types of secondary school. A US *prep school* or *preparatory school* is an independent school funded by tuition fees; the same term is used in the UK for a private school for pupils under thirteen, designed to prepare them for fee-paying public schools. An American *parochial school* covers costs through tuition and has affiliation with a religious institution, most often a Catholic church or diocese. (The term "parochial" is almost never used to describe schools run by fundamentalist Protestant groups.) In England, where the state-funded education system grew from parish schools organized by the local established church, the Church of England (C. of E., or C.E.), and many schools, especially primary schools (up to age 11) retain a church connection and are known as *church schools, C.E. Schools* or *C.E. (Aided) Schools.* There are also *faith schools* associated with the Roman Catholic Church and other major faiths, with a mixture of funding arrangements.

In the US, a *magnet school* receives government funding and has special admission requirements: pupils gain admission through superior performance on admission tests. The UK has city academies, which are independent privately sponsored schools run with public funding and which can select up to 10% of pupils by aptitude. Moreover in the UK 36 Local Education Authorities retain selection by ability at 11. They maintain grammar schools (State funded secondary schools), which admit pupils according to performance in an examination (known as the 11+) and Comprehensive schools that take pupils of all abilities. Grammar schools select the most academically able

10% to 23% of those who sit the exam. Students who fail the exam go to a Secondary modern school sometimes called a high school and increasingly an academy. In areas where there are no grammar schools the comprehensives likewise may term themselves high schools or academies. Nationally only 6% of pupils attend grammar schools, mainly in 4 distinct counties. Some private schools are called grammar schools, chiefly those that were grammar schools long before the advent of state education.

University

In the UK a university student is said to *study*, to *read* or informally simply to *do* a subject. In the recent past the expression 'to read a subject' was more common at the older universities such as Oxford and Cambridge. In the US a student *studies* or *majors in* a subject (although *concentration* or *emphasis* is also used in some US colleges or universities to refer to the major subject of study). *To major in* something refers to the student's principal course of study; *to study* may refer to any class being taken.

BrE:

"She read biology at Cambridge."

"She studied biology at Cambridge."

"She did biology at Cambridge." (informal)

AmE:

"She majored in biology at Harvard."

"She studied biology at Harvard."

"She concentrated in biology at Harvard."

At university level in BrE, each *module* is taught or facilitated by a *lecturer* or *tutor*; *professor* is the job-title of a senior academic. (In AmE, at some universities, the equivalent of the BrE lecturer is instructor, especially when the teacher has a lesser degree or no University degree, though the usage may become confusing according to whether the subject being taught is considered technical or not. Also, it is not to be confused with Adjunct

Instructor/Professor.) In AmE each *class* is generally taught by a *professor* (although some US tertiary educational institutions follow the BrE usage), while the position of *lecturer* is occasionally given to individuals hired on a temporary basis to teach one or more classes and who may or not have a doctoral degree.

The word *course* in American use typically refers to the study of a restricted topic or individual subject (for example, *a course in Early Medieval England, a course in Integral Calculus*) over a limited period of time (such as a semester or term) and is equivalent to a *module* or sometimes *unit* at a British university. In the UK a *course of study* or simply *course* is likely to refer to the entire program of study, which may extend over several years and be made up of any number of *modules,* hence is also practically synonymous to a degree programme.

A *dissertation* in AmE refers to the final written product of a doctoral student to fulfil the requirement of that programme. In BrE, the same word refers to the final written product of a student in an undergraduate or taught master's programme.

General terms

In both the US and the UK, a student *takes* an exam, but in BrE a student can also be said to *sit* an exam. The expression *he sits for* an exam also arises in BrE but only rarely in AmE; American lawyers-to-be *sit for* their bar exams and American master's and doctoral students may *sit for* their comprehensive exams, but in nearly all other instances, Americans *take* their exams. When preparing for an exam students *revise* (BrE)/*review* (AmE) what they have studied; the BrE idiom *to revise for* has the equivalent *to review for* in AmE.

Examinations are supervised by *invigilators* in the UK and *proctors* (or *(exam) supervisors*) in the US (a *proctor* in the UK is an official responsible for student discipline at the University of Oxford or Cambridge). In the UK a teacher *sets* an exam, while in the US, a teacher *writes* (prepares) and then *gives* (administers) an exam.

BrE:

"I sat my Spanish exam yesterday."

"I plan to set a difficult exam for my students, but I don't have it ready yet."

AmE:

"I took my exams at Yale."

"I spent the entire day yesterday writing the exam. I'm almost ready to give it to my students."

In BrE, students are awarded *marks* as credit for requirements (e.g. tests, projects) while in AmE, students are awarded *points* or "grades" for the same. Similarly, in BrE, a candidate's work is being *marked*, while in AmE it is said to be *graded* to determine what mark or grade is given.

Another source of confusion is the different usage of the word *college*. (See a full international discussion of the various meanings at college.) In the US this refers to a post-high school institution that grants either associate's or bachelor's degrees, while in the UK it refers to any post-secondary institution that is not a university (including *Sixth Form College* after the name in secondary education for Years 12 and 13, the *6th form*) where intermediary courses such as A Levels or NVQs can be taken and GCSE courses can be retaken. College may sometimes be used in the UK or in Commonwealth countries as part of the name of a secondary or high school (for example, Dubai College). In the case of Oxford, Cambridge, Aberdeen, London, Lancaster, Durham, Kent and York universities, all members are also members of a college which is part of the university, for example, one is a member of King's College, Cambridge and hence the University.

In both the US and UK *college* can refer to some division within a university that comprises related academic departments such as the "college of business and economics" though in the UK "faculty" is more often used. Institutions in the US that offer two to four years of post-high school education often have the word *college* as part of their name, while those offering more advanced degrees are called a *university*. (There are exceptions: Boston College, Dartmouth College and The College of William & Mary are examples of colleges that offer advanced degrees, while Vincennes University is an unusual example of a "university" that offers only associate degrees in the vast majority of its academic programs.) American students who pursue a *bachelor's degree* (four years of higher education) or an *associate degree* (two years of higher education) are *college students* regardless of whether they attend a college or a university and refer to their educational institutions informally as *colleges*.

A student who pursues a master's degree or a doctorate degree in the arts and sciences is in AmE a *graduate student*; in BrE a *postgraduate student* although *graduate student* is also sometimes used. Students of advanced professional programs are known by their field (*business student, law student, medical student*). Some universities also have a residential college system, the details of which may vary but generally involve common living and dining spaces as well as college-organized activities. Nonetheless, when it comes to the level of education, AmE generally uses the word *college* (e.g. going to college) whereas BrE generally uses the word *university* (e.g. going to university) regardless of the institution's official designation/ status in both countries.

In the context of higher education, the word *school* is used slightly differently in BrE and AmE. In BrE, except for the University of London, the word school is used to refer to an academic department in a university. In AmE, the word school is used to refer to a collection of related academic departments and is headed by a dean. When referring to a division of a university, school is practically synonymous to a college.

"Professor" has different meanings in BrE and AmE. In BrE it is the highest academic rank, followed by Reader, Senior Lecturer and Lecturer. In AmE "Professor" refers to academic staff of all ranks, with (Full) Professor (largely equivalent to the UK meaning) followed by Associate Professor and Assistant Professor.

"Tuition" has traditionally had separate meaning in each variation. In BrE it is the educational content transferred from teacher to student at a university. In AmE it is the money (the fees) paid to receive that education (BrE: Tuition fees).

There is additionally a difference between American and British usage in the word *school*. In British usage "school" by itself refers only to primary (elementary) and secondary (high) schools and to *sixth forms* attached to secondary schools—if one "goes to school", this type of institution is implied. By contrast an American student at a university may talk of "going to school" or "being in school". US law students and medical students almost universally speak in terms of going to "law school" and "med school", respectively. However, the word is used in BrE in the context of higher education to describe a division grouping together several related subjects within a university, for example a "School of European Languages" containing *departments* for each language and also in the term "art school". It is also the name of some of the constituent colleges of the University of London, for example, School of Oriental and African Studies, London School of Economics.

Among high-school and college students in the United States, the words *freshman* (or the gender-neutral term *frosh* or *first year*), *sophomore*, *junior* and *senior* refer to the first, second, third, and fourth years respectively. For first-year students, "frosh" is another gender-neutral term that can be used as a qualifier, for example "Frosh class elections". It is important that the context of either high school or college first be established or else it must be stated direct (that is, *She is a high school freshman. He is a college junior.*). Many institutes in both countries also use the term *first-year* as a gender-neutral replacement for *freshman*, although in the US this is recent usage, formerly referring only to those in the first year as a graduate student. One exception is the University of Virginia; since its founding in 1819 the terms "first-year", "second-year", "third-year", and "fourth-year" have been used to describe undergraduate university students.

At the United States service academies, at least those operated by the federal government directly, a different terminology is used, namely "fourth class", "third class", "second class" and "first class" (the order of numbering being the reverse of the number of years in attendance). In the UK first-year university students are sometimes called *freshers* early in the academic year; however, there are no specific names for those in other years nor for school pupils. Graduate and professional students in the United States are known by their year of study, such as a "second-year medical student" or a "fifth-year doctoral candidate." Law students are often referred to as "1L", "2L", or "3L" rather than "nth-year law students"; similarly, medical students are frequently referred to as "M1", "M2", "M3", or "M4".

While anyone in the US who finishes studying at any educational institution by passing relevant examinations is said to *graduate* and to be a *graduate*, in the UK only degree and above level students can *graduate*. *Student* itself has a wider meaning in AmE, meaning any person of any age studying at any educational institution or level, whereas in BrE it tends to be used for people studying at a post-secondary educational institution and the term *pupil* is more widely used for a young person at primary or secondary school, though the use of "student" for secondary school pupils in the UK is increasingly used, particularly for "sixth form" (years 12 and 13).

The names of individual institutions can be confusing. There are several "University High Schools" in the United States that are not affiliated with any post-secondary institutions and cannot grant degrees, and there is one public high school, Central High School of Philadelphia, which does grant bachelor's degrees to the top ten per cent of graduating seniors. British secondary schools occasionally have the word "college" in their names.

When it comes to the admissions process, applicants are usually asked to solicit *letters of reference* or reference forms from referees in BrE. In AmE, these are called *letters of recommendation* or recommendation forms. Consequently, the writers of these letters are known as *referees* and *recommenders*, respectively.

In the context of education, for AmE, the word *staff* mainly refers to school personnel who are neither administrators nor have teaching loads or academic responsibilities; personnel who have academic responsibilities are referred to as members of their institution's *faculty*. In BrE, the word *staff* refers to both academic and non-academic school personnel. As mentioned previously, the term *faculty* in BrE refers more to a collection of related academic departments.

Politics

In Britain, political candidates *stand for election*, while in the US, they *run for office*. There is virtually no crossover between BrE and AmE in the use of these terms.

Business/Finance

In financial statements, what is referred to in AmE as *revenue* or *sales* is known in BrE as *turnover*.

Employment/Recruitment

In BrE, the term *curriculum vitae* or *CV* is used to describe the document prepared by applicants containing their credentials required for a job. In AmE, the term *résumé* is more commonly used, with *CV* primarily used in academic or research contexts, and is usually more comprehensive than the *résumé*.

Transport/Transportation

Americans refer to *transportation* and British people to *transport*. (*Transportation* in Britain has traditionally meant the punishment of criminals by deporting them to an overseas penal colony.) In AmE, the word *transport* is mainly used only as a verb, seldom as a noun or adjective except in reference to certain specialized objects, such as a *tape transport* or a *military transport* (e.g., a troop transport, a kind of vehicle, not an act of transporting).

Road transport

Differences in terminology are especially obvious in the context of roads. The British term *dual carriageway,* in American parlance, would be *divided highway*. The *central reservation* on a *motorway* or *dual carriageway* in the UK would be the *median* or *center divide* on a *freeway, expressway, highway* or *parkway* in the US. The one-way lanes that make it possible to enter and leave such roads at an intermediate point without disrupting the flow of traffic are known as *slip roads* in the UK but US civil engineers call them *ramps* and both further distinguish between *on-ramps* or *entry-slips* (for entering) and *off-ramps* or *exit-slips* (for leaving). When American engineers speak of *slip roads,* they are referring to a street that runs alongside the main road (separated by a berm) to allow off-the-highway access to the premises that are there, sometimes also known as a frontage road—in both the US and UK this is also known as a *service road*.

In the UK, the term *outside lane* refers to the higher-speed *overtaking lane* (*passing lane* in the US) closest to the centre of the road, while *inside lane* refers to the lane closer to the edge of the road. In the US *outside lane* is used only in the context of a turn, in which case it depends in which direction the road is turning (i.e. if the road bends right the left lane is the "outside lane" but if the road bends left it is the right lane). Both also refer to *slow* and *fast* lanes (even though all actual traffic speeds may be at or around the legal speed limit).

In the UK *drink driving* is against the law, while in the US, where the action is also outlawed, the term is *drunk driving*. The legal term in the US is *driving while intoxicated* (DWI) or *driving under the influence of alcohol* (DUI). The equivalent legal phrase in the UK is *drunk in charge of a motor vehicle* (DIC) or more commonly *driving with excess alcohol*.

Rail transport

There are also differences in terminology in the context of rail transport. The best known is *railway* in Britain and *railroad* in America, but there are several others. A *railway station* in the UK is a *railroad station* or *train station* in the US; trains have *drivers* (often called *engine drivers*) in Britain, while in America trains are driven by *engineers*; trains have *guards* in the UK and *conductors* in the US; a place where two tracks meet is called a set of *points* in the UK and a *switch* in the US; and a place where a road crosses a railway line at ground level is called a *level crossing* in Britain and a *grade crossing* in America. In Britain, the term *sleeper* is used for the devices that bear the weight of the rails and are known as *ties* or *crossties* in the United States. The British term *platform* in the sense "The train is at Platform 1" would be known in the US by the term *track,* and used in the phrase "The train is on Track 1". Also, the British term *Brake Van* or *Guard's Van,* is a *Caboose* in the US. Finally the American English phrase "All aboard!" when getting on a train is rarely used in Britain; the nearest British equivalent is "Take your seats!", and when the train reaches its final stop, in Britain the phrase used by announcers is "All change!" while in America it is "All out!"

Television

Traditionally, a *show* on British television would have referred to a light-entertainment program (BrE *programme*) with one or more performers and a participative audience, whereas in American television, the term is used for any type of program. British English traditionally referred to other types of program by their type, such as drama, serial etc., but the term *show* has now taken on the American meaning. In American television the episodes of a program first broadcast in a particular year constitute a *season,* while the entire run of the program—which may span several seasons—is called a *series*. In British television, on the other hand, the word *series* may apply to the episodes of a program in one particular year, for example, "The 1998 series of *Grange Hill*", as well as to the entire run. However, the entire run may occasionally be referred to as a "show". The term *telecast,* meaning television broadcast, is not used in British English. A television program would be *broadcast, aired* or *shown* in Britain.

Levels of buildings

There are also variations in floor numbering between the US and UK. In most countries, including the UK, the "first floor" is one above the entrance level, while the entrance level is the "ground floor". In the US the ground floor is considered the first floor. In a British lift one would press the "G" or "0" button to return to the ground floor, whereas in an American elevator, one would push the "1", "G", or "L" (for Lobby) button to return to the ground floor. The "L" button (or sometimes "-1") in a British lift would take you to the lower ground floor, which implies that the building is built on a slope and thus there are two ground floors - there would similarly be a "U" button (or "0") for upper ground floor.

American (AmE) *apartment buildings* / (BrE) *blocks of flats* are frequently exceptions to this rule. The ground floor often contains the lobby and parking area for the tenants, while the numbered floors begin one level above and contain only the flats (AmE *apartments*) themselves.

Immigration

In AmE, when immigrants apply for immigration benefits but are unsuccessful, they are said to be *denied* the benefit (e.g. visa application is denied, application for extension of stay is denied, entry to the US is denied). In BrE, those whose applications are unsuccessful are said to be *refused* that benefit (e.g. visa application is refused, entry to the UK is refused).

UNITS AND MEASUREMENT

Numbers

When saying or writing out numbers, the British insert an *and* before the tens and units, as in *one hundred and sixty-two* or *two thousand and three*. In the United States it is considered correct to drop the *and*, as in *one hundred sixty-two* or *two thousand three*.

Some American schools teach students to pronounce decimally written fractions (for example, .5) as though they were longhand fractions (*five tenths*), such as *thirteen and seven tenths* for 13.7. This formality is often dropped in common speech and is steadily disappearing in instruction in mathematics and science as well as in international American schools. In the UK, 13.7 would be read *thirteen point seven*.

In counting, it is common in both varieties of English to count in hundreds up to 1,900—so *1,200* may be *twelve hundred*. However, Americans use this pattern for much higher numbers than is the norm in British English, referring to twenty-four hundred where British English would most often use two thousand four hundred. Even below 2,000, Americans are more likely than the British are to read numbers like 1,234 as *twelve hundred thirty-four*, instead of *one thousand two hundred and thirty-four*.

In the case of years, however, *twelve thirty-four* would be the norm on both sides of the Atlantic for the year 1234. The year 2000 and years beyond it are read as *two thousand, two thousand (and) one* and the like by both British and American speakers. For years after 2009, *twenty ten, twenty twelve* etc. are becoming common.

For the house number (or bus number, etc.) 272, British people tend to say *two seven two* or *two hundred and seventy two*, while Americans tend to say *two seventy-two*.

There is also a historical difference between billions, trillions and so forth. Americans use *billion* to mean one thousand million (1,000,000,000), whereas in the UK, until the latter part of the 20th century, it was used to mean one million million (1,000,000,000,000). In 1974 the British prime minister, Harold Wilson, told the House of Commons that UK government statistics would now use the short scale; followed by the Chancellor, Denis Healey, in 1975, that the treasury would now adopt the US billion version. One thousand million was sometimes described as a *milliard*, the definition adopted by most other European languages. However, the "American" version has since been adopted for all published writing, and the word *milliard* is obsolete in English, as are *billiard* (but not *billiards*, the game), *trilliard*, and so on. All major British publications and broadcasters, including the BBC, which long used *thousand million* to avoid ambiguity, now use *billion* to mean thousand million.

Many people have no direct experience of manipulating numbers this large, and many non-American readers may interpret *billion* as 10 (even if they are young enough to have been taught otherwise at school); moreover usage of the "long" billion is standard in some non-English speaking countries. For these reasons, defining the word may be advisable when writing for the public. See long and short scales for a more detailed discussion of the evolution of these terms in English and other languages.

When referring to the numeral 0, British people would normally use *nought, oh,* or *zero,* although *nil* is common in sports scores. Americans use the term *zero* most frequently; *oh* is also often used (though never when the quantity in question is nothing), and occasionally slang terms such as *zilch* or *zip.* Phrases such as *the team won two–zip* or *the team leads the series two–nothing* are heard when reporting sports scores. In the case of association football—known as "football" in Britain and "soccer" in America—Americans will sometimes use "nil" as in Britain, although this usage is mostly confined to soccer journalists and hardcore fans and is not universal among either group. The digit 0, for example, when a phone or account number is being read aloud, is nearly always pronounced *oh* in both language varieties for the sake of convenience. In the internet age the use of the term *oh* can cause certain inconveniences when one is referencing an email address, causing confusion as to whether the character in question is a zero or the letter O.

When reading numbers in a sequence, such as a telephone or serial number, British people will usually use the terms *double* followed by the repeated number. Hence 007 is *double oh seven.* Exceptions are the emergency telephone number 999, which is always *nine nine nine* and the apocalyptic "Number of the Beast", which is always *six six six.* In the US 911 (the US emergency telephone number) is usually read *nine one one,* while 9/11 (in reference to the September 11, 2001 attacks) is usually read *nine eleven.*

Monetary amounts

- Monetary amounts in the range of one to two major currency units are often spoken differently. In AmE one may say *a dollar fifty* or *a pound eighty*, whereas in BrE these amounts would be expressed *one dollar fifty* and *one pound eighty*. For amounts over a dollar an American will generally either drop denominations or give both dollars and cents, as in *two-twenty* or *two dollars and twenty cents* for $2.20. An American would not say *two dollars twenty*. On the other hand, in BrE, *two-twenty* or *two pounds twenty* would be most common.
- It is more common to hear a British-English speaker say *one thousand two hundred dollars* than *a thousand and two hundred dollars,* although the latter construct is common in AmE. The term *twelve hundred dollars*, popular in AmE, is frequently used in BrE but only for exact multiples of 100 up to 1900. Speakers of BrE very rarely hear amounts over 1900 expressed in hundreds, for example twenty-three hundred.
- In BrE, particularly in television or radio advertisements, integers can be pronounced individually in the expression of amounts. For example, *on sale for £399* might be expressed *on sale for three nine nine,* though the full *Three hundred and ninety-nine pounds* is at least as common. An American advertiser would almost always say *on sale for three ninety-nine,* with context distinguishing $399 from $3.99. In British English the latter pronunciation implies a value in pounds and pence, so *three ninety-nine* would be understood as £3.99.
- The BrE slang term *quid* is roughly equivalent to the AmE *buck* and is often used informally for whole (*round*) pound / dollar amounts, as in *fifty-three quid* for £53 and *forty-seven bucks* for $47. *A hundred and fifty grand* in either dialect could refer to £150,000 or $150,000 depending on context. *Quid* was formerly also used in Ireland for the punt and today is used for the euro. "Quid" does not (generally) have a plural

form but "buck" does (aside from the expression quids in—meaning having made or won a lot of money).

- A user of AmE may hand-write the mixed monetary amount $3.24 as $3 or $3 (often seen for extra clarity on a check); BrE users will write this as £3.24 or sometimes £3 24. There may or may not be a space after the currency symbol, or the currency symbols may be omitted depending on context.
- In order to make explicit the amount in words on a check (BrE cheque), Americans write *three and D* $_{100}$ (using this solidus construction or with a horizontal division line): they do not need to write the word *dollars* as it is usually already printed on the check. On a cheque UK residents would write *three pounds and 24 pence, three pounds 24* or *three pounds 24p* since the currency unit is not preprinted. To make unauthorized amendment difficult, it is useful to have an expression terminator even when a whole number of dollars/pounds is in use: thus, Americans would write *three and D* $_{100}$ or *three and D* $_{100}$ on a three-dollar check (so that it cannot easily be changed to, for example, *three million*), and UK residents would write *three pounds only*.
- The term *pound sign* in BrE always refers to the currency symbol £ whereas in AmE *pound sign* means the number sign, which the British call the *hash* symbol, #. (From the 1960s to the 1990s the British telephone company, the GPO and its successors Post Office Telecommunications and British Telecom referred to this as *gate* on telephone keypads.)
- In spoken BrE the word *pound* is sometimes colloquially used for the plural as well. For example *three pound forty* and *twenty pound a week* are both heard in British English. Some other currencies do not change in the plural; yen and rand being examples. This is in addition to normal adjectival use, as in *a twenty-pound-a-week pay-rise*. The euro most often takes a regular plural -s in practice despite the EU dictum that it should remain invariable in formal contexts; the

invariable usage is more common in Ireland, where it is the official currency.

- In BrE the use of *p* instead of *pence* is common in spoken usage. Each of the following has equal legitimacy: *3 pounds 12 p; 3 pounds and 12 p; 3 pounds 12 pence; 3 pounds and 12 pence;* as well as just *8 p* or *8 pence.*
- AmE uses words such as *nickel, dime,* and *quarter* for small coins. In BrE the usual usage is *a 10-pence piece* or *a 10p piece* or simply *a 10p,* for any coin below £1, but *pound coin* and *two-pound coin.* BrE did have specific words for a number of coins before decimalisation. Formal coin names such as *half crown* (2/6) and *florin* (2/-), as well as slang or familiar names such as *bob* (1/-) and *tanner* (6d) for pre-decimalization coins are still familiar to older BrE speakers but they are not used for modern coins. In older terms like *two-bob bit* (2/-) and *thrupenny bit* (3d), the word *bit* had common usage before decimalisation similar to that of *piece* today.

Dates

Dates are usually written differently in the short (numerical) form. Christmas Day 2000, for example, is 25/12/00 or 25.12.00 in the UK and 12/25/00 in the US, although the formats 25/12/2000, 25.12.2000, and 12/25/2000 now have more currency than they had before the Year 2000 problem. Occasionally other formats are encountered, such as the ISO 8601 2000-12-25, popular among programmers, scientists and others seeking to avoid ambiguity, and to make alphanumerical order coincide with chronological order. The difference in short-form date order can lead to misunderstanding. For example 06/04/05 could mean either June 4, 2005 (if read as US format), 6 April 2005 (if seen as in UK format) or even 5 April 2006 if taken to be an older ISO 8601-style format where 2-digit years were allowed.

A consequence of the different short-form of dates is that in the UK, many people are reluctant to refer to "9/11", although its meaning is instantly understood. On the BBC "September the 11th" is generally used in preference to 9/11. However, 9/

11 is commonplace in the British press to refer to the events of September 11, 2001.

When using the name of the month rather than the number to write a date in the UK, the predominant modern, style is for the day to precede the month, e. g., 21 April. Month preceding date is almost invariably the style in the US. British usage often changes the day from an integer to an ordinal, i.e. 21st instead of 21. In speech, "of" and "the" are used in the UK, as in "the 21st of April". In written language, the words "the" and "of" may be and are usually dropped, i.e. 21 April. Meanwhile, the US would say this as "April 21st". One of the few exceptions in American English is saying "the Fourth of July", which is an abbreviation for the national holiday Independence Day.

Phrases such as the following are common in Britain but are generally unknown in the US: "A week today", "a week tomorrow", "a week Tuesday" and "Tuesday week" (although this is also used in central Texas); these all refer to a day more than a week in the future. "A fortnight Friday" and "Friday fortnight" refer to a day two weeks after the coming Friday). "A week on Tuesday" and "a fortnight on Friday" could refer either to a day in the past ("it's a week on Tuesday, you need to get another one") or in the future ("see you a week on Tuesday"), depending on context. In the US the standard construction is "a week from today", "a week from tomorrow", etc. BrE speakers may also say "Thursday last" or "Thursday gone" where AmE would prefer "last Thursday". "I'll see you (on) Thursday coming" or "let's meet this coming Thursday" in BrE refer to a meeting later this week, while "not until Thursday next" would refer to next week.

Time

The 24-hour clock (*18:00, 18.00* or *1800*) is considered normal in the UK and Europe in many applications including air, rail and bus timetables; it is largely unused in the US outside of military, police, aviation and medical applications. British English tends to use the full stop or period (.) when telling time, compared to American English which uses Colons (:) (i.e. 11:15 PM or 23:15 for AmE and 11.15 pm or 23.15 for BrE).

Fifteen minutes after the hour is called *quarter past* in British usage and *a quarter after* or, less commonly, *a quarter past* in American usage. Fifteen minutes before the hour is usually called *quarter to* in British usage and *a quarter of, a quarter to* or *a quarter 'til* in American usage; the form *a quarter to* is associated with parts of the Northern United States, while *a quarter 'til* is found chiefly in the Appalachian region. Thirty minutes after the hour is commonly called *half past* in both BrE and AmE; *half after* used to be more common in the US. In informal British speech, the preposition is sometimes omitted, so that 5:30 may be referred to as *half five*. The AmE formations *top of the hour* and *bottom of the hour* are not used in BrE. Forms such as *eleven forty* are common in both dialects.

Mass

In British usage, human body mass is colloquially expressed in stones (equal to 14 pounds). People normally describe themselves as weighing, for example, "11 stone 4" (11 stones and 4 pounds) and not "158 pounds" (the conventional way of expressing the same weight in the United States). Stones are never used in the United States, and most Americans are unfamiliar with the term. Kilogrammes (note the difference from the U.S. spelling, *kilograms*) are the official measurement in the United Kingdom, although very few people know their weight in kilogrammes. This is rarely noticed by the British (one such occasion might be a weight measurement at a hospital).

When used as the unit of measurement the plural form of *stone* is correctly *stone* (as in "11 stone"). When describing the units, the correct plural is *stones* (as in "Please enter your weight in stones and pounds").

Mathematics

Besides the differences between the shorthand word for the subject itself (i.e. *Maths* for BrE and *Math* for AmE), there are also differences in terms within the subject.

In geometry, what is referred to as a *trapezoid* (a quadrilateral with exactly 1 pair of parallel sides) in US textbooks is a *trapezium* in its UK counterparts. The *slope* of the line in AmE is said to be the *gradient* of a line in BrE. The skill of *factoring* polynomials in AmE is called *factorisation* in BrE; likewise, the words *factor* and *factorise*, respectively refer to their present tense forms.

In BrE the term mathematics is not commonly used for simple arithmetic. $2 + 2 = 4$ is referred as arithmetic, not mathematics.

Holiday greetings

When people greet one another with Christmas in North America, they say, *Merry Christmas!*. In the UK *Happy Christmas!* is also heard. It is increasingly common for Americans to say *Happy Holidays*, referring to all northern winter holidays (Christmas, Thanksgiving, New Year's Day, Hanukkah, Winter solstice, Kwanzaa, etc.), although this is rarely heard in the UK. *Season's Greetings* is a common phrase printed in greetings cards in both America and Britain. In Britain the term *Holiday Season* or *Holiday Period* refers to the period in the summer when most people take their major annual holiday, and many people are absent from work.

Idiosyncratic differences

Figures of speech

Both BrE and AmE use the expression "I couldn't care less" to mean the speaker does not care at all. Many Americans use "I could care less" to mean the same thing. This variant is frequently derided as sloppy, as the literal meaning of the words is that the speaker *does* care to some extent.

In both areas, saying, "I don't mind" often means, "I'm not annoyed" (for example, by someone's smoking), while "I don't care" often means, "The matter is trivial or boring". However, in answering a question such as "Tea or coffee?", if either alternative is equally acceptable an American may answer, "I don't care", while a British person may answer, "I don't mind". Either sounds odd to the other.

In BrE the phrase *I can't be arsed (to do something)* is a recent vulgar equivalent to the British or American *I can't be bothered (to do it)*. To non-BrE speakers this may be confused with the Southern English pronunciation of *I can't be asked (to do that thing)*, which sounds either defiantly rude or nonsensical.

BrE uses the exclamation "No fear!" where current AmE has "No way!" An example from Dorothy L. Sayers:

Q.: Wilt thou be baptized in this faith?

A.: No fear!

— from *Creed or chaos? : And other essays in popular theology*

This usage may confuse users of AmE, who are likely to interpret and even use "No fear!" as enthusiastic willingness to move forward (because the speaker has "no fear" of doing so!).

Equivalent idioms

A number of English idioms that have essentially the same meaning show lexical differences between the British and the American version; for instance:

Writing

Spelling

Before the early 18th century English spelling was not standardized. Different standards became noticeable after the publishing of influential dictionaries. For the most part current BrE spellings follow those of Samuel Johnson's *Dictionary of the English Language* (1755). Among the advocates of spelling reform in England, the influences of those who preferred the Norman (or Anglo-French) spellings of certain words proved decisive. In many cases AmE deviated in the 19th century from mainstream British spelling; on the other hand it has also often retained older forms. Many of the now characteristic AmE spellings were introduced, although often not created, by Noah Webster in his *An American Dictionary of the English Language* of

1828. Webster was a strong proponent of spelling reform for reasons both philological and nationalistic. Many other spelling changes proposed in the US by Webster himself and by the Simplified Spelling Board in the early 20th century never caught on. Subsequent spelling adjustments in the UK had little effect on present-day US spelling, and vice versa.

Punctuation

Full stops and periods in abbreviations

Americans tend to write *Mr., Mrs., St., Dr.* whereas British "open punctuation" style will write *Mr, Mrs, St, Dr,* following the rule that a full stop/period is used only when the last letter of the abbreviation is not the last letter of the complete word. This kind of abbreviation is known as a *contraction* in the UK. The use of full stops/periods after most abbreviations was once standard in the UK, but current publications generally tend to follow the modern open style. Unit symbols such as *kg* and *Hz* are never punctuated.

Restrictive and non-restrictive modifiers

In American English, restrictive and non-restrictive modifying phrases require different words and sentence structures. In particular, a non-restrictive modifying phrase must be set off by commas, and it generally uses "which" as its pronoun. A restrictive modifying phrase, by contrast, is not set off by commas, and uses the pronoun "that." An example of the first in American English is: "The dog, which bit the man, was brown." In that sentence the phrase "which bit the man" is non-restrictive: it is merely providing background information about a dog whose identity is otherwise not in question. The contrasting sentence in American English would be: "The dog that bit the man was brown." In this sentence, the phrase "that bit the man" is restrictive: it tells the reader that, of several dogs that might have bitten the man, the actual biter was brown. Interchanging the two structures is grammatically incorrect in American English because they have different meanings.

British English, by contrast, generally does not require its writers to construct sentences in a manner that distinguishes between the restrictive and non-restrictive forms of modifiers. Thus, a writer of British English might write: "The dog which bit the man was brown." In this sentence, it is ambiguous whether the phrase "which bit the man" is serving to identify a particular dog among several candidates or just to provide background information about a dog whose identity is otherwise not in doubt. The reader must try to infer the distinction from context or from his own knowledge.

Quoting

Americans begin their quotations with double quotation marks (") and use single quotation marks (') for quotations within quotations. BrE usage varies, with some authoritative sources such as *The Economist* and *The Times* recommending the same usage as in the US, whereas other authoritative sources, such as *The King's English*, recommend single quotation marks. In journals and newspapers, quotation mark double/single use depends on the individual publication's house style.

Quotation usage

Americans almost always place commas and periods inside adjacent quotation marks. Specific exceptions are made for cases in which the addition of a period or comma could create confusion, such as the quotation of web addresses or certain types of data strings. In both styles, question marks and exclamation marks are placed inside the quotation marks if they belong to the quotation and outside otherwise. With narration of direct speech, both styles retain punctuation inside the quotation marks, with a full stop changing into a comma if followed by explanatory text, also known as a dialogue tag. Americans tend to apply quotations when signifying doubt of veracity (sarcastically or seriously), to imply another meaning to a word or to imply a cynical take on a paraphrased quotation, without punctuation at all.

- Carefree means "free from care or anxiety." (American style)

- Carefree means 'free from care or anxiety'. (British style, optional use of single quotes)
- "Hello, John," I said. (both styles)
- Did you say, "I'm shot"? No, I said, "Why not?" (Both styles)
- To use a long dash on Wikipedia, type in "—". (exception under American style)
- My "friend" just told the whole school my secret. (American style, but also common in British English)

The American style is used by most American newspapers, publishing houses and style guides in the United States and Canada (including the Modern Language Association's *MLA Style Manual*, the American Psychological Association's *APA Publication Manual*, the University of Chicago's *The Chicago Manual of Style*, the American Institute of Physics's *AIP Style Manual*, the American Medical Association's *AMA Manual of Style*, the American Political Science Association's *APSA Style Manual*, the Associated Press' *The AP Guide to Punctuation* and the Canadian Public Works' *The Canadian Style*).

Hart's Rules and the *Oxford Dictionary for Writers and Editors* call the British style "new" quoting. It is also similar to the use of quotation marks in many other languages (including Portuguese, Spanish, French, Italian, Catalan, Dutch and German). A few US professional societies whose professions frequently employ various non-word characters, such as chemistry and computer programming, use the British form in their style guides (see *ACS Style Guide*). According to the *Jargon File*, American hackers switched to what they later discovered to be the British quotation system because placing a period inside a quotation mark can change the meaning of data strings that are meant to be typed character-for-character. (It may be noted that the current American system places periods and commas outside the quotation marks in these cases anyway.)

Parentheses/brackets

In British English, "( )" marks are often referred to as brackets, whereas "[ ]" are called square brackets and "{ }" are called curly brackets. In formal British English and in American English "( )" marks are parentheses (singular: parenthesis), "[ ]" are called brackets, and "{ }" can often be called curly braces. In both countries, standard usage is to place punctuation outside the parenthesis, unless the entire sentence is contained within them:

- "I am going to the store (if it is still open)."
- (This page is intentionally blank.)

In the case of a parenthetical expression which is itself a complete sentence, the final punctuation may be placed inside the parenthesis, particularly if not a period:

- "I am going to the store (Is it still open?)"
- "I am going to the store (I hope it's still open!)"

Titles and headlines

Use of capitalisation varies.

Sometimes the words in titles of publications and newspaper headlines as well as chapter and section headings are capitalised in the same manner as in normal sentences (sentence case). That is, only the first letter of the first word is capitalised, along with proper nouns, etc.

However, publishers sometimes require additional words in titles and headlines to have the initial capital, for added emphasis, as it is often perceived as appearing more professional. In AmE this is common in titles but less so in newspaper headlines. The exact rules differ between publishers and are often ambiguous; a typical approach is to capitalise all words other than short articles, prepositions, and conjunctions. This should probably be regarded as a common stylistic difference rather than a linguistic difference, as neither form would be considered incorrect or unusual in either the UK or the US. Many British tabloid newspapers (such as *The Sun, The Daily Sport*) use fully capitalised headlines for impact as opposed to readability (for example, BERLIN WALL FALLS or BIRD FLU PANIC). On the other hand the broadsheets (such as *The Guardian, The Times,* and *The Independent*) usually follow the sentence style of having only the first letter of the first word capitalised.

American newspapers commonly use a comma as a shorthand for "and" in headlines. For example, *The Washington Post* had the headline "A TRUE CONSERVATIVE: For McCain, Bush Has Both Praise, Advice."

5

English Literature

The focus of this article is literature in the English language from anywhere, not just the literature of England, so that it includes writers from Scotland, the whole of Ireland, Wales, as well as literature in English from former British colonies, including the US. But until the early 19th century, it just deals with literature from Britain and Ireland written in English; then America starts to produce major writers. In the 20th century America and Ireland produced many of the most significant works of literature in English, and after World War II writers from the former British Empire also began to produce major works of literature.

- A fuller discussion of literature in English from countries other than the UK and Ireland can be found in see also below.
- For a discussion of literature from England in other languages than English, see British literature.

OLD ENGLISH LITERATURE: C.658-1100

Old English literature, or Anglo-Saxon literature, encompasses the surviving literature written in Old English in Anglo-Saxon England, in the period after the settlement of the Saxons and other Germanic tribes in England, as the Jutes and the Angles, c.450, after the withdrawal of the Romans, and "ending soon after the Norman Conquest" in 1066; that is, c. 1100–50. These works include genres such as epic poetry, hagiography, sermons, Bible translations, legal works, chronicles, riddles, and others. In all there are about 400 surviving manuscripts from the period. The earliest surviving work of literature in Old English is Caedmon's Hymn, which was probably composed between 658-680.

Oral tradition was very strong in early English culture and most literary works were written to be performed. Epic poems were thus very popular, and some, including *Beowulf*, have survived to the present day. Much Old English verse in the extant manuscripts is probably adapted from the earlier Germanic war poems from the continent. When such poetry was brought to England it was still being handed down orally from one generation to another.

Old English poetry falls broadly into two styles or fields of reference, the heroic Germanic and the Christian. The Anglo-Saxons were converted to Christianity after their arrival in England. The most popular and well-known of Old English poetry is alliterative verse, which uses accent, alliteration, the quantity of vowels, and patterns of syllabic accentuation. It consists of five permutations on a base verse scheme; any one of the five types can be used in any verse. The system was inherited from and exists in one form or another in all of the older Germanic languages.

The epic poem *Beowulf*, of 3182 alliterative lines, is the most famous work in Old English and has achieved national epic status in England, despite being set in Scandinavia. The only surviving manuscript is the Nowell Codex, the precise date of which is debated, but most estimates place it close to the year 1000. Beowulf is the conventional title, and its composition by an anonymous Anglo-Saxon poet, who is commonly referred to as the "*Beowulf* poet", is dated between the 8th and the early 11th century.

In the poem, Beowulf, a hero of the Geats in Scandinavia, comes to the help of Hroðgar, the king of the Danes, whose mead hall (in Heorot) has been under attack by a monster known as Grendel. After Beowulf slays him, Grendel's mother attacks the hall and is then also defeated. Victorious, Beowulf goes home to Geatland in Sweden and later becomes king of the Geats. After a period of fifty years has passed, Beowulf defeats a dragon, but is fatally wounded in the battle. After his death, his attendants bury him in a tumulus, a burial mound, in Geatland.

Found in the same manuscript as the heroic poem Beowulf, the Nowell Codex, is the poem *Judith*, a retelling of the story found in the Latin Vulgate Bible's Book of Judith about the beheader of the Assyrian general Holofernes. The *Old English Martyrology* is a Mercian collection of hagiographies. Ælfric of Eynsham was a prolific 10th-century writer of hagiographies and homilies.

Nearly all Anglo-Saxon authors are anonymous: twelve are known by name from Medieval sources, but only four of those are known by their vernacular works with any certainty: Caedmon, Bede, Alfred the Great, and Cynewulf. Cædmon is the earliest English poet whose name is known. Cædmon's only known surviving work is *Cædmon's Hymn*, which probably dates from the late 7th century. The *Hymn* itself was composed between 658 and 680, recorded in the earlier part of the 8th century, and survives today in at least 14 verified manuscript copies. The poem is one of the earliest attested examples of Old English and is, with the runic Ruthwell Cross and Franks Casket inscriptions, one of three candidates for the earliest attested example of Old English poetry. It is also one of the earliest recorded examples of sustained poetry in a Germanic language. The poem, *The Dream of the Rood*, was inscribed upon the Ruthwell Cross.

Chronicles contained a range of historical and literary accounts, and a notable example is the *Anglo-Saxon Chronicle*. This is a collection of annals in Old English chronicling the history of the Anglo-Saxons. Nine manuscripts survive in whole or in part, though not all are of equal historical value and none of them is the original version. The oldest seems to have been started towards the end of King Alfred's reign in the 9th century, and the most recent was written at Peterborough Abbey in 1116.

Almost all of the material in the *Chronicle* is in the form of annals by year, the earliest being dated at 60 BC (the annals' date for Caesar's invasions of Britain), and historical material follows up to the year in which the chronicle was written, at which point contemporary records begin.

The poem Battle of Maldon also deals with history. This is the name given to a work, of uncertain date, celebrating the real Battle of Maldon of 991, at which the Anglo-Saxons failed to prevent a Viking invasion. Only 325 lines of the poem are extant; both the beginning and the ending are lost.

The Wanderer is an Old English poem preserved only in an anthology known as the Exeter Book, a manuscript dating from the late 10th century. It counts 115 lines of alliterative verse. As often the case in Anglo-Saxon verse, the composer and compiler are anonymous, and within the manuscript the poem is untitled. The Wanderer conveys the meditations of a solitary exile on his past glories as a warrior in his lord's band of retainers, his present hardships and the values of forbearance and faith in the heavenly Lord. Another poem with a religious theme, The Seafarer is also recorded in the Exeter Book, one of the four surviving manuscripts, and consists of 124 lines, followed by the single word "Amen".

In the past it has been frequently referred to as an elegy, a poem that mourns a loss, or has the more general meaning of a simply sorrowful piece of writing. Some scholars, however, have argued that the content of the poem also links it with Sapiential Books, or Wisdom Literature. In his account of the poem in the *Cambridge Old English Reader*, published in 2004, Richard Marsden writes, "It is an exhortatory and didactic poem, in which the miseries of winter seafaring are used as a metaphor for the challenge faced by the committed Christian [...]" (p. 221).

Classical antiquity was not forgotten in Anglo-Saxon England and several Old English poems are adaptations of late classical philosophical texts. The longest is King Alfred's (849–899) 9th-century translation of Boethius' *Consolation of Philosophy*. The *Metres of Boethius* are a series of Old English alliterative poems adapted from the Latin *metra* of the *Consolation of Philosophy* soon after Alfred's prose translation.

MIDDLE ENGLISH LITERATURE: 1100–1500

After the Norman conquest of England in 1066, the written form of the Anglo-Saxon language became less common, and under the influence of the new aristocracy, Law French became the standard language of courts, parliament, and polite society. As the invaders integrated, their language and literature mingled with that of the natives and the Norman dialects of the ruling classes became Anglo-Norman. At the same time Anglo-Saxon underwent a gradual transition into Middle English. Political power was no longer in English hands, so that the West Saxon literary language had no more influence than any other dialect and Middle English literature was written in the many dialects that correspond to the region, history, culture, and background of individual writers.

In this period religious literature continued to enjoy popularity and Hagiographies were written, adapted and translated, for example, *The Life of Saint Audrey*, Eadmer's (c. 1060 – c. 1126) contemporary biography of Anselm of Canterbury, and the *South English Legendary*. At the end of the 12th century, Layamon's *Brut* adapted Wace to make the first English-language work to discuss the legends of Arthur and the Knights of the Round Table. It was also the first historiography written in English since the Anglo-Saxon Chronicle. In this century a new form of English now known as Middle English evolved. This is the earliest form of English which is comprehensible to modern readers and listeners, albeit not easily.

Middle English Bible translations, notably Wyclif's Bible, helped to establish English as a literary language. Wycliffe's Bible is the name now given to a group of Bible translations into Middle English, that were made under the direction of, or at the instigation of John Wycliffe. They appeared between approximately 1382 and 1395. These Bible translations were the chief inspiration and chief cause of the Lollard movement, a pre-Reformation movement that rejected many of the distinctive teachings of the Roman Catholic Church.

The term "Lollard" refers to the followers of John Wycliffe, a prominent theologian who was dismissed from the University of Oxford in 1381 for criticism of the Church. In the Middle Ages most Western Christian people encountered the Bible only in the form of oral versions of scriptures, verses and homilies in Latin (other sources were mystery plays, usually conducted in the vernacular, and popular iconography). Though relatively few people could read at this time, Wycliffe's idea was to translate the Bible into the vernacular, saying "it helpeth Christian men to study the Gospel in that tongue in which they know best Christ's sentence". Although unauthorized, the work was popular and Wycliffite Bible texts are the most common manuscript literature in Middle English and almost 200 manuscripts of the Wycliffite Bible survive.

Another literary genre, that of Romances, appear in English from the 13th century, with *King Horn* and *Havelock the Dane*, based on Anglo-Norman originals such as the *Romance of Horn* (ca.1170), but it was in the 14th century that major writers in English first appeared. These are William Langland, Geoffrey Chaucer and the so-called 'Pearl Poet', whose most famous work is *Sir Gawain and the Green Knight*.

Langland's *Piers Plowman* (written ca. 1360–1387) or *Visio Willelmi de Petro Plowman* (*William's Vision of Piers Plowman*) is a Middle English allegorical narrative poem, written in unrhymed alliterative verse.

Sir Gawain and the Green Knight is a late-14th-century Middle English alliterative romance. It is one of the better-known Arthurian stories of an established type known as the "beheading game". Developing from Welsh, Irish and English tradition, *Sir Gawain* highlights the importance of honour and chivalry. It is an important poem in the romance genre, which typically involves a hero who goes on a quest that tests his prowess. "Preserved in the same manuscript with Sir Gawayne were three other poems, now generally accepted as the work of its author. These are two alliterative poems of moral teaching,

"Patience" and "Purity", and an intricate elegiac poem, *Pearl.* The author of *Sir Gawayne* and the other poems is frequently referred to as 'the Pearl Poet'. " The English dialect of these poems from the Midlands is markedly different from that of the London-based Chaucer and, though influenced by French in the scenes at court in *Sir Gawain,* there are in the poems also many dialect words, often of Scandinavian origin, that belonged to northwest England.Middle English lasts up until the 1470s, when the Chancery Standard, a form of London-based English, became widespread and the printing press regularized the language. The prolific Geoffrey Chaucer (c. 1343 – 1400), whose works were written in Chancery Standard, was the first poet to have been buried in Poet's Corner of Westminster Abbey. Among his many works, which include *The Book of the Duchess,* the *House of Fame,* the *Legend of Good Women* and *Troilus and Criseyde,* Chaucer is best known today for *The Canterbury Tales.* This is a collection of stories written in Middle English (mostly written in verse although some are in prose), that are presented as part of a story-telling contest by a group of pilgrims as they travel together on a journey from Southwark to the shrine of Saint Thomas Becket at Canterbury Cathedral. The prize for this contest is a free meal at the Tabard Inn at Southwark on their return. Chaucer is a significant figure in developing the legitimacy of the vernacular, Middle English, at a time when the dominant literary languages in England were still French and Latin. The first recorded association of Valentine's Day with romantic love is in Chaucer's *Parlement of Foules* of 1382.

At this time literature was being written in various languages in England, including Latin, Norman-French, English, and the multilingual nature of the audience for literature in the 14th century can be illustrated by the example of John Gower (c. 1330 – October 1408). A contemporary of William Langland and a personal friend of Geoffrey Chaucer, Gower is remembered primarily for three major works, the *Mirroir de l'Omme, Vox Clamantis,* and *Confessio Amantis,* three long poems written in Anglo-Norman, Latin and, Middle English respectively, which are united by common moral and political themes.

Significant religious works were also created in the 14th century, including works by an anonymous author in the manuscript called the Katherine Group, and by Julian of Norwich (ca.1342 – ca. 1416), and Richard Rolle. Julian's *Revelations of Divine Love* (circa 1393) is believed to be the first published book written by a woman in the English language; it chronicles, to some extent, her extensive pilgrimages to various holy sites in Europe and Asia.

A major work from the 15th century is *Le Morte d'Arthur* by Sir Thomas Malory, which was printed by Caxton in 1485. This is compilation of some French and English Arthurian romances, and was among the earliest books printed in England. it was popular and influential in the later revival of interest in the Arthurian legends.

Medieval theatre

In the Middle Ages, drama in the vernacular languages of Europe may have emerged from religious enactments of the liturgy. Mystery plays were presented on the porch of the cathedrals or by strolling players on feast days. Miracle and mystery plays, along with moralities and interludes, later evolved into more elaborate forms of drama, such as was seen on the Elizabethan stages. Another form of medieval theatre was the mummers' plays, a form of early street theatre associated with the Morris dance, concentrating on themes such as Saint George and the Dragon and Robin Hood. These were folk tales re-telling old stories, and the actors travelled from town to town performing these for their audiences in return for money and hospitality.

Mystery plays and miracle plays (sometimes distinguished as two different forms, although the terms are often used interchangeably) are among the earliest formally developed plays in medieval Europe. Medieval mystery plays focused on the representation of Bible stories in churches as tableaux with accompanying antiphonal song. They developed from the 10th to the 16th century, reaching the height of their popularity in the 15th century before being rendered obsolete by the rise of professional theatre. The name derives from *mystery* used in its sense of *miracle,* but an occasionally quoted derivation is from *misterium,* meaning *craft,* a play performed by the craft guilds.

There are four complete or nearly complete extant English biblical collections of plays from the late medieval period; although these collections are sometimes referred to as "cycles," it is now believed that this term may attribute to these collections more coherence than they in fact possess. The most complete is the *York cycle* of forty-eight pageants. They were performed in the city of York, from the middle of the fourteenth century until 1569. There are also the *Towneley plays* of thirty-two pageants, once thought to have been a true 'cycle' of plays and most likely performed around the Feast of Corpus Christi probably in the town of Wakefield, England during the late Middle Ages until 1576. Besides the Middle English drama, there are three surviving plays in Cornish known as the Ordinalia.

These biblical plays differ widely in content. Most contain episodes such as the *Fall of Lucifer*, the *Creation and Fall of Man, Cain and Abel, Noah and the Flood, Abraham and Isaac*, the *Nativity*, the *Raising of Lazarus*, the *Passion*, and the *Resurrection*. Other pageants included the story of *Moses*, the *Procession of the Prophets, Christ's Baptism*, the *Temptation in the Wilderness*, and the *Assumption and Coronation of the Virgin*. In given cycles, the plays came to be sponsored by the newly emerging Medieval craft guilds.

Having grown out of the religiously based mystery plays of the Middle Ages, the morality play is a genre of Medieval and earl*y* Tudor theatrical entertainment, which represented a shift towards a more secular base for European theatre. In their own time, these plays were known as "interludes", a broader term given to dramas with or without a moral theme. Morality plays are a type of allegory in which the protagonist is met by personifications of various moral attributes who try to prompt him to choose a Godly life over one of evil. The plays were most popular in Europe during the 15th and 16th centuries.

The Somonyng of Everyman (*The Summoning of Everyman*) (c. 1509 – 1519), usually referred to simply as *Everyman*, is a late

15th-century English morality play. Like John Bunyan's allegory *Pilgrim's Progress* (1678), *Everyman* examines the question of Christian salvation through the use of allegorical characters. The play is the allegorical accounting of the life of Everyman, who represents all mankind. All the characters are also allegorical, each personifying an abstract idea such as Fellowship, (material) Goods, and Knowledge and the conflict between good and evil is dramatized by the interactions between characters.

English Renaissance: 1500–1660

Following the introduction of a printing press into England by William Caxton in 1476, vernacular literature flourished. The Reformation inspired the production of vernacular liturgy which led to the Book of Common Prayer, a lasting influence on literary language. The English Renaissance was a cultural and artistic movement in England dating from the late 15th and early 16th centuries to the 17th century. It is associated with the pan-European Renaissance that is usually regarded as beginning in Italy in the late 14th century. Like most of northern Europe, England saw little of these developments until more than a century later. Renaissance style and ideas, however, were slow in penetrating England, and the Elizabethan era in the second half of the 16th century is usually regarded as the height of the English Renaissance.

Elizabethan and Jacobean period (1558–1625)

During the reign of Elizabeth I (1558–1603) and then James I (1603–25), in the late 16th and early 17th century, a London-centred culture, that was both courtly and popular, produced great poetry and drama. English playwrights combined the influence of the Medieval theatre with the Renaissance's rediscovery of the Roman dramatists, Seneca, for tragedy, and Plautus and Terence, for comedy. Italy was an important source for Renaissance ideas in England and the linguist and lexicographer John Florio (1553–1625), whose father was Italian, was a royal language tutor at the Court of James I, had furthermore brought much of the Italian language and culture to England. He was also the translator of Frenchman Montaigne into English. This Italian influence can also be found in the poetry of Thomas Wyatt (1503–1542), one of the earliest English Renaissance poets. He was responsible for many innovations in English poetry and, alongside Henry Howard, Earl of Surrey (1516/1517–1547), introduced the sonnet from Italy into England in the early 16th century. Wyatt's professed object was to experiment with the English tongue, to civilise it, to raise its powers to those of its neighbours. While a significant amount of his literary output consists of translations and imitations of sonnets by the Italian poet Petrarch, he also wrote sonnets of his own. Wyatt took subject matter from Petrarch's sonnets, but his rhyme schemes make a significant departure. Petrarch's sonnets consist of an "octave", rhyming *abba abba*, followed, after a turn (volta) in the sense, by a sestet with various rhyme schemes, however his poems never ended in a rhyming couplet. Wyatt employs the Petrarchan octave, but his most common sestet scheme is *cddc ee*. This marks the beginnings of English sonnet with 3 quatrains and a closing couplet.

Edmund Spenser (c. 1552–1599) was one of the most important poets of this period, author of *The Faerie Queene* (1590 and 1596), an epic poem and fantastical allegory celebrating the Tudor dynasty and Elizabeth I. Another major figure was Sir Philip Sidney (1554–1586) was an English poet, courtier and soldier, and is remembered as one of the most prominent figures of the Elizabethan Age. His works include *Astrophel and Stella, The Defence of Poetry,* and *The Countess of Pembroke's Arcadia.* Poems intended to be set to music as songs, such as by Thomas Campion (1567–1620), became popular as printed literature was disseminated more widely in households. *See English Madrigal School.*

The earliest Elizabethan plays includes *Gorboduc* (1561) by Sackville and Norton and Thomas Kyd's (1558–94) *The Spanish Tragedy* (1592). *Gorboduc* is notable especially as the first verse drama in English to employ blank verse, and for the way it developed elements, from the earlier morality plays and Senecan tragedy, in the direction which would be followed by later playwrights. *The Spanish Tragedy, or Hieronimo is Mad Again* is an Elizabethan tragedy written by Thomas Kyd between 1582 and 1592. Highly popular and influential in its time, *The Spanish Tragedy* established a new genre in English literature theatre, the revenge play or revenge tragedy.

Its plot contains several violent murders and includes as one of its characters a personification of Revenge. *The Spanish Tragedy* was often referred to, or parodied, in works written by other Elizabethan playwrights, including William Shakespeare, Ben Jonson, and Christopher Marlowe. Many elements of *The Spanish Tragedy,* such as the play-within-a-play used to trap a murderer and a ghost intent on vengeance, appear in Shakespeare's *Hamlet.* Thomas Kyd is frequently proposed as the author of the hypothetical *Ur-Hamlet* that may have been one of Shakespeare's primary sources for *Hamlet.*

William Shakespeare (1564–1616) stands out in this period as a poet and playwright as yet unsurpassed. Shakespeare was not a man of letters by profession, and probably had only some grammar school education. He was neither a lawyer, nor an aristocrat, like the "university wits" who monopolised the English stage when he started writing. But he was very gifted and versatile, and he surpassed the "professionals", like Robert Greene, who mocked this "Shake-scene" of low origins. Shakespeare wrote plays in a variety of genres, including histories, tragedies, comedies and the late romances, or tragicomedies. His early classical and Italianate comedies, like *A Comedy of Errors,* containing tight double plots and precise comic sequences, give way in the mid-1590s to the romantic atmosphere of his greatest comedies. *A Midsummer Night's Dream* is a witty mixture of romance, fairy magic, and rustic comic scenes. Shakespeare's next comedy, the equally romantic *Merchant of Venice,* can be problematic because of how it portrays Shylock, a vengeful Jewish moneylender. The wit and wordplay of *Much Ado About Nothing,* the charming rural setting of *As You Like It,* and the lively merrymaking of *Twelfth Night* complete Shakespeare's sequence of great comedies.

After the lyrical *Richard II,* written almost entirely in verse, Shakespeare introduced prose comedy into the histories of the late 1590s, *Henry IV, parts 1* and 2, and *Henry V*. His characters become more complex and tender as he switches deftly between comic and serious scenes, prose and poetry, and achieves the narrative variety of his mature work. This period begins and ends with two tragedies: *Romeo and Juliet*, the famous romantic tragedy of sexually charged adolescence, love, and death; and *Julius Caesar*, based on Sir Thomas North's 1579 translation of Plutarch's *Parallel Lives*, which introduced a new kind of drama. In the early 17th century, Shakespeare wrote the so-called "problem plays", *Measure for Measure, Troilus and Cressida*, and *All's Well That Ends Well*, as well as a number of his best known tragedies, including *Hamlet, Othello, Macbeth, King Lear* and *Anthony and Cleopatra*.

The plots of Shakespeare's tragedies often hinge on such fatal errors or flaws, which overturn order and destroy the hero and those he loves. In his final period, Shakespeare turned to romance or tragicomedy and completed three more major plays: *Cymbeline, The Winter's Tale* and *The Tempest*, as well as the collaboration, *Pericles, Prince of Tyre*. Less bleak than the tragedies, these four plays are graver in tone than the comedies of the 1590s, but they end with reconciliation and the forgiveness of potentially tragic errors. Some commentators have seen this change in mood as evidence of a more serene view of life on Shakespeare's part, but it may merely reflect the theatrical fashion of the day. Shakespeare collaborated on two further surviving plays, *Henry VIII* and *The Two Noble Kinsmen*, probably with John Fletcher.

Shakespeare also popularized the English sonnet, which made significant changes to Petrarch's model. A collection of 154 by sonnets, dealing with themes such as the passage of time, love, beauty and mortality, were first published in a 1609 quarto entitled *SHAKE-SPEARES SONNETS: Never before imprinted*. (although sonnets 138 and 144 had previously been published in the 1599 miscellany *The Passionate Pilgrim*). The first 17 poems, traditionally called the procreation sonnets, are addressed to a young man urging him to marry and have children in order to immortalize his beauty by passing it to the next generation. Other sonnets express the speaker's love for a young man; brood upon loneliness, death, and the transience of life; seem to criticise the young man for preferring a rival poet; express ambiguous feelings for the speaker's mistress; and pun on the poet's name. The final two sonnets are allegorical treatments of Greek epigrams referring to the "little love-god" Cupid.

Other important figures in Elizabethan theatre include Christopher Marlowe, and Ben Jonson, Thomas Dekker, John Fletcher and Francis Beaumont.

Marlowe's (1564–1593) subject matter is different from Shakespeare's as it focuses more on the moral drama of the Renaissance man than any other thing. Drawing on German lore, Marlowe introduced the story of Faust to England in his play Doctor Faustus (c. 1592), about a scientist and magician who, obsessed by the thirst of knowledge and the desire to push man's technological power to its limits, sells his soul to the Devil. *Faustus* makes use of "the dramatic framework of the morality plays in its presentation of a story of temptation, fall, and damnation, and its free use of morality figures such as the good angel and the bad angel and the seven deadly sins, along with the devils Lucifer and Mephistopheles."

Thomas Dekker (c. 1570–1632) was, between 1598 and 1602, involved in about forty plays, usually in collaboration. He is particularly remembered for *The Shoemaker's Holiday* (1599), a work where he appears to be the sole author. Dekker is noted for his "realistic portrayal of daily London life and for "his sympathy for the poor and oppressed".

After Shakespeare's death, the poet and dramatist Ben Jonson (1572–1637) was the leading literary figure of the Jacobean era. Jonson's aesthetics hark back to the Middle Ages and his characters embody the theory of humours. According to this contemporary medical theory, behavioral differences result from a prevalence of one of the body's four "humours" (blood, phlegm, black bile, and yellow bile) over the other three; these humours correspond with the four elements of the universe: air, water, fire, and earth. However, the stock types of Latin literature were an equal influence. Jonson therefore tends to create types or caricatures. However, in his best work, characters are "so vitally rendered as to take on a being that transcends the type". Jonson's famous comedy *Volpone* (1605 or 1606)) shows how a group of scammers are fooled by a top con-artist, vice being punished by vice. Other major plays by Jonson are *Epicoene* (1609), *The Alchemist* (1610), and *Bartholomew Fair* (1614).

Others who followed Jonson's style include Beaumont and Fletcher, who wrote the popular comedy, *The Knight of the Burning Pestle* (probably 1607–08), a satire of the rising middle class, especially of those nouveaux riches who pretend to dictate literary taste without knowing much literature at all. In the story, a couple of grocers wrangle with professional actors to have their illiterate son play a leading role in a drama. He becomes a knight-errant wearing, appropriately, a burning pestle on his shield. Seeking to win a princesses' heart, the young man is ridiculed much in the way Don Quixote was. One of Beaumont and Fletcher's skills was that of portraying of how feudalism and chivalry had turned into snobbery and make-believe and that new social classes were on the rise.

Another popular style of theatre during Jacobean times was the revenge play, which was popularized in the Elizabethan era by Thomas Kyd (1558–94), and then further developed later by John Webster (?1578-?1632). Webster's most famous plays are *The White Devil* (1612) and *The Duchess of Malfi* (1613). Other revenge tragedies include *The Changeling* written by Thomas Middleton and William Rowley, *The Atheist's Tragedy* by Cyril Tourneur, first published in 1611, Christopher Marlow's *The Jew of Malta*, *The Revenge of Bussy D'Ambois* by George Chapman, *The Malcontent* (ca. 1603) of John Marston and John Ford's *'Tis Pity She's a Whore*. Besides *Hamlet*, Shakespeare's *Titus Andronicus* is a revenge tragedy.

George Chapman (?1559-?1634) also wrote a couple revenge tragedies, but today he is remembered chiefly for his famous translation in 1616 of Homer's Iliad and Odyssey into English verse. This was the first ever complete translations of either poem into the English language. The translation had a profound influence on English literature and inspired John Keats's famous sonnet "On First Looking into Chapman's Homer" (1816).

The most important prose work of the early 17th century was the King James Bible. This, one of the most massive translation projects in the history of English up to this time, was started in 1604 and completed in 1611. This represents the culmination of a tradition of Bible translation into English that began with the work of William Tyndale, and it became the standard Bible of the Church of England. The project was headed by James I himself, who supervised the work of forty-seven scholars.

Besides Shakespeare and Ben Jonson, the major poets of the early 17th century included the Metaphysical poets: John Donne (1572–1631), George Herbert (1593–1633), Henry Vaughan, Andrew Marvell, and Richard Crashaw. Their style was characterized by wit and metaphysical conceits, that is far-fetched or unusual similes or metaphors, such as in Andrew Marvell's comparison of the soul with a drop of dew, in an expanded epigram format, with the use of simple verse forms, octosyllabic couplets, quatrains or stanzas in which length of line and rhyme scheme enforce the sense. The specific definition of wit which Johnson applied to the school was: "a kind of *discordia concors*; a combination of dissimilar images, or discovery of occult resemblances in things apparently unlike." Their poetry diverged from the style of their times, containing neither images of nature nor allusions to classical mythology, as were common, and there are often allusions to scientific or geographical discoveries. There is also a frequent concern with religious subjects in their poetry

Late Renaissance: 1625–1660

The Metaphysical poets John Donne (1572–1631) and George Herbert (1593–1633 were still alive after 1625, and later in the 17th century a second generation of metaphysical poets were writing, including Richard Crashaw (1613–49), Andrew Marvell (1621–1678), Thomas Traherne (1636 or 1637–1674) and Henry Vaughan (1622–1695). The Cavalier poets were another important group of 17th-century poets, who came from the classes that supported King Charles I during the English Civil War (1642–51). (King Charles reigned from 1625 and was executed 1649). The best known of the Cavalier poets are Robert Herrick, Richard Lovelace, Thomas Carew and Sir John Suckling. They "were not a formal group, but all were influenced by" Ben Jonson. Most of the Cavalier poets were courtiers, with notable exceptions. For example, Robert Herrick was not a courtier, but his style marks him as a Cavalier poet. Cavalier works make use of allegory and classical allusions, and are influence by Latin authors Horace, Cicero and Ovid. John Milton (1608–74) "was the last great poet of the English Renaissance" and published a number of works before 1660, including A *L'Allegro*,1631; *Il Penseroso*, 1634; *Comus* (a masque), 1638; and *Lycidas*, (1638). However, his major epic works, including *Paradise Lost* (1667) were published in the Restoration period.

Neo-Classical Period: 1660–1798

Restoration Age: 1660–1700

Restoration literature includes both *Paradise Lost* and the Earl of Rochester's *Sodom*, the high spirited sexual comedy of *The Country Wife* and the moral wisdom of *Pilgrim's Progress*. It saw Locke's *Two Treatises on Government*, the founding of the Royal Society, the experiments and the holy meditations of Robert Boyle, the hysterical attacks on theatres from Jeremy Collier, the pioneering of literary criticism from Dryden, and the first newspapers. The official break in literary culture caused by censorship and radically moralist standards under Cromwell's Puritan regime created a gap in literary tradition, allowing a seemingly fresh start for all forms of literature after the Restoration. During the Interregnum, the royalist forces attached to the court of Charles I went into exile with the twenty-year-old Charles II. The nobility who travelled with Charles II were therefore lodged for over a decade in the midst of the continent's literary scene. Charles spent his time attending plays in France, and he developed a taste for Spanish plays. Those nobles living in Holland began to learn about mercantile exchange as well as the tolerant, rationalist prose debates that circulated in that officially tolerant nation.

John Milton is one of the greatest English poets, wrote at this time of religious flux and political upheaval. Milton best known for his epic poem Paradise Lost (1671). Among other important poems are: *L'Allegro*,1631; *Il Penseroso* 1634; *Comus* (a masque), 1638; *Lycidas*; *Paradise Regained*, 1671; Samson Agonistes, 1671. Milton's poetry and prose reflect deep personal convictions, a passion for freedom and self-determination, and the urgent issues and political turbulence of his day. Writing in English, Latin, and Italian, he achieved international renown within his lifetime, and his celebrated Areopagitica, written in condemnation of pre-publication censorship, is among history's most influential and impassioned defenses of free speech and freedom of the press. William Hayley's 1796 biography called him the "greatest English author", and he remains generally regarded "as one of the preeminent writers in the English language".

The largest and most important poetic form of the era was satire. In general, publication of satire was done anonymously. There were great dangers in being associated with a satire. On the one hand, defamation law was a wide net, and it was difficult for a satirist to avoid prosecution if he were proven to have written a piece that seemed to criticize a noble. On the other hand, wealthy individuals would respond to satire as often as not by having the suspected poet physically attacked by ruffians. John Dryden was set upon for being merely *suspected* of having written the *Satire on Mankind*. A consequence of this anonymity is that a great many poems, some of them of merit, are unpublished and largely unknown.

John Dryden (1631–1700) was an influential English poet, literary critic, translator, and playwright who dominated the literary life of Restoration England to such a point that the period came to be known in literary circles as the Age of Dryden. He established the heroic couplet as a standard form of English poetry by writing successful satires, religious pieces, fables, epigrams, compliments, prologues, and plays with it; he also introduced the alexandrine and triplet into the form. In his poems, translations, and criticism, he established a poetic diction appropriate to the heroic couplet. Dryden's greatest achievements were in satiric verse in works like the mock-heroic *MacFlecknoe* (1682). W. H. Auden referred to him as "the master of the middle style" that was a model for his contemporaries and for much of the 18th century. The considerable loss felt by the English literary community at his death was evident from the elegies that it inspired. Alexander Pope (1688–1744) was heavily influenced by Dryden, and often borrowed from him; other writers in the 18th century were equally influenced by both Dryden and Pope. Though Ben Jonson had been poet laureate to James I, this was not then a formal position and the formal title of Poet Laureate, as a royal office, was first conferred by letters patent on John Dryden in 1670. The post then became a regular British institution.

Prose in the Restoration period is dominated by Christian religious writing, but the Restoration also saw the beginnings of two genres that would dominate later periods: fiction and journalism. Religious writing often strayed into political and economic writing, just as political and economic writing implied or directly addressed religion. The Restoration was also the time when John Locke wrote many of his philosophical works. Locke's empiricism was an attempt at understanding the basis of human understanding itself and thereby devising a proper manner for making sound decisions.

These same scientific methods led Locke to his two *Treatises on Government*, which later inspired the thinkers in the American Revolution. As with his work on understanding, Locke moves from the most basic units of society toward the more elaborate, and, like Thomas Hobbes, he emphasizes the plastic nature of the social contract. For an age that had seen absolute monarchy overthrown, democracy attempted, democracy corrupted, and limited monarchy restored, only a flexible basis for government could be satisfying.

The Restoration moderated most of the more strident sectarian writing, but radicalism persisted after the Restoration. Puritan authors such as John Milton were forced to retire from public life or adapt, and those Digger, Fifth Monarchist, Leveller, Quaker, and Anabaptist authors who had preached against monarchy and who had participated directly in the regicide of Charles I were partially suppressed. Consequently, violent writings were forced underground, and many of those who had served in the Interregnum attenuated their positions in the Restoration. John Bunyan stands out beyond other religious authors of the period. Bunyan's *The Pilgrim's Progress* is an allegory of personal salvation and a guide to the Christian life. Instead of any focus on eschatology or divine retribution, Bunyan instead writes about how the individual saint can prevail against the temptations of mind and body that threaten damnation. The book is written in a straightforward narrative and shows influence from both drama and biography, and yet it also shows an awareness of the grand allegorical tradition found in Edmund Spenser. During the Restoration period, the most common manner of getting news would have been a broadsheet publication.

A single, large sheet of paper might have a written, usually partisan, account of an event. However, the period saw the beginnings of the first professional and periodical (meaning that the publication was regular) journalism in England. Journalism develops late, generally around the time of William of Orange's claiming the throne in 1689. Coincidentally or by design, England began to have newspapers just when William came to court from Amsterdam, where there were already newspapers being published. It is impossible to satisfactorily date the beginning of the novel in English. However, long fiction and fictional biographies began to distinguish themselves from other forms in England during the Restoration period. An existing tradition of *Romance* fiction in France and Spain was popular in England. The "Romance" was considered a feminine form, and women were taxed with reading "novels" as a vice. One of the most significant figures in the rise of the novel in the Restoration period is Aphra Behn. She was not only the first professional female novelist, but she may be among the first professional novelists of either sex in England. Behn's most famous novel was *Oroonoko* in 1688. This was a biography of an entirely fictional African king who had been enslaved in Suriname. Behn's novels show the influence of tragedy and her experiences as a dramatist.

As soon as the previous Puritan regime's ban on public stage representations was lifted, the drama recreated itself quickly and abundantly. The most famous plays of the early Restoration period are the unsentimental or "hard" comedies of John Dryden, William Wycherley, and George Etherege, which reflect the atmosphere at Court, and celebrate an aristocratic macho lifestyle of unremitting sexual intrigue and conquest. After a sharp drop in both quality and quantity in the 1680s, the mid-1690s saw a brief second flowering of the drama, especially comedy. Comedies like William Congreve's *The Way of the World* (1700), and John Vanbrugh's *The Relapse* (1696) and *The Provoked Wife* (1697) were "softer" and more middle-class in ethos, very different from the aristocratic extravaganza twenty years earlier, and aimed at a wider audience. The playwrights of the 1690s set out to appeal to more socially mixed audiences with a strong middle-class element, and to female spectators, for instance by moving the war between the sexes from the arena of intrigue into that of marriage. The focus in comedy is less on young lovers outwitting the older generation, more on marital relations.

Augustan literature (1700–1750)

During the 18th century literature reflected the worldview of the Age of Enlightenment (or Age of Reason): a rational and scientific approach to religious, social, political, and economic issues that promoted a secular view of the world and a general sense of progress and perfectibility. Led by the philosophers who were inspired by the discoveries of the previous century by people like Isaac Newton and the writings of Descartes, John Locke and Francis Bacon. They sought to discover and to act upon universally valid principles governing humanity, nature, and society. They variously attacked spiritual and scientific authority, dogmatism, intolerance, censorship, and economic and social restraints. They considered the state the proper and rational instrument of progress. The extreme rationalism and skepticism of the age led naturally to deism; the same qualities played a part in bringing the later reaction of romanticism. The Encyclopédie of Denis Diderot epitomized the spirit of the age.

The term Augustan literature derives from authors of the 1720s and 1730s themselves, who responded to a term that George I of England preferred for himself. While George I meant the title to reflect his might, they instead saw in it a reflection of Ancient Rome's transition from rough and ready literature to highly political and highly polished literature. Because of the aptness of the metaphor, the period from 1689 to 1750 was called "the Augustan Age" by critics throughout the 18th century (including Voltaire and Oliver Goldsmith). The literature of the period is overtly political and thoroughly aware of critical dictates for literature. It is an age of exuberance and scandal, of enormous energy and inventiveness and outrage, that reflected an era when English, Scottish, and Irish people found themselves in the midst of an expanding economy, lowering barriers to education, and the stirrings of the Industrial Revolution.

It was during this time that poet James Thomson (1700–48) produced his melancholy *The Seasons* (1728–30) and Edward Young (1681–1765) wrote his poem *Night Thoughts* (1742), though the most outstanding poet of the age is Alexander Pope (1688–1744). It is also the era that saw a serious competition over the proper model for the pastoral. In criticism, poets struggled with a doctrine of *decorum*, of matching proper words with proper sense and of achieving a diction that matched the gravity of a subject. At the same time, the mock-heroic was at its zenith. Pope's *Rape of the Lock* (1712–17) and *The Dunciad* (1728–43) are still the greatest mock-heroic poems ever written. Pope also translated the *Iliad* (1715–20) and the *Odyssey* (1725–26). Since his death, Pope has been in a constant state of re-evaluation. His high artifice, strict prosody, and, at times, the sheer cruelty of his satire were an object of derision for the Romantic poets, and it was not until the 1930s that his reputation was revived. Pope is now considered the dominant poetic voice of his century, a model of prosodic elegance, biting wit, and an enduring, demanding moral force.

In prose, the earlier part of the period was overshadowed by the development of the English essay. Joseph Addison and Richard Steele's *The Spectator* established the form of the British periodical essay, inventing the pose of the detached observer of human life who can meditate upon the world without advocating any specific changes in it. Periodical essays bloomed into journalistic writings; such as Samuel Johnson's "Reports of the Debates of the Senate of Lilliput", titled to disguise the actual proceeding of parliament as it was illegal for any Parliamentary Reports to be reproduced in print. However, this was also the time when the English novel, first emerging in the Restoration, developed into a major art form. Daniel Defoe turned from journalism and writing criminal lives for the press to writing fictional criminal lives with *Roxana* and *Moll Flanders.* He also wrote a fictional treatment of the travels of Alexander Selkirk called *Robinson Crusoe* (1719). The novel would benefit indirectly from a tragedy of the stage, and in mid-century many more authors would begin to write novels.

If Addison and Steele were dominant in one type of prose, then Jonathan Swift was in another. Swift's prose style is unmannered and direct, with a clarity that few contemporaries matched. He was a profound skeptic about the modern world, but he was similarly profoundly distrustful of nostalgia. He saw in history a record of lies and vanity, and he saw in the present a madness of vanity and lies. He believed that Christian values were essential, but these values had to be muscular and assertive and developed by constant rejection of the games of confidence men and their gulls. Swift's *A Tale of a Tub* announced his skeptical analysis of the claims of the modern world, and his later prose works, such as his war with Patridge the astrologer, and most of all his attacks on pride in *Gulliver's Travels,* only left safe the individual who was in constant fear and humility. After his "exile" to Ireland, Swift reluctantly began defending the Irish people from the predations of colonialism. His *A Modest Proposal* and the Drapier Letters provoked riots and arrests, but Swift, who had no love of Irish Roman Catholics, was outraged by the abuses and barbarity he saw around him.

Drama in the early part of the period featured the last plays of John Vanbrugh and William Congreve, both of whom carried on the Restoration comedy with some alterations. However, the majority of stagings were of lower farces and much more serious and domestic tragedies. George Lillo and Richard Steele both produced highly moral forms of tragedy, where the characters and the concerns of the characters were wholly middle class or working class. This reflected a marked change in the audience for plays, as royal patronage was no longer the important part of theatrical success. Additionally, Colley Cibber and John Rich began to battle each other for greater and greater spectacles to present on stage. The figure of Harlequin was introduced, and pantomime theatre began to be staged. This "low" comedy was quite popular, and the plays became tertiary to the staging. Opera also began to be popular in London, and there was significant literary resistance to this Italian incursion. This trend was broken only by a few attempts at a new type of comedy. Pope and John Arbuthnot and John Gay attempted a play entitled *Three Hours After Marriage* that failed. In 1728, however, John Gay returned to the playhouse with *The Beggar's Opera.* Gay's opera was in English and retold the story of Jack Sheppard and Jonathan Wild. However, it seemed to be an allegory based on Robert Walpole and the directors of the South Sea Company, and so Gay's follow up opera was banned without a performance. The Licensing Act 1737 brought an abrupt halt to much of the period's drama, as the theatres were once again brought under state control.

An effect of the Licensing Act of 1737 was to cause more than one aspiring playwright to switch over to writing novels. Henry Fielding (1707–54) began to write prose satire and novels after his plays could not pass the censors. In the interim, Samuel Richardson (1689–1761) had produced a novel intended to counter the deleterious effects of novels in *Pamela, or Virtue Rewarded* (1740). Henry Fielding attacked the absurdity of this novel with two of his own works, *Joseph Andrews* (1742) and *Shamela,* and then countered Richardson's *Clarissa* (1748) with *Tom Jones* (1749). Tobias Smollett (1721–71) elevated the picaresque novel with works such as Roderick Random (1748) and Peregrine Pickle (1751). Each of these novels represents a formal and thematic divergence from the others. Each novelist was in dialogue and competition with the others, and, in a sense, the novel established itself as a diverse and open-formed genre in this explosion of creativity. The most lasting effects of the experimentation would be the psychological realism of Richardson, the bemused narrative voice of Fielding.

Age of sensibility: 1750–1798

This period is also sometimes described as the "Age of Johnson". Samuel Johnson (1709–1784), often referred to as Dr Johnson, was an English author who made lasting contributions to English literature as a poet, essayist, moralist, literary critic, biographer, editor and lexicographer. Johnson has been described as "arguably the most distinguished man of letters in English history". He is also the subject of "the most famous single work of biographical art in the whole of literature": James Boswell's *Life of Samuel Johnson* (1791). His early works include the poems "London" and "his most impressive poem" "The Vanity of Human Wishes" (1749). Both poems are modelled on Juvenal's satires. After nine years of work, Johnson's *A Dictionary of the English Language* was published in 1755; it had a far-reaching effect on Modern English and has been described as "one of the greatest single achievements of scholarship." This work brought Johnson popularity and success. Until the completion of the *Oxford English Dictionary* 150 years later, Johnson's was viewed as the pre-eminent British dictionary. His later works included essays, an influential annotated edition of William Shakespeare's plays (1765), and the widely read tale *Rasselas* (1759). In 1763, he befriended James Boswell, with whom he later travelled to Scotland; Johnson described their travels in *A Journey to the Western Islands of Scotland* (1786). Towards the end of his life, he produced the massive and influential *Lives of the Most Eminent English Poets* (1779–81), a collection of biographies and evaluations of 17th- and 18th-century poets. Through works such as the "Dictionary, his edition of Shakespeare, and his *Lives of the Poets* in particular, he helped invent what we now call English Literature".

The second half of the 18th century saw the emergence of three major Irish authors Oliver Goldsmith (1728–1774), Richard Brinsley Sheridan (1751–1816) and Laurence Sterne (1713–68). Goldsmith settled in London in 1756, where he published the novel *The Vicar of Wakefield* (1766), a pastoral poem *The Deserted Village* (1770) and two plays, *The Good-Natur'd Man* 1768 and *She Stoops to Conquer* 1773. This latter was a huge success and is still regularly revived. Sheridan was born in Dublin into a family with a strong literary and theatrical tradition. The family moved to England in the 1750s. His first play, *The Rivals* 1775, was performed at Covent Garden and was an instant success. He went on to become the most significant London playwright of the late 18th century with plays like *The School for Scandal* and *The Critic*. Both Goldsmith and Sheridan reacted against the sentimental comedy of the 18th-century theatre, writing plays closer to the style of Restoration comedy. Sterne published his famous novel *Tristram Shandy* in parts between 1759 and 1767.

The sentimental novel or the novel of sensibility is a genre which developed during the second half of the 18th century. It celebrates the emotional and intellectual concepts of sentiment, sentimentalism, and sensibility. Sentimentalism, which is to be distinguished from sensibility, was a fashion in both poetry and prose fiction beginning in the eighteenth century in reaction to the rationalism of the Augustan Age. Sentimental novels relied on emotional response, both from their readers and characters. They feature scenes of distress and tenderness, and the plot is arranged to advance emotions rather than action. The result is a valorization of "fine feeling," displaying the characters as a model for refined, sensitive emotional effect. The ability to display feelings was thought to show character and experience, and to shape social life and relations. Among the most famous sentimental novels in English are Samuel Richardson's *Pamela, or Virtue Rewarded* (1740), Oliver Goldsmith's *Vicar of Wakefield* (1766), Laurence Sterne's *Tristram Shandy* (1759–67), *Sentimental Journey* (1768), Henry Brooke's *The Fool of Quality* (1765–70), Henry Mackenzie's *The Man of Feeling* (1771) and Maria Edgeworth's *Castle Rackrent* (1800).

Another novel genre also developed in this period. In 1778, Frances Burney (1752–1840) wrote *Evelina*, one of the first novels of manners. Social behaviour in public and private settings accounts for much of the plot of *Evelina*. This is mirrored in other novels that were particularly popular at the beginning of the 19th century, especially those of Jane Austen. Fanny Burney's novels indeed "were enjoyed and sadmired by Jane Austen".

The Romantic movement in English literature of the early 19th century has its roots in 18th-century poetry, the Gothic novel and the novel of sensibility. This includes the graveyard poets, who were a number of pre-Romantic English poets, writing in the 1740s and later, whose works are characterised by their gloomy meditations on mortality, "skulls and coffins, epitaphs and worms" in the context of the graveyard. To this was added, by later practitioners, a feeling for the 'sublime' and uncanny, and an interest in ancient English poetic forms and folk poetry. They are often considered precursors of the Gothic genre. The poets include; Thomas Gray (1716–71), whose *Elegy Written in a Country Churchyard* (1751) is "the best known product of this kind of sensibility"; William Cowper (1731–1800); Christopher Smart (1722–71); Thomas Chatterton (1752–70); Robert Blair (1699–1746), author of *The Grave* (1743), "which celebrates the horror of death"; and Edward Young (1683–1765), whose *The Complaint, or Night Thoughts on Life, Death and Immortality* (1742–45), is another "noted example of the graveyard genre". Other precursors of Romanticism are the poets James Thomson (1700–48) and James Macpherson (1736–96).

James Macpherson (1736–96) was the first Scottish poet to gain an international reputation. Claiming to have found poetry written by the ancient bard Ossian, he published translations that acquired international popularity, being proclaimed as a Celtic equivalent of the Classical epics. *Fingal,* written in 1762, was speedily translated into many European languages, and its appreciation of natural beauty and treatment of the ancient legend has been credited more than any single work with bringing about the Romantic movement in European, and especially in German literature, through its influence on Johann Gottfried von Herder and Johann Wolfgang von Goethe. It was also popularised in France by figures that included Napoleon. Eventually it became clear that the poems were not direct translations from the Gaelic, but flowery adaptations made to suit the aesthetic expectations of his audience. Both Robert Burns (1759–96) and Walter Scott (1771–1832) were highly influenced by the Ossian cycle.

Significant foreign influences were the Germans Goethe, Schiller and August Wilhelm Schlegel and French philosopher and writer Jean-Jacques Rousseau (1712–78). Edmund Burke's *A Philosophical Enquiry into the Origin of Our Ideas of the Sublime and Beautiful* (1757) is another important influence. The changing landscape, brought about by the industrial and agricultural revolutions, with the expansion of the city and depopulation of the countryside, was another influence on the growth of the Romantic movement in Britain. The poor condition of workers, the new class conflicts and the pollution of the environment, led to a reaction against urbanism and industrialization and a new emphasis on the beauty and value of nature.

During the end of the 18th century, Horace Walpole's 1764 novel *The Castle of Otranto*, created the Gothic fiction genre, that combines elements of horror and romance. The pioneering gothic novelist Ann Radcliffe introduced the brooding figure of the gothic villain which developed into the Byronic hero. Her most popular and influential work *The Mysteries of Udolpho* 1795, is frequently cited as the archetypal Gothic novel. *Vathek* 1786 by William Beckford, and *The Monk* 1796 by Matthew Lewis, were further notable early works in both the gothic and horror literary genres. The first short stories in the United Kingdom were gothic tales like Richard Cumberland's "remarkable narrative" "The Poisoner of Montremos" (1791).

19TH-CENTURY LITERATURE

Romanticism (1798–1837)

Romanticism was an artistic, literary, and intellectual movement that originated in Europe toward the end of the 18th century. Various dates are given for the Romantic period in British literature, but here the publishing of *Lyrical Ballads* in 1798 is taken as the beginning, and the crowning of Queen Victoria in 1837 as its end, even though, for example, William

Wordsworth lived until 1850 and both Robert Burns and William Blake published before 1798. The writers of this period, however, "did not think of themselves as 'Romantics' ", and the term was first used by critics of the Victorian period. Romanticism arrived later in other parts of the English-speaking world.

The Romantic period was one of major social change in England, because of the depopulation of the countryside and the rapid development of overcrowded industrial cities, that took place in the period roughly between 1750 and 1850. The movement of so many people in England was the result of two forces: the Agricultural Revolution, that involved the Enclosure of the land, drove workers off the land, and the Industrial Revolution which provided them employment, "in the factories and mills, operated by machines driven by steam-power". Indeed Romanticism may be seen in part as a reaction to the Industrial Revolution, though it was also a revolt against aristocratic social and political norms of the Age of Enlightenment, as well a reaction against the scientific rationalization of nature. The French Revolution was an especially important influence on the political thinking of many of the Romantic poets.

The landscape is often prominent in the poetry of this period, so that it the Romantics, especially perhaps Wordsworth, are often described as 'nature poets'. However, the longer Romantic 'nature poems' have a wider concern because they are usually meditations on "an emotional problem or personal crisis".

Robert Burns (1759–1796) was a pioneer of the Romantic movement, and after his death he became a cultural icon in Scotland. As well as writing poems, Burns also collected folk songs from across Scotland, often revising or adapting them. His *Poems, chiefly in the Scottish Dialect* was published in 1786. Among poems and songs of Burns that remain well known across the world are, "Auld Lang Syne", "A Red, Red Rose", "A Man's A Man for A' That", "To a Louse", "To a Mouse", "The Battle of Sherramuir", "Tam o' Shanter" and "Ae Fond Kiss".

The poet, painter, and printmaker William Blake (1757–1827) was another the early Romantic poets. Largely disconnected from the major streams of the literature of the time, Blake was generally unrecognised during his lifetime, but is now considered a seminal figure in the history of both the poetry and visual arts of the Romantic Age. Considered mad by contemporaries for his idiosyncratic views, Blake is held in high regard by later critics for his expressiveness and creativity, and for the philosophical and mystical undercurrents within his work. Among his most important works are *Songs of Innocence* (1789) and *Songs of Experience* (1794) "and profound and difficult 'prophecies' " such as *Visions of the Daughters of Albion* (1793), *The First Book of Urizen* (1794), *Milton* (1804–?11), and "Jerusalem: the Emanation of the Giant Albion" (1804–?20).

After Blake, among the earliest Romantics were the Lake Poets, a small group of friends, including William Wordsworth (1770–1850), Samuel Taylor Coleridge (1772–1834), Robert Southey (1774–1843) and journalist Thomas de Quincey (1785–1859). However, at the time Walter Scott (1771–1832) was the most famous poet. Scott achieved immediate success with his long narrative poem *The Lay of the Last Minstrel* in 1805, followed by the full epic poem *Marmion* in 1808. Both were set in the distant Scottish past.

The early Romantic Poets brought a new emotionalism and introspection, and their emergence is marked by the first romantic manifesto in English literature, the "Preface" to *Lyrical Ballads* (1798). In it Wordsworth discusses what he sees as the elements of a new type of poetry, one based on the "real language of men", and which avoids the poetic diction of much 18th-century poetry. Here, Wordsworth gives his famous definition of poetry, as "the spontaneous overflow of powerful feelings" which "takes its origin from emotion recollected in tranquility." The poems in *Lyrical Ballads* were mostly by Wordsworth, though Coleridge contributed, one of the great poems of English literature, the long "Rime of the Ancient Mariner", a tragic ballad about the survival of one sailor through a series of supernatural events on his voyage through the South

Seas, and which involves the symbolically significant slaying of an albatross. Coleridge is also especially remembered for "Kubla Khan", "Frost at Midnight", "Dejection: an Ode", "Christabel", as well as the major prose work *Biographia Literaria*.

His critical work, especially on Shakespeare, was highly influential, and he helped introduce German idealist philosophy to English-speaking culture. Coleridge and Wordsworth, along with Carlyle, were a major influence, through Emerson, on American transcendentalism. Among Wordsworth's most important poems, are "Michael", "Lines Composed a Few Miles Above Tintern Abbey", "Resolution and Independence", "Ode: Intimations of Immortality from Recollections of Early Childhood" and the long, autobiographical, epic *The Prelude*. *The Prelude* was begun in 1799 but published posthumously in 1850. Wordsworth's poetry is noteworthy for how he "inverted the traditional hierarchy of poetic genres, subjects, and style by elevating humble and rustic life and the plain [...] into the main subject and medium of poetry in general", and how, in Coleridge's words, he awakens in the reader "freshness of sensation" in his depiction of familiar, commonplace objects.

Robert Southey (1774–1843) was another of the so-called "Lake Poets", and Poet Laureate for 30 years from 1813 to his death in 1843. Although his fame has been long eclipsed by that of his contemporaries and friends William Wordsworth and Samuel Taylor Coleridge. Thomas De Quincey (1785–1859) was an English essayist, best known for his *Confessions of an English Opium-Eater* (1821), an autobiographical account of his laudanum use and its effect on his life. William Hazlitt (1778–1830), friend of both Coleridge and Wordsworth, is another important essayist at this time, though today he is best known for his literary criticism, especially *Characters of Shakespeare's Plays* (1817–18).

The second generation of Romantic poets includes Lord Byron (1788–1824), Percy Bysshe Shelley (1792–1822) and John Keats (1795–1821). Byron, however, was still influenced by 18th-century satirists and was, perhaps the least 'romantic' of the three, preferring "the brilliant wit of Pope to what he called the 'wrong poetical system' of his Romantic contemporaries". Byron achieved enormous fame and influence throughout Europe with works exploiting the violence and drama of their exotic and historical settings. Goethe called Byron "undoubtedly the greatest genius of our century". A trip to Europe resulted in the first two cantos of Childe Harold's Pilgrimage (1812), a mock-heroic epic of a young man's adventures in Europe, but also a sharp satire against London society. The poem contains elements thought to be autobiographical, as Byron generated some of the storyline from experience gained during his travels between 1809 and 1811.

However, despite the success of *Childe Harold* and other works, Byron was forced to leave England for good in 1816 and seek asylum on the Continent, because, among other things, of his alleged incestuous affair with his half-sister Augusta Leigh. Here he joined Percy Bysshe and Mary Shelley, with his secretary John William Polidori on the shores of Lake Geneva, during the 'year without a summer'. Polidori's *The Vampyre* was published in 1819, creating the literary vampire genre. This short story was inspired by the life of Lord Byron and his poem *The Giaour* (1813). Between 1819 and 1824 Byron published his unfinished epic satire *Don Juan*, which, though initially condemned by the critics, "was much admired by Goethe who translated part of it".

Shelley is perhaps best known for poems such as *Ozymandias, Ode to the West Wind, To a Skylark, Music, When Soft Voices Die, The Cloud, The Masque of Anarchy* and *Adonaïs*, an elegy written on the death of Keats. Shelley's early profession of atheism, in the tract "The Necessity of Atheism", led to his expulsion from Oxford, and branded him as a radical agitator and thinker, setting an early pattern of marginalization and ostracism from the intellectual and political circles of his time. His close circle of admirers, however, included the most progressive thinkers of the day, including his future father-in-law, philosopher William Godwin. A work like *Queen Mab* (1813) reveal Shelley, "as the direct heir to the French and British revolutionary intellectuals of the 1790s. Shelley became an idol of the next three or four generations of poets, including important Victorian and Pre-Raphaelite poets such as Robert Browning, and Dante Gabriel Rossetti, as well as later W. B. Yeats. Shelley's influential poem *The Masque of Anarchy* (1819) calls for nonviolence in protest and political action. It is perhaps the first modern statement of the principle of nonviolent protest. Mahatma Gandhi's passive resistance was influenced and inspired by Shelley's verse, and Gandhi would often quote the poem to vast audiences.

Mary Shelley (1797–1851) is remembered as the author of *Frankenstein* (1818). The plot of this is said to have come from a waking dream she had, in the company of Percy Shelley, Lord Byron, and John Polidori, following a conversation about galvanism and the feasibility of returning a corpse or assembled body parts to life, and on the experiments of the 18th-century natural philosopher and poet Erasmus Darwin, who was said to have animated dead matter. Sitting around a log fire at Byron's villa, the company also amused themselves by reading German ghost stories, prompting Byron to suggest they each write their own supernatural tale.

Though John Keats shared Byron and Shelley's radical politics, "his best poetry is not political", but is especially noted for its sensuous music and imagery, along with a concern with material beauty and the transience of life. Among his most famous works are: "The Eve of St Agnes", "Ode to Psyche", "La Belle Dame sans Merci", "Ode to a Nightingale", "Ode on a Grecian Urn", "Ode on Melancholy", "To Autumn" and the incomplete *Hyperion*, a 'philosophical' poem in blank verse, which was "conceived on the model of Milton's *Paradise Lost* ". Keats' letters "are among the finest in English" and important "for their discussion of his aesthetic ideas", including 'negative capability' ". Keats has always been regarded as a major Romantic, "and his stature as a poet has grown steadily through all changes of fashion".

Another important poet in this period was John Clare (1793–1864), Clare was the son of a farm labourer, who came to be known for his celebratory representations of the English countryside and his lamentation for the changes taking place in rural England. His poetry underwent a major re-evaluation in the late 20th century and he is often now considered to be among the most important 19th-century poets. His biographer Jonathan Bate states that Clare was "the greatest labouring-class poet that England has ever produced. No one has ever written more powerfully of nature, of a rural childhood, and of the alienated and unstable self".

George Crabbe (1754–1832) was an English poet who, during the Romantic period, wrote "closely observed, realistic portraits of rural life [...] in the heroic couplets of the Augustan age". Lord Byron who was an admirer of Crabbe's poetry, described him as "nature's sternest painter, yet the best". Modern critic Frank Whitehead has said that "Crabbe, in his verse tales in particular, is an important–indeed, a major–poet whose work has been and still is seriously undervalued." Crabbe's works include *The Village* (1783), *Poems* (1807), *The Borough* (1810), and his poetry collections *Tales* (1812) and *Tales of the Hall* (1819).

One of the most popular novelist of the era was Sir Walter Scott, whose historical romances inspired a generation of painters, composers, and writers throughout Europe, including Franz Schubert, Felix Mendelssohn and J. M. W. Turner. His novels also inspired many operas, of which the most famous are *Lucia di Lammermoor* (1835) by Donizetti and Bizet's, *La jolie fille de Perth, The Fair Maid of Perth* (1867). Scott's novel-writing career was launched in 1814 with *Waverley*, often called the first historical novel, and was followed by *Ivanhoe*. His popularity in England and further abroad did much to form the modern stereotype of Scottish culture. The Waverley Novels, including *The Antiquary, Old Mortality, The Heart of Midlothian*, are now generally regarded as Scott's masterpieces.

Jane Austen's works critique the novels of sensibility of the second half of the 18th century and are part of the transition to 19th-century realism. Her plots, though fundamentally comic, highlight the dependence of women on marriage to secure social standing and economic security. Austen brings to light the hardships women faced, who usually did not inherit money, could not work and where their only chance in life depended on the man they married. She reveals not only the difficulties women faced in her day, but also what was expected of men and of the careers they had to follow. This she does with wit and humour and with endings where all characters, good or bad, receive exactly what they deserve. Her work brought her little personal fame and only a few positive reviews during her lifetime, but the publication in 1869 of her nephew's *A Memoir of Jane Austen* introduced her to a wider public, and by the 1940s she had become accepted as a major writer. The second half of the 20th century saw a proliferation of Austen scholarship and the emergence of a Janeite fan culture. Austen's works include *Sense and Sensibility* (1811), *Pride and Prejudice* (1813), *Mansfield Park*(1814), *Emma* (1815), *Northanger Abbey* (1817) and *Persuasion* (1817).

Romanticism in America

The European Romantic movement reached America in the early 19th century. American Romanticism was just as multifaceted and individualistic as it was in Europe. Like the Europeans, the American Romantics demonstrated a high level of moral enthusiasm, commitment to individualism and the unfolding of the self, an emphasis on intuitive perception, and the assumption that the natural world was inherently good, while human society was filled with corruption. Romanticism became popular in American politics, philosophy and art. The movement appealed to the revolutionary spirit of America as well as to those longing to break free of the strict religious traditions of early settlement. The Romantics rejected rationalism and religious intellect. It appealed to those in opposition of Calvinism, which includes the belief that the destiny of each individual is preordained.

Romantic Gothic literature made an early appearance with Washington Irving's *The Legend of Sleepy Hollow* (1820) and *Rip Van Winkle* (1819), There are picturesque "local color" elements in Washington Irving's essays and especially his travel books. From 1823 the prolific and popular novelist James Fenimore Cooper (1789–1851) began publishing his historical romances of frontier and Indian life, to create a unique form of American literature. Cooper is best remembered for his numerous sea-stories and the historical novels known as the *Leatherstocking Tales,* with their emphasis on heroic simplicity and their fervent landscape descriptions of an already-exotic mythicized frontier peopled by "noble savages", exemplified by Uncas, from *The Last of the Mohicans* (1826) show the influence of Rousseau's (1712–78) philosophy. Edgar Allan Poe's tales of the macabre that first appeared in the early 1830s, and his balladic poetry were more influential in France than at home.

The Romantic movement in America continued well into the 19th-century and writers like Hawthorne and Melville are discussed in the next section.

VICTORIAN LITERATURE (1837–1901)

Also American literature (sections 4–6)

The Victorian novel

It was in the Victorian era (1837–1901) that the novel became the leading literary genre in English. Women played an important part in this rising popularity both as authors and as readers. Monthly serializing of fiction encouraged this surge in popularity, due to a combination of the rise of literacy, technological advances in printing, and improved economics of distribution. Charles Dickens' *Pickwick Papers,* was published in twenty parts between April 1836 and November 1837. Both Dickens and Thackeray frequently published this way. However, the standard practice of publishing three volume editions continued until the end of the 19th century. Circulating libraries, that allowed books to be borrowed for an annual subscription, were a further factor in the rising popularity of the novel.

The 1830s and 1840s saw the rise of social novel, that "arose out of the social and political upheavals which followed the Reform Act of 1832". This was in many ways a reaction to rapid industrialization, and the social, political and economic issues associated with it, and was a means of commenting on abuses of government and industry and the suffering of the poor, who were not profiting from England's economic prosperity. Stories of the working class poor were directed toward middle class to help create sympathy and promote change. An early example is Charles Dickens' *Oliver Twist* (1837–38). Other significant early example of this genre are *Sybil, or The Two Nations*, a novel by Benjamin Disraeli (1804–81) and Charles Kingsley's (1819–75) Alton Locke (1849).

Charles Dickens (1812–70) emerged on the literary scene in the late 1830s and soon became probably the most famous novelist in the history of English literature. One of his most popular works to this day is *A Christmas Carol* (1843). Dickens fiercely satirized various aspects of society, including the workhouse in *Oliver Twist*, the failures of the legal system in *Bleak House*, the dehumanizing effect of money in *Dombey and Son* and the influence of the philosophy of utilitarianism in factories, education etc., in *Hard Times*. However some critics have suggested that Dickens' sentimentality blunts the impact of his satire. In more recent years Dickens has been most admired for his later novels, such as *Dombey and Son* (1846–48), *Bleak House* (1852–53) and *Little Dorrit* (1855–57), *Great Expectations* (1860–61), and *Our Mutual Friend* (1864–65). An early rival to Dickens was William Makepeace Thackeray (1811–63), who during the Victorian period ranked second only to him, but he is now much less read and is known almost exclusively for *Vanity Fair* (1847). In that novel he satirizes whole swaths of humanity while retaining a light touch. It features his most memorable character, the engagingly roguish Becky Sharp.

The Brontë sisters, Emily, Charlotte and Anne, were other significant novelists in the 1840s and 1850s. Their novels caused a sensation when they were first published but were subsequently accepted as classics. They had written compulsively from early childhood and were first published, at their own expense, in 1846 as poets under the pseudonyms Currer, Ellis and Acton Bell. The following year the three sisters each published a novel. Charlotte Brontë's (1816–55) work was *Jane Eyre*, which is written in an innovative style that combines naturalism with gothic melodrama, and broke new ground in being written from an intensely first-person female perspective. Emily Brontë's (1818–48) novel was *Wuthering Heights* and, according to Juliet Gardiner, "the vivid sexual passion and power of its language and imagery impressed, bewildered and appalled reviewers," and led the Victorian public and many early reviewers to think that it had been written by a man. Even though it received mixed reviews when it first came out, and was often condemned for its portrayal of amoral passion, the book subsequently became an English literary classic. The third Brontë novel of 1847 was Anne Brontë's (1820–49) *Agnes Grey*, which deals with the lonely life of a governess. Anne Brontë's second novel, *The Tenant of Wildfell Hall* (1848), is perhaps the most shocking of the Brontës' novels. In seeking to present the truth in literature, Anne's depiction of alcoholism and debauchery was profoundly disturbing to 19th-century sensibilities. Charlotte Brontë's *Shirley* was published in 1849, *Villette* in 1853, and *The Professor* in 1857.

Elizabeth Gaskell (1810–65) was also a successful writer and her first novel, *Mary Barton*, was published anonymously in 1848. Gaskell's *North and South* contrasts the lifestyle in the industrial north of England with the wealthier south. Even though her writing conforms to Victorian conventions, Gaskell usually frames her stories as critiques of contemporary attitudes, and her early works focused on factory work in the Midlands. She always emphasised the role of women, with complex narratives and dynamic female characters.

Anthony Trollope's (1815–82) was one of the most successful, prolific and respected English novelists of the Victorian era. Some of his best-loved works are set in the imaginary west country county of Barsetshire, including *The Warden* (1855) and *Barchester Towers* (1857). Trollope's novels portray the lives of the landowning and professional classes of early Victorian England. Henry James suggested that Trollope's greatest achievement was "great apprehension of the real", and that "what made him so interesting, came through his desire to satisfy us on this point".

George Eliot's (Mary Ann Evans (1819–80) first novel *Adam Bede* was published in 1859, and she was a major novelist of the mid-Victorian period. Her works, especially *Middlemarch* (1871–72), are important examples of literary realism, and are admired for their combination of high Victorian literary detail, with an intellectual breadth that removes them from the narrow geographic confines they often depict, that has led to comparisons with Tolstoy. While her reputation declined somewhat after her death, in the 20th century she was championed by a new breed of critics, most notably by Virginia Woolf, who called *Middlemarch* "one of the few English novels written for grown-up people". Various film and television adaptations of Eliot's books have also introduced her to a wider readership.

George Meredith (1828–1909) is best remembered for his novels *The Ordeal of Richard Fevered* (1859) and *The Egotist* (1879). "His reputation stood very high well into" the 20th-century but then seriously declined.

An interest in rural matters and the changing social and economic situation of the countryside is seen in the novels of Thomas Hardy (1840–1928). A Victorian realist, in the tradition of George Eliot, he was also influenced both in his novels and poetry by Romanticism, especially by William Wordsworth. Charles Darwin is another important influence on Thomas Hardy. Like Charles Dickens he was also highly critical of much in Victorian society, though Hardy focussed more on a declining rural society. While Hardy wrote poetry throughout his life, and regarded himself primarily as a poet, his first collection was not published until 1898, so that initially he gained fame as the author of such novels as, *Far from the Madding Crowd* (1874), *The Mayor of Casterbridge* (1886), *Tess of the d'Urbervilles* (1891), and *Jude the Obscure* (1895). He ceased writing novels following adverse criticism of this last novel. In novels such as *The Mayor of Casterbridge* and *Tess of the d'Urbervilles* Hardy attempts to create modern works in the genre of tragedy, that are modelled on the Greek drama, especially Aeschylus and Sophocles, though in prose, not poetry, fiction, not a play, and with characters of low social standing, not nobility. Another significant late-19th-century novelist is George Robert Gissing (1857–1903), who published 23 novels between 1880 and 1903.

His best known novel is *New Grub Street* (1891). Important developments occurred in genre fiction in this era.

Although pre-dated by John Ruskin's *The King of the Golden River* in 1841, the history of the modern fantasy genre is generally said to begin with George MacDonald, the influential author of *The Princess and the Goblin* and *Phantastes* (1858). William Morris was a popular English poet who also wrote several fantasy novels during the latter part of the 19th century. Wilkie Collins' epistolary novel *The Moonstone* (1868), is generally considered the first detective novel in the English language, while *The Woman in White* is regarded as one of the finest sensation novels. H. G. Wells's (1866–1946) writing career began in the 1890s with science fiction novels like *The Time Machine* (1895), and *The War of the Worlds* (1898) which describes an invasion of late Victorian England by Martians, and Wells is seen, along with Frenchman Jules Verne (1828–1905), as a major figure in the development of the science fiction genre. He also wrote realistic fiction about the lower middle class in novels like *Kipps* (1905) and *The History of Mr Polly* (1910).

American novel (From Romanticism to realism)

By the mid-19th century, the pre-eminence of literature from the British Isles began to be challenged by writers from the former American colonies. This included one of the creators of the new genre of the short story, and inventor of the detective story Edgar Allan Poe (1809–49). A major influence on American writers at this time was Romanticism. The Romantic movement gave rise to New England Transcendentalism, which portrayed a less restrictive relationship between God and Universe. The publication of Ralph Waldo Emerson's 1836 essay *Nature* is usually considered the watershed moment at which transcendentalism became a major cultural movement. The new philosophy presented the individual with a more personal relationship with God. Transcendentalism and Romanticism appealed to Americans in a similar fashion, for both privileged feeling over reason, individual freedom of expression over the restraints of tradition and custom. It often involved a rapturous response to nature. It encouraged the rejection of harsh, rigid

Calvinism, and promised a new blossoming of American culture. Other significant transcendentalists were Henry David Thoreau (1817–1862), the naturalist John Muir, (1838–1914), and Louisa May Alcott (1832–1888) author of *Little Women*.In 1837, the young Nathaniel Hawthorne (1804–1864) collected some of his stories as *Twice-Told Tales*, a volume rich in symbolism and occult incidents. Hawthorne went on to write full-length "romances", quasi-allegorical novels that explore such themes as guilt, pride, and emotional repression in his native New England. The romantic American novel developed fully with Hawthorne's *The Scarlet Letter* (1850), a stark drama of a woman cast out of her community for committing adultery. Hawthorne's fiction had a profound impact on his friend Herman Melville (1819–1891). Melville first made a name for himself by turning material from his seafaring days into exotic and sensational sea narrative novels. Inspired by Hawthorne's focus on allegories and dark psychology, Melville went on to write romances replete with philosophical speculation. In *Moby-Dick* (1851), an adventurous whaling voyage becomes the vehicle for examining such themes as obsession, the nature of evil, and human struggle against the elements. In another important work, the short novel *Billy Budd*, Melville dramatizes the conflicting claims of duty and compassion on board a ship in time of war. His books sold poorly, and he had been long forgotten by the time of his death, but Melville was rediscovered in the early decades of the 20th century. Later Transcendentalist writers are Henry David Thoreau *Walden*, (1854) and poets Walt Whitman and Emily Dickinson. By the 1880s, however, psychological and social realism were competing with Romanticism in the novel.

American realist fiction has its beginnings in the 1870s with the works of Twain, Howell and James.

Mark Twain (the pen name used by Samuel Langhorne Clemens, 1835–1910) was the first major American writer to be born away from the East Coast – in the border state of Missouri. His regional masterpieces were the memoir *Life on the Mississippi* and the novels *Adventures of Tom Sawyer* (1876) and *Adventures of Huckleberry Finn* (1884). Twain's style – influenced by journalism, wedded to the vernacular, direct and unadorned but also highly evocative and irreverently humorous – changed the way Americans write their language. His characters speak like real people and sound distinctively American, using local dialects, newly invented words, and regional accents. William Dean Howells also represented the realist tradition through his novels, including *The Rise of Silas Lapham* (1885). Realism also influenced American drama of the period, in part through the works of Howells but also through the works of such Europeans as Ibsen and Zola.

The most significant American novelist of the late 19th-century was Henry James (1843–1916). Although born in New York City, he spent most of his adult years in England. Many of his novels centre on Americans who live in or travel to Europe. James confronted the Old World-New World dilemma by writing directly about it. The first period of James's fiction, usually considered to have culminated in *The Portrait of a Lady*, concentrated on the contrast between Europe and America. The style of these novels is generally straightforward and, though personally characteristic, well within the norms of 19th-century fiction. *Roderick Hudson* (1875) is a Künstlerroman that traces the development of the title character, an extremely talented sculptor. Although *Roderick Hudson* featured mostly American characters in a European setting, James made the Europe–America contrast even more explicit in his next novel. In fact, the contrast could be considered the leading theme of *The American* (1877). Other works of James first period include *Washington Square* (1880), *The Portrait of a Lady* (1881), and James concluded the first phase of his career with a novel that remains his most popular piece of long fiction. Later works of James second period, that have a more involved, psychological approach, include *The Bostonians* (1886), *The Princess Casamassima* (1886), and *What Maisie Knew* (1897).

Genre fiction

The premier ghost story writer of the 19th century was Sheridan Le Fanu. His works include the macabre mystery novel *Uncle Silas* (1865), and his Gothic novella *Carmilla* (1872), tells the story of a young woman's susceptibility to the attentions of a female vampire. Bram Stoker's horror story *Dracula* (1897), belongs to a number of literary genres, including vampire literature, horror fiction, gothic novel and invasion literature.

Arthur Conan Doyle's Sherlock Holmes is a brilliant London-based "consulting detective", famous for his intellectual prowess. Conan Doyle wrote four novels and fifty-six short stories featuring Holmes, from 1880 up to 1907, with a final case in 1914. All but four Conan Doyle stories are narrated by Holmes' friend, assistant, and biographer, Dr. Watson. The Lost World literary genre was inspired by real stories of archaeological discoveries by imperial adventurers. H. Rider Haggard wrote one of the earliest examples, *King Solomon's Mines*, in 1885. Contemporary European politics and diplomatic manoeuvrings informed Anthony Hope's swashbuckling Ruritanian adventure novel *The Prisoner of Zenda* (1894).

Literature for children developed as a separate genre. Some works become internationally known, such as those of Lewis Carroll, *Alice's Adventures in Wonderland* (1865) and its sequel *Through the Looking-Glass*. Adventure novels, such as those of Robert Louis Stevenson (1850–94), are generally classified as for children. Stevenson's *Strange Case of Dr Jekyll and Mr Hyde* (1886), depicts the dual personality of a kind and intelligent physician who turns into a psychopathic monster after imbibing a drug intended to separate good from evil in a personality. His *Kidnapped* (1886) is a fast-paced historical novel set in the aftermath of the Jacobite rising of 1745, and *Treasure Island* 1883, is the classic pirate adventure. At the end of the Victorian era and leading into the Edwardian era, Beatrix Potter was an author and illustrator, best known for her children's books, which featured animal characters. In her thirties, Potter published the highly successful children's book *The Tale of Peter Rabbit* in 1902. Potter eventually went on to published 23 children's books and become a wealthly woman.

Victorian poetry

The leading poets during the Victorian period were Alfred, Lord Tennyson (1809–1892), Robert Browning (1812–89),

Elizabeth Barrett Browning (1806–61), and Matthew Arnold (1822–88). The poetry of this period was heavily influenced by the Romantics, but also went off in its own directions. Particularly notable was the development of the dramatic monologue, a form used by many poets in this period, but perfected by Browning. Literary criticism in the 20th century gradually drew attention to the links between Victorian poetry and modernism.

Tennyson was Poet Laureate of the United Kingdom during much of Queen Victoria's reign. He was described by T. S. Eliot, as "the greatest master of metrics as well as melancholia", and as having "the finest ear of any English poet since Milton". Browning main achievement was in dramatic monologues such as "My Last Duchess", "Andrea del Sarto" and "The Bishop Orders his Tomb", which were published in his two-volume *Men and Women* in 1855. In his introduction to the Oxford University Press edition of Browning's *Poems 1833–1864*, Ian Jack comments, that Thomas Hardy, Rudyard Kipling, Ezra Pound and T S Eliot "all learned from Browning's exploration of the possibilities of dramatic poetry and of colloquial idiom". Tennyson was also a pioneer in the use of the dramatic monologue, in "The Lotus-Eaters" (1833), "Ulysses" (1842), and '"Tithonus" (1860). While Elizabeth Barrett Browning was the wife of Robert Browning she had established her reputation as a major poet before she met him. Her most famous work is the sequence of 44 sonnets "Sonnets from the Portuguese" published in *Poems* (1850). Matthew Arnold's reputation as a poet has "within the past few decades [...] plunged drastically," and he is best remembered now for his critical works, like *Culture and Anarchy* (1869), and his 1867 poem "Dover Beach". This poem depicts a nightmarish world from which the old religious verities have receded. It is sometimes held up as an early, if not the first, example of the modern sensibility. Arnold was both an admirer and a critic of Romantic poetry, and has been seen as another a bridge between Romanticism and Modernism. In many of his poems can be seen the psychological and emotional conflicts, the uncertainty of purpose, above all the feeling of disunity within oneself or of the individual's estrangement from society which is today called alienation and is thought of as a modern phenomenon. As Kenneth Allott said in 1954: "If a poet can ever teach us to understand what we feel, and how to live with our feelings, then Arnold is a contemporary."

Dante Gabriel Rossetti (1828–1882) was a poet, illustrator, painter and translator. He founded the Pre-Raphaelite Brotherhood in 1848 with William Holman Hunt and John Everett Millais, and was later to be the main inspiration for a second generation of artists and writers influenced by the movement, most notably William Morris and Edward Burne-Jones. Rossetti's art was characterised by its sensuality and its medieval revivalism. Poetry and image are closely entwined in Rossetti's work and he frequently wrote sonnets to accompany his pictures. He also illustrated poems by his sister Christina Rossetti such as *Goblin Market*.

While Arthur Clough (1819–1861) was a more minor figure of this era, he has been described as "a fine poet whose experiments in extending the range of literary language and subject were ahead of his time". Clough has been regarded as one of the most forward-looking English poets of the 19th century, in part due to a sexual frankness that shocked his contemporaries. He often went against the popular religious and social ideals of his day, and his verse is said to have the melancholy and the perplexity of an age of transition, although *Through a Glass Darkly* suggests that he did not lack certain religious beliefs of his own.

George Meredith (1828–1909) was an English novelist and poet, who is remembered for his innovative collection of poems *Modern Love* (1862).

Towards the end of the 19th century, English poets began to take an interest in French Symbolism and Victorian poetry entered a decadent *fin-de-siècle* phase. Two groups of poets emerged in the 1890s, the *Yellow Book* poets who adhered to the tenets of Aestheticism, including Algernon Charles Swinburne, Oscar Wilde and Arthur Symons and the Rhymers' Club group, that included Ernest Dowson, Lionel Johnson and Irishman

William Butler Yeats. Yeats went on to become an important modernist in the 20th century. Also in the 1890s A. E. Housman published at his own expense *A Shropshire Lad*, a cycle of 63 poems, because he could not find a publisher. At first selling slowly, it rapidly became a lasting success, and its appeal to English musicians had helped to make it widely known before World War I, when its themes struck a powerful chord with English readers. *A Shropshire Lad* has been in print continuously since May 1896. The poems are pervaded by deep pessimism and preoccupation with death, without religious consolation. Housman wrote most of them while living in Highgate, London, before ever visiting that part of Shropshire (about thirty miles from his birthplace), which he presented in an idealised pastoral light, as his 'land of lost content'.

The nonsense verse of Edward Lear, along with the novels and poems of Lewis Carroll, is regarded as a precursor of surrealism. In 1846 Lear published *A Book of Nonsense*, a volume of limericks that went through three editions and helped popularise the form. In 1865 *The History of the Seven Families of the Lake Pipple-Popple* was published, and in 1867 his most famous piece of nonsense, *The Owl and the Pussycat*, which he wrote for the children of his patron Edward Stanley, 13th Earl of Derby. Many other works followed. Lewis Carroll's most famous writings are *Alice's Adventures in Wonderland* (1865) and its sequel *Through the Looking-Glass*, as well as the poems "The Hunting of the Snark" and "Jabberwocky".

Writers of comic verse included the dramatist, librettist, poet and illustrator W. S. Gilbert (1836–1911), who is best known for his fourteen comic operas produced in collaboration with the composer Sir Arthur Sullivan, of which the most famous include *H.M.S. Pinafore*, *The Pirates of Penzance* and one of the most frequently performed works in the history of musical theatre, *The Mikado*.

In the 21st century two Victorian poets who published little in the 19th century, Thomas Hardy (1840–1928) and Gerard Manley Hopkins (1844–89), are now regarded as major poets. While Hardy first established his reputation the late 19th century with novels, he also wrote poetry throughout his career. However he did not publish his first collection until 1898, so that he tends to be treated as a 20th-century poet. Hopkins *Poems* were published posthumously by Robert Bridges in 1918. Hopkins' poem "The Wreck of the Deutschland", written in 1875, first introduced what Hopkins called "sprung rhythm." As well as developing new rhythmic effects, Hopkins "was also very interested in ways of rejuvenating poetic language" and frequently "employed compound and unusual word combinations". Several 20th-century poets, including W.H. Auden, Dylan Thomas, and American Charles Wright, "turned to his work for its inventiveness and rich aural patterning".

American poets

America also produced major poets in the 19th century, such as Emily Dickinson (1830–86) and Walt Whitman (1819–92). America's two greatest 19th-century poets could hardly have been more different in temperament and style. Walt Whitman (1819–1892) was a working man, a traveler, a self-appointed nurse during the American Civil War (1861–1865), and a poetic innovator. His major work was *Leaves of Grass*, in which he uses a free-flowing verse and lines of irregular length to depict the all-inclusiveness of American democracy. Whitman was also a poet of the body, or "the body electric," as he called it. In *Studies in Classic American Literature*, the English novelist D. H. Lawrence wrote that Whitman "was the first to smash the old moral conception that the soul of man is something 'superior' and 'above' the flesh". Emily Dickinson (1830–1886), on the other hand, lived the sheltered life of a genteel, unmarried woman in small-town Amherst, Massachusetts. Within its formal structure, her poetry is ingenious, witty, exquisitely wrought, and psychologically penetrating. Her work was unconventional for its day, and little of it was published during her lifetime. Many of her poems dwell on death, often with a mischievous twist. One, "Because I could not stop for Death", begins, "He kindly stopped for me." The opening of another Dickinson poem toys with her position as a woman in a male-dominated society and an unrecognized poet: "I'm nobody! Who are you? / Are you nobody too?"

Victorian drama

A change came in the Victorian era with a profusion on the London stage of farces, musical burlesques, extravaganzas and comic operas that competed with productions of Shakespeare's plays and serious drama by dramatists like of James Planché and Thomas William Robertson. In 1855, the German Reed Entertainments began a process of elevating the level of (formerly risqué) musical theatre in Britain that culminated in the famous series of comic operas by Gilbert and Sullivan and were followed by the 1890s with the first Edwardian musical comedies. The length of runs in the theatre changed rapidly during the Victorian period. As transportation improved, poverty in London diminished, and street lighting made for safer travel at night, the number of potential patrons for the growing number of theatres increased enormously. Plays could run longer and still draw in the audiences, leading to better profits and improved production values.

The first play to achieve 500 consecutive performances was the London comedy *Our Boys*, opening in 1875. Its astonishing new record of 1,362 performances was bested in 1892 by *Charley's Aunt*. Several of Gilbert and Sullivan's comic operas broke the 500-performance barrier, beginning with *H.M.S. Pinafore* in 1878, and Alfred Cellier and B. C. Stephenson's 1886 hit, *Dorothy*, ran for 931 performances. After W. S. Gilbert, Oscar Wilde became the leading poet and dramatist of the late Victorian period. Wilde's plays, in particular, stand apart from the many now forgotten plays of Victorian times and have a much closer relationship to those of the Edwardian dramatists such as Irish playwright George Bernard Shaw (1856–1950), whose career began in the last decade of the 19th century, Wilde's 1895 comic masterpiece, *The Importance of Being Earnest*, holds an ironic mirror to the aristocracy and displays a mastery of wit and paradoxical wisdom.

ENGLISH LITERATURE SINCE 1901

1901–1939 Modernism

A major British lyric poet of the first decades of the 20th century was Thomas Hardy (1840–1928). Though not a modernist, Hardy was an important transitional figure between the Victorian era and the 20th century. A major novelist of the late 19th century, Hardy lived well into the third decade of the 20th century, but because of the adverse criticism of his last novel, *Jude the Obscure,* in 1895, from that time Hardy concentrated on publishing poetry. On the other hand another significant transitional figure between Victorians and modernists, the late-19th-century novelist, Henry James (1843–1916), continued to publish major works into the 20th century. James had lived in Europe since 1875 and became a British citizen, but this was only in 1915, and he was born in America and spent his formative years there. Another immigrant, Polish-born modernist novelist Joseph Conrad (1857–1924) published his first important work, *Heart of Darkness* in 1899 and Lord Jim in 1900. The American exponent of Naturalism Theodore Dreiser's (1871–1945) *Sister Carrie* was also published in 1900. However, the Victorian Gerard Manley Hopkins's (1844–89) highly original poetry was not published until 1918, long after his death, while another major modernist poet, Irishman W. B. Yeats's (1865–1939), career began late in the Victorian era. Yeats was one of the foremost figures of 20th-century literature. A pillar of both the Irish and British literary establishments, in his later years he served as an Irish Senator for two terms. Yeats was a driving force behind the Irish Literary Revival. In 1923 he was awarded the Nobel Prize in Literature as the first Irishman so honoured Yeats is generally considered one of the few writers who completed their greatest works after being awarded the Nobel Prize; such works include *The Tower* (1928) and *The Winding Stair and Other Poems* (1929).

But while modernism was to become an important literary movement in the early decades of the new century, there were also many fine writers who, like Thomas Hardy, were not modernists. During the early decades of the 20th century the Georgian poets like Rupert Brooke (1887–1915), Walter de la Mare (1873–1956), John Masefield (1878–1967, Poet Laureate from 1930) maintained a conservative approach to poetry by combining romanticism, sentimentality and hedonism, sandwiched as they were between the Victorian era, with its strict classicism, and Modernism, with its strident rejection of pure aestheticism. Edward Thomas (1878–1917) is sometimes treated as another Georgian poet. Thomas enlisted in 1915 and is one of the First World War poets along with Wilfred Owen (1893–1918), Rupert Brooke (1887–1915), Isaac Rosenberg (1890–1917), Edmund Blunden (1896–1974) and Siegfried Sassoon (1886–1967). Irish playwrights George Bernard Shaw (1856–1950) and J.M. Synge (1871–1909) were influential in British drama. Shaw's career began in the last decade of the 19th century, while Synge's plays belong to the first decade of the 20th century. Synge's most famous play, *The Playboy of the Western World*, "caused outrage and riots when it was first performed" in Dublin in 1907. George Bernard Shaw turned the Edwardian theatre into an arena for debate about important political and social issues, like marriage, class, "the morality of armaments and war" and the rights of women. An important dramatist in the 1920s, and later, was Irishman Sean O'Casey (1880–1964). Also in the 1920s and later Noël Coward (1899–1973) achieved enduring success as a playwright, publishing more than 50 plays from his teens onwards. Many of his works, such as *Hay Fever* (1925), *Private Lives* (1930), *Design for Living* (1932), *Present Laughter* (1942) and *Blithe Spirit* (1941), have remained in the regular theatre repertoire.

Novelists who are not considered modernists include: Rudyard Kipling (1865–1936) who was also a successful poet; H. G. Wells (1866–1946); John Galsworthy (1867–1933), (Nobel Prize in Literature, 1932) whose works include a sequence of novels, collectively called *The Forsyte Saga* (1906–21); Arnold Bennett (1867–1931) author of *The Old Wives' Tale* (1908); G. K. Chesterton (1874–1936); and E.M. Forster's (1879–1970), though Forster's work is "frequently regarded as containing both modernist and Victorian elements". H. G. Wells was a prolific author who is now best known for his science fiction novels. His most notable science fiction works include *The War of the Worlds, The Time Machine, The Invisible Man* and *The Island of Doctor Moreau* all written in the 1890s. Other novels include *Kipps* (1905) and *Mr Polly* (1910). Forster's most famous work, *A Passage to India* 1924, reflected challenges to imperialism, while his earlier novels, such as *A Room with a View* (1908) and *Howards End* (1910), examined the restrictions and hypocrisy of Edwardian society in England. The most popular British writer of the early years of the 20th century was arguably Rudyard Kipling, a highly versatile writer of novels, short stories and poems, and to date the youngest ever recipient of the Nobel Prize for Literature (1907). Kipling's works include *The Jungle Books* (1894–95), *The Man Who Would Be King* and *Kim* (1901), while his inspirational poem "If—" (1895) is a national favourite and a memorable evocation of Victorian stoicism. Kipling's reputation declined during his lifetime, but more recently postcolonial studies has "rekindled an intense interest in his work, viewing it as both symptomatic and critical of imperialist attitudes".

Strongly influenced by his Christian faith, G. K. Chesterton was a prolific and hugely influential writer with a diverse output. His best-known character is the priest-detective Father Brown, who appeared only in short stories, while *The Man Who Was Thursday* published in 1908 is arguably his best-known novel. Of his nonfiction, *Charles Dickens: A Critical Study* (1906) has received some of the broadest-based praise. Another major work of science fiction, from the early 20th century, is *A Voyage to Arcturus* by Scottish writer David Lindsay, first published in 1920. It combines fantasy, philosophy, and science fiction in an exploration of the nature of good and evil and their relationship with existence. It has been described by writer Colin Wilson as the "greatest novel of the twentieth century", and was a central influence on C. S. Lewis's *Space Trilogy*. Also J. R. R. Tolkien said he read the book "with avidity", and praised it as a work of philosophy, religion, and morality. It was made widely available in paperback form when published as one of the precursor volumes to the Ballantine Adult Fantasy series in 1968.

Alongside the more conservative writers mentioned, English literary modernism developed in the early 20th-century out of a general sense of disillusionment with Victorian era attitudes of certainty, conservatism, and belief in the idea of objective truth. The movement was influenced by the ideas of Charles Darwin (1809–82) (*On Origin of Species*) (1859), Ernst Mach (1838–1916), Henri Bergson (1859–1941), Friedrich Nietzsche (1844–1900), James G. Frazer (1854–1941), Karl Marx (1818–83) (*Das Kapital*, 1867), and the psychoanalytic theories of Sigmund Freud (1856–1939), among others. The continental art movements of Impressionism, and later Cubism, were also important inspirations for modernist writers. Important literary precursors of modernism, were: Fyodor Dostoevsky (1821–81) (*Crime and Punishment* (1866), *The Brothers Karamazov* (1880); Walt Whitman (1819–92) (*Leaves of Grass*) (1855–91); Charles Baudelaire (1821–67) (*Les Fleurs du mal*), Rimbaud (1854–91) (*Illuminations*, 1874); August Strindberg (1849–1912), especially his later plays.

In addition to W. B. Yeats other important early modernists poets were the American poets T. S. Eliot (1888–1965) and Ezra Pound (1885–1972). Eliot became a British citizen in 1927 but was born and educated in America. His most famous works are: "Prufrock" (1915), *The Wasteland* (1921) and *Four Quartets* (1935–42). Ezra Pound was not only a major poet, first publishing part of *The Cantos* in 1917, but an important mentor for other poets, most significantly in his editorial advice for Eliot's poem *The Wasteland*. Other important American poets writing early in the 20th century were William Carlos Williams (1883–1963), Robert Frost (1874–1963), who published his first collection in England in 1913, and H.D. (1886–1961). Gertrude Stein (1874–1946), an American expatriate living in Paris, famous for her line "Rose is a rose is a rose is a rose," was also an important literary force during this time period. American poet Marianne Moore (1887–1972) published from the 1920s to the 1960s.

Amongst the novelists, after Joseph Conrad, other important early modernist include Dorothy Richardson (1873–1957), whose novel *Pointed Roof* (1915), is one of the earliest example of the stream of consciousness technique, and D. H. Lawrence (1885–1930), who published *The Rainbow* in 1915, though it was immediately seized by the police. Then in 1922 Irishman James Joyce's important modernist novel *Ulysses* appeared. *Ulysses* has been called "a demonstration and summation of the entire movement". Set during one day in Dublin, in it Joyce creates parallels with Homer's epic poem the Odyssey. William Faulkner's *The Sound and the Fury* (1929) is another significant modernist novel, that uses the stream of consciousness technique.

The modernist movement continued through the 1920s and 1930s and beyond. During the period between the World Wars, American drama came to maturity, thanks in large part to the works of Eugene O'Neill (1888–1953). O'Neill's experiments with theatrical form and his use of both Naturalist and Expressionist techniques had a major influence on American dramatists. His best-known plays include *Anna Christie* (Pulitzer Prize 1922), *Desire Under the Elms* (1924), *Strange Interlude* (Pulitzer Prize 1928), *Mourning Becomes Electra* (1931). In poetry Hart Crane published *The Bridge* in 1930 and E. E. Cummings and Wallace Stevens were publishing from the 1920s until the 1950s. Similarly William Faulkner continued to publish until the 1950s and was awarded a Nobel Prize in 1949. However, not all those writing in these years were modernists, this includes Americans novelists Theodore Dreiser, Dos Passos, Ernest Hemingway, Scott Fitzgerald (*The Great Gatsby* 1925), and John Steinbeck.

Important British writers between the World Wars, include the Scottish poet Hugh MacDiarmid (1892–1978), who began publishing in the 1920s, and novelists Virginia Woolf (1882–1941), E. M. Forster (1879–1970) (*A Passage to India*, 1924), Evelyn Waugh (1903–66), P. G. Wodehouse (1881–1975) (who was not a modernist) and D. H. Lawrence. Lawrence's *Lady Chatterley's Lover* was published privately in Florence in 1928, though the unexpurgated version was not published in Britain until 1959. Woolf was an influential feminist, and a major stylistic innovator associated with the stream-of-consciousness technique in novels like *Mrs Dalloway* (1925) and *To the Lighthouse* (1927). Her 1929 essay *A Room of One's Own* contains her famous dictum; "A woman must have money and a room of her own if she is to write fiction". In the 1930s W. H. Auden and Christopher Isherwood co-authored verse dramas, of which The Ascent of F6 (1936) is the most notable, that owed much to Bertolt Brecht. T. S. Eliot had begun this attempt to revive poetic drama with *Sweeney Agonistes* in 1932, and this was followed by *The Rock* (1934), *Murder in the Cathedral* (1935) and *Family Reunion* (1939). There were three further plays after the war. *In Parenthesis*, a modernist epic poem by David Jones (1895–1974) first published in 1937, is probably the best known contribution from Wales to the literature of the First World War.

An important development, beginning really in the 1930s and 1940s was a tradition of working class novels that were actually written by writers who had a working-class background. Among these were coal miner Jack Jones, James Hanley, whose father was a stoker and who also went to sea as a young man, and other coal miner authors' Lewis Jones from South Wales and Harold Heslop from County Durham.

Aldous Huxley (1894–1963) published his famous dystopia *Brave New World* in 1932, the same year as John Cowper Powys's *A Glastonbury Romance*. Henry Miller's *Tropic of Cancer* then appeared in 1934, though it was banned for many years in both Britain and America. Samuel Beckett (1906–89) published his first major work, the novel *Murphy* in 1938. This same year Graham Greene's (1904–91) first major novel *Brighton Rock* was published. Then in 1939 James Joyce's published *Finnegans Wake*. In this work Joyce creates a special language to express the consciousness of a character who is dreaming. It was also in 1939 that another Irish modernist poet, W. B. Yeats, died. British poet W. H. Auden was another significant modernists in the 1930s.

1940 to the 21st century

Though some have seen modernism ending by around 1939, with regard to English literature, "When (if) modernism petered out and postmodernism began has been contested almost as hotly as when the transition from Victorianism to modernism occurred". In fact a number of modernists were still living and publishing in the 1950s and 1960, including T. S. Eliot, William Faulkner, Dorothy Richardson, and Ezra Pound. Furthermore Basil Bunting, born in 1901, published little until *Briggflatts* in 1965 and Samuel Beckett, born in Ireland in 1906, continued to produce significant works until the 1980s, including *Waiting for Godot* (1953), *Happy Days* (1961), *Rockaby* (1981), though some view him as a post-modernist.

Among British writers in the 1940s and 1950s were novelist Graham Greene whose works span the 1930s to the 1980s and poet Dylan Thomas, while Evelyn Waugh, W.H. Auden and T. S. Eliot continued publishing significant work. In 1947 Malcolm Lowry published *Under the Volcano*, while George Orwell's satire of totalitarianism, *1984*, was published in 1949. One of the most influential novels of the immediate post-war period was William Cooper's naturalistic *Scenes from Provincial Life*, a conscious rejection of the modernist tradition. Graham Greene was a convert to Catholicism and his novels explore the ambivalent moral and political issues of the modern world. Notable for an ability to combine serious literary acclaim with broad popularity, his novels include *Brighton Rock* (1938), *The Power and the Glory* (1940), *The Heart of the Matter* (1948), *A Burnt-Out Case* (1961), and *The Human Factor* (1978). Other novelists writing in the 1950s and later were: Anthony Powell whose twelve-volume cycle of novels *A Dance to the Music of Time*, is a comic examination of movements and manners, power and passivity in English political, cultural and military life in the mid-20th century; comic novelist Kingsley Amis is best known for his academic satire *Lucky Jim* (1954); Nobel Prize laureate William Golding's allegorical novel *Lord of the Flies* 1954, explores how culture created by man fails, using as an example a group of British schoolboys marooned on a deserted island who try to govern themselves, but with disastrous results.

Philosopher Iris Murdoch was a prolific writer of novels throughout the second half of the 20th century, that deal especially with sexual relationships, morality, and the power of the unconscious, including *Under the Net* (1954), *The Black Prince* (1973) and *The Green Knight* (1993). Scottish writer Muriel Spark pushed the boundaries of realism in her novels. Her first, *The Comforters* (1957) concerns a woman who becomes aware that she is a character in a novel; *The Prime of Miss Jean Brodie* (1961), at times takes the reader briefly into the distant future, to see the various fates that befall its characters. Anthony Burgess is especially remembered for his dystopian novel *A Clockwork Orange* (1962), set in the not-too-distant future, which was made into a film by Stanley Kubrick in 1971. In the entirely different genre of Gothic fantasy Mervyn Peake (1911–68) published his highly successful Gormenghast trilogy between 1946 and 1959.

Doris Lessing from Southern Rhodesia (now Zimbabwe), published her first novel *The Grass is Singing* in 1950, after immigrating to England. She initially wrote about her African experiences. Lessing soon became a dominant presence in the English literary scene, frequently publishing right through the century, and won the nobel prize for literature in 2007. Other works by her include a sequence of five novels collectively called *Children of Violence* (1952–69), *The Golden Notebook* (1962), *The Good Terrorist* (1985), and a sequence of five science fiction novels the *Canopus in Argos: Archives* (1979–1983). Indeed from 1950 on a significant number of major writers came from countries that had over the centuries been settled by the British, other than America which had been producing significant writers from at least the Victorian period. There had of course been a few important works in English prior to 1950 from the then British Empire. Olive Schreiner's famous novel *The Story of an African Farm* was published in 1883 and New Zealander Katherine Mansfield published her first collection of short stories, *In a German Pension*, in 1911. The first major novelist, writing in English, from the Indian sub-continent, R. K. Narayan, began publishing in England in the 1930s, thanks to the encouragement of English novelist Graham Greene. Caribbean writer Jean Rhys's writing career began as early as 1928, though her most famous work, *Wide Sargasso Sea*, was not published until 1966. Alan Paton's famous *Cry, the Beloved Country* dates from 1948.

From Nigeria a number of writers have achieved an international reputation for works in English, including novelist Chinua Achebe, who published *Things Fall Apart* in 1958, as well as playwright Wole Soyinka and novelist Buchi Emecheta. Soyinka won the Nobel Prize for literature in 1986, as did South African novelist Nadine Gordimer in 1995. Other South African writers in English are novelist J.M. Coetzee (Nobel Prize 2003) and playwright Athol Fugard. Kenya's most internationally renown author is Ngig) wa Thiong'o who has written novels, plays and short stories in English. Poet Derek Walcott, from St Lucia in the Caribbean, was another Nobel Prize winner in 1992. Two Irishmen and an Australian were also winners in the period after 1940: novelist and playwright, Samuel Beckett (1969); poet Seamus Heaney (1995); Patrick White (1973) a major novelist in this period, whose first work was published in 1939. Another noteworthy Australian writer at the end of this period is poet Les Murray. Northern Ireland has produced major poets, including Paul Muldoon and Derek Mahon. While Scotland has in the late 20th century produced several important novelists, including James Kelman who like Samuel Beckett can create humour out of the most grim situations. *How Late it Was, How Late*, 1994, won the Booker Prize that year; A. L. Kennedy whose 2007 novel *Day* was named Book of the Year in the Costa Book Awards. In 2007 she won the Austrian State Prize for European Literature; Alasdair Gray whose *Lanark: A Life in Four Books* (1981) is a dystopian fantasy set in his home town Glasgow.

Among Canadian writers who have achieved an international reputation, are novelist and poet Margaret Atwood, poet, song writer and novelist Leonard Cohen, short story writer Alice Munro, and more recently poet Anne Carson. Another admired Canadian novelist and poet is Michael Ondaatje, who was born in Sri Lanka.

An important cultural movement in the British theatre which developed in the late 1950s and early 1960s was Kitchen sink realism (or "kitchen sink drama"), a term coined to describe art (the term itself derives from an expressionist painting by John Bratby), novels, film and television plays. The term angry young men was often applied members of this artistic movement. It used a style of social realism which depicts the domestic lives of the working class, to explore social issues and political issues. The drawing room plays of the post war period, typical of dramatists like Terence Rattigan and Noël Coward were challenged in the 1950s by these Angry Young Men, in plays like John Osborne's *Look Back in Anger* (1956). Arnold Wesker and Nell Dunn also brought social concerns to the stage.

Again In the 1950s, the absurdist play *Waiting for Godot* (1955) (originally *En attendant Godot*, 1952), by Irish writer Samuel Beckett profoundly affected British drama. The Theatre of the Absurd influenced Harold Pinter (born 1930), (The Birthday Party, 1958), whose works are often characterised by menace or claustrophobia. Beckett also influenced Tom Stoppard (born 1937) (*Rosencrantz and Guildenstern are Dead*,1966). Stoppard's works are however also notable for their high-spirited wit and the great range of intellectual issues which he tackles in different plays. Both Pinter and Stoppard continued to have new plays produced into the 1990s. Michael Frayn (born 1933) is among other playwrights noted for their use of language and ideas. He is also a novelist.

Other Important playwrights whose careers began later in the century are: Caryl Churchill (*Top Girls*, 1982) and Alan Ayckbourn (*Absurd Person Singular*, 1972).

An important new element in the world of British drama, from the beginnings of radio in the 1920s, was the commissioning of plays, or the adaption of existing plays, by BBC radio. This was especially important in the 1950s and 1960s (and from the 1960s for television). Many major British playwrights in fact, either effectively began their careers with the BBC, or had works adapted for radio. Most of playwright Caryl Churchill's early experiences with professional drama production were as a radio playwright and, starting in 1962 with *The Ants*, there were nine productions with BBC radio drama up until 1973 when her stage work began to be recognised at the Royal Court Theatre. Joe Orton's dramatic debut in 1963 was the radio play *The Ruffian on the Stair*, which was broadcast on 31 August 1964. Tom Stoppard's "first professional production was in the fifteen-minute *Just Before Midnight* programme on BBC Radio, which showcased new dramatists". John Mortimer made his radio debut as a dramatist in 1955, with his adaptation of his own novel *Like Men Betrayed* for the BBC Light Programme.

But he made his debut as an original playwright with *The Dock Brief,* starring Michael Hordern as a hapless barrister, first broadcast in 1957 on BBC Radio's Third Programme, later televised with the same cast, and subsequently presented in a double bill with *What Shall We Tell Caroline?* at the Lyric Hammersmith in April 1958, before transferring to the Garrick Theatre. Mortimer is most famous for Rumpole of the Bailey a British television series which starred Leo McKern as Horace Rumpole, an aging London barrister who defends any and all clients. It has been spun off into a series of short stories, novels, and radio programmes.

Other notable radio dramatists included Brendan Behan, and novelist Angela Carter. Novelist Susan Hill also wrote for BBC radio, from the early 1970s. Irish playwright Brendan Behan, author of *The Quare Fellow* (1954), was commissioned by the BBC to write a radio play *The Big House* (1956); prior to this he had written two plays *Moving Out*and *A Garden Party* for Irish radio.

Among the most famous works created for radio, are Dylan Thomas's *Under Milk Wood* (1954), Samuel Beckett's *All That Fall* (1957), Harold Pinter's *A Slight Ache* (1959) and Robert Bolt's *A Man for All Seasons* (1954). Samuel Beckett wrote a number of short radio plays in the 1950s and 1960s, and later for television. Beckett's radio play *Embers* was first broadcast on the BBC Third Programme on 24 June 1959, and won the RAI prize at the Prix Italia awards later that year.

While poets T. S. Eliot, W. H. Auden and Dylan Thomas were still publishing in this period, new poets starting their careers in the 1950s and 1960s included Philip Larkin (1922–85) (*The Whitsun Weddings*,1964), Ted Hughes (1930–98) (*The Hawk in the Rain*,1957) and Irishman (Northern Ireland)Seamus Heaney (born 1939) (*Death of a Naturalist*, 1966). Northern Ireland has also produced a number of other significant poets, including Derek Mahon and Paul Muldoon. In the 1960s and 1970s Martian poetry aimed to break the grip of 'the familiar', by describing ordinary things in unfamiliar ways, as though, for example, through the eyes of a Martian. Poets most closely associated with it are Craig Raine and Christopher Reid. Martin Amis, an important contemporary novelist, carried into fiction this drive to make the familiar strange.

Another literary movement in this period was the British Poetry Revival was a wide-reaching collection of groupings and subgroupings that embraces performance, sound and concrete poetry. Leading poets associated with this movement include J. H. Prynne, Eric Mottram, Tom Raworth, Denise Riley and Lee Harwood. The Mersey Beat poets were Adrian Henri, Brian Patten and Roger McGough. Their work was a self-conscious attempt at creating an English equivalent to the Beats. Many of their poems were written in protest against the established social order and, particularly, the threat of nuclear war. Other noteworthy later 20th-century poets are Welshman R. S. Thomas, Geoffrey Hill, Charles Tomlinson and Carol Ann Duffy, who is the current poet laureate. Geoffrey Hill (born 1932) is considered one of the most distinguished English poets of his generation, Although frequently described as a "difficult" poet, Hill has retorted that poetry supposed to be difficult can be "the most democratic because you are doing your audience the honour of supposing they are intelligent human beings". Charles Tomlinson (born 1927) is another important English poet of an older generation, though "since his first publication in 1951, has built a career that has seen more notice in the international scene than in his native England; this may explain, and be explained by, his international vision of poetry". The critic Michael Hennessy has described Tomlinson as "the most international and least provincial English poet of his generation". His poetry has won international recognition and has received many prizes in Europe and the United States.

One of Penguin Books most successful publications in the 1970s was Richard Adams's heroic fantasy *Watership Down* (1972). Evoking epic themes, it recounts the odyssey of a group of rabbits seeking to establish a new home. Another successful novel of the same era was John Fowles' *The French Lieutenant's Woman* (1969), with a narrator who freely admits the fictive nature of his story, and its famous alternative endings. This was made into a film in 1981 with a screenplay by Harold Pinter. Angela Carter (1940–1992) was a novelist and journalist, known for her feminist, magical realism, and picaresque works. Writing from the 1960s until the 1980s, her novels include, *The Infernal Desire Machines of Doctor Hoffman* 1972 and *Nights at the Circus* 1984. Margaret Drabble (born 1939) is a novelist, biographer and critic, who published from the 1960s into the 21st century. Her older sister, A. S. Byatt (born 1936) is best known for *Possession* published in 1990.

Salman Rushdie is among a number of post Second World War writers from the former British colonies who permanently settled in Britain. Rushdie achieved fame with *Midnight's Children* 1981, which was awarded both the James Tait Black Memorial Prize and Booker prize, and was named Booker of Bookers in 1993. His most controversial novel *The Satanic Verses* 1989, was inspired in part by the life of Muhammad. V. S. Naipaul (born 1932), born in Trinidad, was another immigrant, who wrote among other things *A House for Mr Biswas* (1961) and *A Bend in the River* (1979). Naipaul won the Nobel Prize in Literature. Also from the West Indies is George Lamming (born 1927), who wrote *In the Castle of the Skin* (1953), while from Pakistan, came Hanif Kureshi (born 1954), a playwright, screenwriter, filmmaker, novelist and short story writer. His book *The Buddha of Suburbia* (1990) won the Whitbread Award for the best first novel, and was also made into a BBC television series. Another important immigrant writer Kazuo Ishiguro (born 1954) was born in Japan, but his parents immigrated to Britain when he was six. His works include, *The Remains of the Day* 1989, *Never Let Me Go* 2005.

Martin Amis (1949) is one of the most prominent of contemporary British novelists. His best-known novels are *Money* (1984) and *London Fields* (1989). Pat Barker (born 1943) has won many awards for her fiction. English novelist and screenwriter Ian McEwan (born 1948) is another of contemporary Britain's most highly regarded writers. His works include *The Cement Garden* (1978) and *Enduring Love* (1997), which was made into a film. In 1998 McEwan won the Man Booker Prize with *Amsterdam. Atonement* (2001) was made into an Oscar-winning film. McEwan was awarded the Jerusalem Prize in 2011. Zadie Smith's Whitbread Book Award winning novel *White Teeth* (2000), mixes pathos and humour, focusing on the later lives of two war time friends in London. Julian Barnes (born 1946) is another successful living novelist, who won the 2011 Man Booker Prize for his book *The Sense of an Ending*, while three of his earlier books had been shortlisted for the Booker Prize: *Flaubert's Parrot* (1984), *England, England* (1998), and *Arthur & George* (2005). He has also written crime fiction under the pseudonym Dan Kavanagh.

Two significant contemporary Irish novelists are John Banville (born 1945) and Colm Tóibín (born 1955). Banville is also adapter of dramas, and screenwriter and writes detective novels under the pseudonym Benjamin Black. Banville has won numerous awards: *The Book of Evidence* was shortlisted for the Booker Prize and won the Guinness Peat Aviation award in 1989; his eighteenth novel, *The Sea*, won the Booker Prize in 2005; he was awarded the Franz Kafka Prize in 2011. Colm Tóibín (Irish),1955) is a novelist, short story writer, essayist, playwright, journalist, critic, and, most recently, poet. The contemporary Australian novelist Peter Carey (born 1943) is one of only two writers to have won the Booker Prize twice.

AMERICAN

From 1940 into the 21st century, American playwrights, poets and novelists have continued to be internationally prominent. The following is a list of some of the more important writers (along with some important early works):

Novelists: Russian-born Vladimir Nabokov (*Lolita*, 1956), John Updike (*Rabbit Run*, 1960), Thomas Pynchon (*V*, 1963), Richard Ford, Eudora Welty (mainly short stories), Richard Wright, James Baldwin (*Go Tell it on the Mountain*, (1953), Saul

Bellow (*Herzog* 1964)*, Bernard Malamud (*The Fixer*, 1967), Joyce Carol Oates, Cynthia Ozick, Toni Morrison*, Philip Roth (*Portnoy's Complaint*, 1969), Don DeLillo, Jane Smiley, David Foster Wallace, Isaac Bashevis Singer.*

Playwrights: Arthur Miller (*Death of a Salesman*, 1949), Tennessee Williams (*A Streetcar Named Desire*, 1947), Edward Albee (*Who's Afraid of Virginia Woolf?*, 1962), David Mamet.

Poets: John Ashberry, Robert Lowell (*Life Studies*, 1959), Charles Olson, Louise Glück, Elizabeth Bishop (*North and South*, 1946), Alan Ginsberg (*Howl*, 1956), Robert Bly (*Silence in the Snowy Fields*, 1962), Richard Wilbur, Sylvia Plath (*Ariel*, 1965), Amy Clampitt, Robert Pinsky, Mary Oliver, James Wright, Billy Collins.

- Nobel Prize winners

Post-modern literature

The term Postmodern literature is used to describe certain tendencies in post-World War II literature. It is both a continuation of the experimentation championed by writers of the modernist period (relying heavily, for example, on fragmentation, paradox, questionable narrators, etc.) and a reaction against Enlightenment ideas implicit in Modernist literature. Postmodern literature, like postmodernism as a whole, is difficult to define and there is little agreement on the exact characteristics, scope, and importance of postmodern literature. Among postmodern writers are the Americans Henry Miller, William S. Burroughs, Joseph Heller, Kurt Vonnegut, Hunter S. Thompson, Truman Capote and Thomas Pynchon.

20th-century genre literature

Agatha Christie (1890–1976) was a crime writer of novels, short stories and plays, who is best remembered for her 80 detective novels as well as her successful plays for the West End theatre. Christie's works, particularly those featuring the detectives Hercule Poirot or Miss Marple, have given her the title the 'Queen of Crime' and she was one of the most important and innovative writers in this genre. Christie's novels include,

Murder on the Orient Express, Death on the Nile and *And Then There Were None*. Another popular writer during the Golden Age of detective fiction was Dorothy L. Sayers (1893–1957). Other recent noteworthy writers in this genre are Ruth Rendell, P. D. James and Scot Ian Rankin.

Erskine Childers *The Riddle of the Sands* 1903, is an early example of the spy novel. A noted writer in the spy novel genre was John le Carré, while in thriller writing, Ian Fleming created the character James Bond 007 in January 1952, while on holiday at his Jamaican estate, Goldeneye. Fleming chronicled Bond's adventures in twelve novels, including *Casino Royale* (1953), *Live and Let Die* (1954), *Dr. No* (1958), *Goldfinger* (1959), *Thunderball* (1961), and nine short story works.

Hungarian-born Baroness Emma Orczy's (1865–1947) original play, *The Scarlet Pimpernel*, opened in October 1903 at Nottingham's Theatre Royal and was not a success. However, with a rewritten last act, it opened at the New Theatre in London in January 1905. The premier of the London production was enthusiastically received by the audience, running 122 performances and enjoying numerous revivals. *The Scarlet Pimpernel* became a favourite of London audiences, playing more than 2,000 performances and becoming one of the most popular shows staged in England to that date. The novel *The Scarlet Pimpernel* was published soon after the play opened and was an immediate success. Orczy gained a following of readers in Britain and throughout the world. The popularity of the novel encouraged her to write a number of sequels for her "reckless daredevil" over the next 35 years. The play was performed to great acclaim in France, Italy, Germany and Spain, while the novel was translated into 16 languages. Subsequently, the story has been adapted for television, film, a musical and other media.

John Buchan (1875–1940) published the adventure novel *The Thirty-Nine Steps* in 1915.

The novelist Georgette Heyer created the historical romance genre.

The Kailyard school of Scottish writers, notably J. M. Barrie (1869–1937), creator of *Peter Pan* (1904), presented an idealised version of society and brought of fantasy and folklore back into fashion. In 1908, Kenneth Grahame (1859–1932) wrote the children's classic *The Wind in the Willows*. An informal literary discussion group associated with the English faculty at the University of Oxford, were the "Inklings". Its leading members were the major fantasy novelists; C.S. Lewis and J.R.R. Tolkien. Lewis is especially known for *The Chronicles of Narnia*, while Tolkien is best known as the author of *The Hobbit* and *The Lord of the Rings*. Another significant writer is Alan Garner author of *Elidor* (1965), while Terry Pratchett is a more recent fantasy writer. Roald Dahl rose to prominence with his children's fantasy novels, such as *James and the Giant Peach* and *Charlie and the Chocolate Factory*, often inspired by experiences from his childhood, which are notable for their often unexpected endings, and unsentimental, dark humour. J. K. Rowling author of the highly successful *Harry Potter* series and Philip Pullman famous for his *His Dark Materials* trilogy are other significant authors of fantasy novels for younger readers.

Noted writers in the field of comic books are Neil Gaiman, and Alan Moore; Gaiman also produces graphic novels.

In the later decades of the 20th century, the genre of science fiction began to be taken more seriously because of the work of writers such as Arthur C. Clarke's (*2001: A Space Odyssey*), Isaac Asimov, Ursula K. Le Guin, Michael Moorcock and Kim Stanley Robinson. Another prominent writer in this genre, Douglas Adams, is particularly associated with the comic science fiction work, *The Hitchhiker's Guide to the Universe*, which began life as a radio series in 1978. Mainstream novelists such Doris Lessing and Margaret Atwood also wrote works in this genre, while Scottish novelist Ian M. Banks has also achieved a reputation as both a writer of traditional and science fiction novels.

Indian English literature

Indian English literature (IEL) refers to the body of work by writers in India who write in the English language and whose native or co-native language could be one of the numerous languages of India. It is also associated with the works of members of the Indian diaspora, such as V. S. Naipaul, Kiran Desai, Jhumpa Lahiri, Agha Shahid Ali, Rohinton Mistry and Salman Rushdie, who are of Indian descent.

It is frequently referred to as Indo-Anglian literature. (*Indo-Anglian* is a specific term in the sole context of writing that should not be confused with the term *Anglo-Indian*). As a category, this production comes under the broader realm of postcolonial literature- the production from previously colonised countries such as India.

HISTORY

IEL has a relatively recent history, it is only one and a half centuries old. The first book written by an Indian in English was by Sake Dean Mahomet, titled *Travels of Dean Mahomet;* Mahomet's travel narrative was published in 1793 in England. In its early stages it was influenced by the Western art form of the novel. Early Indian writers used English unadulterated by Indian words to convey an experience which was essentially Indian. Raja Rao (1908–2006),Indian philosopher and writer authored *Kanthapura* and *The Serpent and the Rope* which are Indian in terms of its storytelling qualities.Ruskin Bond, winner of sahitya academy award and the author of many novellas including The room on the roof, Flight of pigeons, etc. Rabindranath Tagore (1861–1941) wrote in Bengali and English and was responsible for the translations of his own work into English. Dhan Gopal Mukerji was the first Indian author to win a literary award in the United States. Nirad C. Chaudhuri, a writer of non-fiction, is best known for his *The Autobiography of an Unknown Indian* where he relates his life experiences and influences. P. Lal, a poet, translator, publisher and essayist, founded a press in the 1950s for Indian English writing, Writers Workshop. Ram Nath Kak (1917–1933), a Kashmiri veterinarian wrote his autobiography *Autumn Leaves,* which is one of the most vivid portraits of life in 20th century Kashmir and has become a sort of a classic.

R.K. Narayan is a writer who contributed over many decades and who continued to write till his death recently. He was discovered by Graham Greene in the sense that the latter helped him find a publisher in England. Graham Greene and Narayan remained close friends till the end. Similar to Thomas Hardy's Wessex, Narayan created the fictitious town of Malgudi where he set his novels. Some criticise Narayan for the parochial, detached and closed world that he created in the face of the changing conditions in India at the times in which the stories are set. Others, such as Graham Greene, however, feel that through Malgudi they could vividly understand the Indian experience. Narayan's evocation of small town life and its experiences through the eyes of the endearing child protagonist Swaminathan in *Swami and Friends* is a good sample of his writing style. Simultaneous with Narayan's pastoral idylls, a very different writer, Mulk Raj Anand, was similarly gaining recognition for his writing set in rural India; but his stories were harsher, and engaged, sometimes brutally, with divisions of caste, class and religion.

Later history

Among the later writers, the most notable is Salman Rushdie, born in India, now living in the United Kingdom. Rushdie with his famous work *Midnight's Children* (Booker Prize 1981, Booker of Bookers 1992, and Best of the Bookers 2008) ushered in a new trend of writing. He used a hybrid language – English generously peppered with Indian terms – to convey a theme that could be seen as representing the vast canvas of India. He is usually categorised under the magic realism mode of writing most famously associated with Gabriel García Márquez. Nayantara Sehgal was one of the first female Indian writers in English to receive wide recognition. Her fiction deals with India's elite responding to the crises engendered by political change.

She was awarded the 1986 Sahitya Akademi Award for English, for her novel, Rich Like Us (1985), by the Sahitya Akademi, India's National Academy of Letters. Anita Desai was shortlisted for the Booker Prize three times, received a Sahitya Akademi Award in 1978 for her novel *Fire on the Mountain* and the British Guardian Prize for *The Village by the Sea*. Her daughter Kiran Desai won the 2006 Man Booker Prize for her second novel The Inheritance of Loss. Ruskin Bond received Sahitya Academy Award for his collection of short stories *Our Trees Still Grow in Dehra* in 1992. He is also the author of a historical novel A Flight of Pigeons, which is based on an episode during the Indian Rebellion of 1857.

Vikram Seth, author of *The Golden Gate* (1986) and *A Suitable Boy* (1994) is a writer who uses a purer English and more realistic themes. Being a self-confessed fan of Jane Austen, his attention is on the story, its details and its twists and turns.Vikram Seth is notable both as an accomplished novelist and poet. Vikram Seth's outstanding achievement as a versatile and prolific poet remains largely and unfairly neglected.

Another writer who has contributed immensely to the India English Literature is Amitav Ghosh who is the author of *The Circle of Reason* (his 1986 debut novel), *The Shadow Lines* (1988), *The Calcutta Chromosome* (1995), *The Glass Palace* (2000), *The Hungry Tide* (2004), and *Sea of Poppies* (2008), the first volume of *The Ibis* trilogy, set in the 1830s, just before the Opium War, which encapsulates the colonial history of the East. Ghosh's latest work of fiction is *River of Smoke* (2011), the second volume of *The Ibis* trilogy.

Rohinton Mistry is an India born Canadian author who is a Neustadt International Prize for Literature laureate (2012). His first book Tales from Firozsha Baag (1987) published by Penguin Books Canada is a collection of 11 short stories. His novels Such a Long Journey (1991) and A Fine Balance (1995)earned him great acclaim.

Shashi Tharoor, in his *The Great Indian Novel* (1989), follows a story-telling (though in a satirical) mode as in the Mahabharata drawing his ideas by going back and forth in time. His work as UN official living outside India has given him a vantage point that helps construct an objective Indianness. However, his stint with Congress Party and his nearness to the Gandhi family has led to some critics question his objectivity. His well-known affinity with Rahul Gandhi and one-sided favor of Congress

Party with all its scandals, has also put the objectivity of his books into question. Vikram Chandra is another author who shuffles between India and the United States and has received critical acclaim for his first novel *Red Earth and Pouring Rain* (1995) and collection of short stories *Love and Longing in Bombay* (1997). His namesake Vikram A. Chandra is a renowned journalist and the author of *The Srinagar Conspiracy* (2000). Suketu Mehta is another writer currently based in the United States who authored Maximum City (2004), an autobiographical account of his experiences in the city of Mumbai. In 2008, Arvind Adiga received the Man Booker Prize for his debut novel The White Tiger.

Recent writers in India such as Arundhati Roy and David Davidar show a direction towards contextuality and rootedness in their works. Arundhati Roy, a trained architect and the 1997 Booker prize winner for her *The God of Small Things*, calls herself a "home grown" writer. Her award winning book is set in the immensely physical landscape of Kerala. Davidar sets his *The House of Blue Mangoes* in Southern Tamil Nadu. In both the books, geography and politics are integral to the narrative. In his novel Lament of Mohini (2000), Shreekumar Varma touches upon the unique matriarchal system and the *sammandham* system of marriage as he writes about the Namboodiris and the aristocrats of Kerala. Jahnavi Barua, a Bangalore based author from Assam has set her critically acclaimed collection of short stories *Next Door* on the social scenario in Assam with insurgency as the background. Another author Aruni Kashyap has also based his first novel *The House with A Thousand Stories* on the society and psyche of the people of Assam at the backdrop of insurgency.

As for the history of the gradual development of Indian drama in English, one may consult Pinaki Roy's essay "*Dramatic Chronicle*: A Very Brief Review of the Growth of Indian English Plays", included in *Indian Drama in English: Some Perspectives* (ISBN 978-81-269-1772-3) (pp. 272-87), edited by Abha Shukla Kaushik, and published by the New Delhi-based *Atlantic Publishers and Distributors Pvt. Ltd.* in 2013. G. S. Amur has also written extensively on Indian authors including those who write in English.

Debates

One of the key issues raised in this context is the superiority/inferiority of IWE (Indian Writing in English) as opposed to the literary production in the various languages of India. Key polar concepts bandied in this context are superficial/authentic, imitative/creative, shallow/deep, critical/uncritical, elitist/parochial and so on.

The views of Salman Rushdie and Amit Chaudhuri expressed through their books *The Vintage Book of Indian Writing* and *The Picador Book of Modern Indian Literature* respectively essentialise this battle.

Rushdie's statement in his book – "the ironic proposition that India's best writing since independence may have been done in the language of the departed imperialists is simply too much for some folks to bear" – created a lot of resentment among many writers, including writers in English. In his book, Amit Chaudhuri questions – "Can it be true that Indian writing, that endlessly rich, complex and problematic entity, is to be represented by a handful of writers who write in English, who live in England or America and whom one might have met at a party?"

Chaudhuri feels that after Rushdie, IWE started employing magical realism, bagginess, non-linear narrative and hybrid language to sustain themes seen as microcosms of India and supposedly reflecting Indian conditions. He contrasts this with the works of earlier writers such as Narayan where the use of English is pure, but the deciphering of meaning needs cultural familiarity. He also feels that Indianness is a theme constructed only in IWE and does not articulate itself in the vernacular literatures. He further adds "the post-colonial novel, becomes a trope for an ideal hybridity by which the West celebrates not so much Indianness, whatever that infinitely complex thing is, but its own historical quest, its reinterpretation of itself".

Some of these arguments form an integral part of what is called postcolonial theory. The very categorisation of IWE – as IWE or under post-colonial literature – is seen by some as limiting. Amitav Ghosh made his views on this very clear by refusing to accept the Eurasian Commonwealth Writers Prize for his book *The Glass Palace* in 2001 and withdrawing it from the subsequent stage.

The renowned writer V. S. Naipaul, a third generation Indian from Trinidad and Tobago and a Nobel prize laureate, is a person who belongs to the world and usually not classified under IWE. Naipaul evokes ideas of homeland, rootlessness and his own personal feelings towards India in many of his books.

Jhumpa Lahiri, a Pulitzer prize winner from the U.S., is a writer uncomfortable under the label of IWE.

Poetry

An overlooked category of Indian writing in English is poetry. Rabindranath Tagore wrote in Bengali and English and was responsible for the translations of his own work into English. Other early notable poets in English include Derozio, Michael Madhusudan Dutt, Toru Dutt, Romesh Chunder Dutt, Sri Aurobindo, Sarojini Naidu, and her brother Harindranath Chattopadhyay. "Sarojini Naidu and her art of poetry" is one of the finest efforts made by Dr. Deobrata Prasad in order to bring forth the real psyche of Sarojini Naidu through her poetry.This book was published by Delhi-based Capital Publishing House in 1988 in field of 'women and Anglo-Indian literature'.Dr Deobrata Prasad has very carefully taken into account all the nuances of Sarojini Naidu's poetry.The significance of this work towards Indian English Literature was first brought into perspective by University of Michigan.such a systematic work is rare to single out in today's era. Notable 20th Century authors of English poetry in India include Dilip Chitre, Kamala Das, Eunice De Souza, Nissim Ezekiel, Kersy Katrak, Arun Kolatkar, P. Lal, Jayanta Mahapatra, Dom Moraes, Gieve Patel, and A. K. Ramanujan, and among several others.

The younger generation of poets writing in English include Smita Agarwal, Makarand Paranjape, Arundhathi Subramaniam, Ranjit Hoskote, Sudeep Sen, Jeet Thayil, Mani Rao, Jerry Pinto, Meena Kandasamy, Gopi Kottoor, Dr Tapan

Kumar Pradhan, Rukmini Bhaya Nair, Jaydeep Sarangi, Anju Makhija and K Srilata among others.

Modern expatriate Indian poets writing in English include Agha Shahid Ali, Sujata Bhatt, Richard Crasta, Yuyutsu Sharma Shampa Sinha, Tabish Khair Vikram Seth and [Dharmendra kumar.he is trainor of english from (up)kanpur.he started to writting and teaching when he has compleated high school in 2006].

Alternative writing

India's experimental and avant garde counterculture is symbolized in the Prakalpana Movement. During the last four decades this bilingual literary movement has included Richard Kostelanetz, John M. Bennett, Don Webb, Sheila Murphy and many others worldwide and their Indian counterparts. Vattacharja Chandan is a central figure who contrived the movement. Prakalpana fiction is a fusion of prose, poetry, play, essay, and pictures. An example of a Prakalpana work is Chandan's bilingual *Cosmosphere 1* (2011).

Some bilingual writers have also made significant contributions, such as Paigham Afaqui with his novel *Makaan* in 1989.

6

Grammar Translation Method

The grammar translation method is a method of teaching foreign languages derived from the classical (sometimes called traditional) method of teaching Greek and Latin. In grammar-translation classes, students learn grammatical rules and then apply those rules by translating sentences between the target language and the native language. Advanced students may be required to translate whole texts word-for-word. The method has two main goals: to enable students to read and translate literature written in the target language, and to further students' general intellectual development.

HISTORY AND PHILOSOPHY

The grammar-translation method originated from the practice of teaching Latin. In the early 1500s, Latin was the most widely-studied foreign language due to its prominence in government, academia, and business.However, during the course of the century the use of Latin dwindled, and it was gradually replaced by English, French, and Italian. After the decline of Latin, the purpose of learning it in schools changed. Whereas previously students had learned Latin for the purpose of communication, it came to be learned as a purely academic subject.

Throughout Europe in the 18th and 19th centuries, the education system was formed primarily around a concept called faculty psychology. This theory dictated that the body and mind were separate and the mind consisted of three parts: the will, emotion, and intellect. It was believed that the intellect could be sharpened enough to eventually control the will and emotions. The way to do this was through learning classical literature of the Greeks and Romans, as well as mathematics. Additionally, an adult with such an education was considered mentally prepared for the world and its challenges.

At first it was believed that teaching modern languages was not useful for the development of mental discipline and thus they were left out of the curriculum. When modern languages did begin to appear in school curricula in the 19th century, teachers taught them with the same grammar-translation method as was used for classical Latin and Greek. As a result, textbooks were essentially copied for the modern language classroom. In the United States of America, the basic foundations of this method were used in most high school and college foreign language classrooms.

Principles and goals

There are two main goals to grammar-translation classes. One is to develop students' reading ability to a level where they can read literature in the target language. The other is to develop students' general mental discipline. The users of foreign language wanted simply to note things of their interest in the literature of foreign languages. Therefore, this method focuses on reading and writing and has developed techniques which facilitate more or less the learning of reading and writing only. As a result, speaking and listening are overlooked.

Method

Grammar-translation classes are usually conducted in the students' native language. Grammar rules are learned deductively; students learn grammar rules by rote, and then practice the rules by doing grammar drills and translating sentences to and from the target language. More attention is paid to the form of the sentences being translated than to their content. When students reach more advanced levels of achievement, they may translate entire texts from the target language. Tests often consist of the translation of classical texts.

There is not usually any listening or speaking practice, and very little attention is placed on pronunciation or any communicative aspects of the language. The skill exercised is reading, and then only in the context of translation.

Materials

The mainstay of classroom materials for the grammar-translation method is the textbook. Textbooks in the 19th century attempted to codify the grammar of the target language into discrete rules for students to learn and memorize. A chapter in a typical grammar-translation textbook would begin with a bilingual vocabulary list, after which there would be grammar rules for students to study and sentences for them to translate. Some typical sentences from 19th-century textbooks are as follows:

The philosopher pulled the lower jaw of the hen.

My sons have bought the mirrors of the Duke.

The cat of my aunt is more treacherous than the dog of your uncle.

Reception

The method by definition has a very limited scope. Because speaking or any kind of spontaneous creative output was missing from the curriculum, students would often fail at speaking or even letter writing in the target language. A noteworthy quote describing the effect of this method comes from Bahlsen, who was a student of Plötz, a major proponent of this method in the 19th century. In commenting about writing letters or speaking he said he would be overcome with "a veritable forest of paragraphs, and an impenetrable thicket of grammatical rules."

According to Richards and Rodgers, the grammar-translation has been rejected as a legitimate language teaching method by modern scholars:

[T]hough it may be true to say that the Grammar-Translation Method is still widely practiced, it has no advocates. It is a method for which there is no theory. There is no literature that offers a rationale or justification for it or that attempts to relate it to issues in linguistics, psychology, or educational theory.

Influence

The grammar-translation method was the standard way languages were taught in schools from the 17th to the 19th century. Despite attempts at reform from Roger Ascham, Montaigne, Comenius and John Locke, no other methods gained any significant popularity during this time.

Later, theorists such as Vietor, Passy, Berlitz, and Jespersen began to talk about what a new kind of foreign language instruction needed, shedding light on what the grammar translation was missing. They supported teaching the language, not about the language, and teaching in the target language, emphasizing speech as well as text. Through grammar translation, students lacked an active role in the classroom, often correcting their own work and strictly following the textbook.

The grammar-translation method is still in use today in hybrid forms in many different countries, including many parts of Pakistan and India.

The grammar-translation method of foreign language teaching is one of the most traditional methods, dating back to the late nineteenth and early twentieth centuries. It was originally used to teach 'dead' languages (and literatures) such as Latin and Greek, and this may account for its heavy bias towards written work to the virtual exclusion of oral production. As Omaggio comments, this approach reflected "the view of faculty psychologists that mental discipline was essential for strengthening the powers of the mind." (Omaggio 89) Indeed, the emphasis on achieving 'correct' grammar with little regard for the free application and production of speech is at once the greatest asset and greatest drawback to this approach.

The major characteristic of the grammar-translation method is, precisely as its name suggests, a focus on learning the rules of grammar and their application in translation passages from one language into the other. Vocabulary in the target language is learned through direct translation from the native language, e.g. with vocabulary tests such as:

the house = das Haus

mouse = die Maus

Very little teaching is done in the target language. Instead, readings in the target language are translated directly and then discussed in the native language, often precipitating in-depth comparisons of the two languages themselves. Grammar is taught with extensive explanations in the native language, and only later applied in the production of sentences through translation from one language to the other, e.g.

Do you have my book? = Hast du mein Buch?

Ich weiß nicht, wo dein Buch ist. = I don't know where your book is.

As Omaggio describes is, testing of the students is done almost exclusively through translation: "students had learned the language well if they could translate the passages well." (Omaggio 90)

Obviously, there are many drawbacks to the grammar-translation approach. Virtually no class time is allocated to allow students to produce their own sentences, and even less time is spent on oral practice (whether productive or reproductive). Students may have difficulties "relating" to the language, because the classroom experience keeps them from personalizing it or developing their own style. In addition, there is often little contextualization of the grammar — although this of course depends upon the passages chosen and the teacher's own skills. Culture, when discussed, is communicated through means of reading passages, but there is little direct confrontation with foreign elements. Perhaps most seriously, as Omaggio points out, the type of error correction that this method requires can actually be harmful to the students' learning processes: "students are clearly in a defensive learning environment where right answers are expected." (Omaggio 91)

Despite all of these drawbacks, there are certain positive traits to be found in such a rigid environment. Although far from trying to defend or reinstate this method, I must still say: my highschool German class was almost entirely grammar-translation based, with the exception of a few dialogues from the textbook, and I don't really feel it "harmed" or even hampered my acquisition of the language — and it certainly gave me a strong grounding in German grammar! For left-brained students who respond well to rules, structure and correction, the grammar-translation method can provide a challenging and even intriguing classroom environment. For those students who don't respond well to such structures, however, it is obvious that the grammar-translation method must be tempered with other approaches to create a more flexible and conducive methodology.

At the height of the Communicative Approach to language learning in the 1980s and early 1990s it became fashionable in some quarters to deride so-called "old-fashioned" methods and, in particular, something broadly labelled "Grammar Translation". There were numerous reasons for this but principally it was felt that translation itself was an academic exercise, rather than one which would actually help learners to use language, and an overt focus on grammar was to learn about the target language rather than to learn it.

As with many other methods and approaches, Grammar Translation tended to be referred to in the past tense as if it no longer existed and had died out to be replaced world-wide by the fun and motivation of the communicative classroom. If we examine the principal features of Grammar Translation, however, we will see that not only has it not disappeared but that many of its characteristics have been central to language teaching throughout the ages and are still valid today.

The Grammar Translation method embraces a wide range of approaches but, broadly speaking, foreign language study is seen as a mental discipline, the goal of which may be to read literature in its original form or simply to be a form of intellectual development. The basic approach is to analyze and study the grammatical rules of the language, usually in an order roughly matching the traditional order of the grammar of Latin, and then to practise manipulating grammatical structures through the means of translation both into and from the mother tongue.

The method is very much based on the written word and texts are widely in evidence. A typical approach would be to present the rules of a particular item of grammar, illustrate its use by including the item several times in a text, and practise using the item through writing sentences and translating it into the mother tongue. The text is often accompanied by a vocabulary list consisting of new lexical items used in the text together with the mother tongue translation. Accurate use of language items is central to this approach.

Generally speaking, the medium of instruction is the mother tongue, which is used to explain conceptual problems and to discuss the use of a particular grammatical structure. It all sounds rather dull but it can be argued that the Grammar Translation method has over the years had a remarkable success. Millions of people have successfully learnt foreign languages to a high degree of proficiency and, in numerous cases, without any contact whatsoever with native speakers of the language (as was the case in the former Soviet Union, for example).

There are certain types of learner who respond very positively to a grammatical syllabus as it can give them both a set of clear objectives and a clear sense of achievement. Other learners need the security of the mother tongue and the opportunity to relate grammatical structures to mother tongue equivalents. Above all, this type of approach can give learners a basic foundation upon which they can then build their communicative skills.

Applied wholesale of course, it can also be boring for many learners and a quick look at foreign language course books from the 1950s and 1960s, for example, will soon reveal the non-communicative nature of the language used. Using the more enlightened principles of the Communicative Approach, however, and combining these with the systematic approach of Grammar Translation, may well be the perfect combination for many learners. On the one hand they have motivating communicative activities that help to promote their fluency and, on the other, they gradually acquire a sound and accurate basis in the grammar of the language. This combined approach is reflected in many of the EFL course books currently being published and, amongst other things, suggests that the Grammar Translation method, far from being dead, is very much alive and kicking as we enter the 21st century.

Without a sound knowledge of the grammatical basis of the language it can be argued that the learner is in possession of nothing more than a selection of communicative phrases which are perfectly adequate for basic communication but which will be found wanting when the learner is required to perform any kind of sophisticated linguistic task

7

History of Linguistic

Linguistics as a study endeavors to describe and explain the human faculty of language.

In ancient civilization, linguistic study was originally motivated by the correct description of classical liturgical language, notably that of Sanskrit grammar beginning in about the 6th century BCE, or by the development of logic and rhetoric in ancient Greece, leading to a grammatical tradition in Hellenism. Beginning around the 4th century BCE, China also developed its own grammatical traditions. Traditions of Arabic grammar and Hebrew grammar developed during the Middle Ages, also in a religious context.

Modern linguistics began to develop in the 18th century, reaching the "golden age of philology" in the 19th century. The first half of the 20th century was marked by the structuralist school, based on the work of Ferdinand de Saussure in Europe and Edward Sapir and Leonard Bloomfield in the United States. The 1960s saw the rise of many new fields in linguistics, such as Noam Chomsky's generative grammar, William Labov's sociolinguistics, Michael Halliday's systemic functional linguistics and also modern psycholinguistics.

ANTIQUITY

Across cultures, the early history of linguistics is associated with a need to disambiguate discourse, especially for ritual texts or in arguments. This often led to explorations of sound-meaning mappings, and the debate over conventional versus naturalistic origins for these symbols. Finally this led to the processes by which larger structures are formed from units.

India

Linguistics in ancient India derives its impetus from the need to correctly recite and interpret the Vedic texts. Already in the oldest Indian text, the Rigveda, *vâk* ("speech") is deified. By 1200 BCE, the oral performance of these texts becomes standardized, and treatises on ritual recitation suggest splitting up the Sanskrit compounds into words, stems, and phonetic units, providing an impetus for morphology and phonetics. Over the next few centuries, clarity was reached in the organization of sound units, and the stop consonants were organized in a 5x5 square (c. 800 BCE, Pratisakhyas), eventually leading to a systematic alphabet, Brâhmî, by the 3rd century BCE.

In semantics, the early Sanskrit grammarian Úâkamâyana (before c. 500 BCE) proposes that verbs represent ontologically prior categories, and that all nouns are etymologically derived from actions. The etymologist Yâska (c. 5th century BCE) posits that meaning inheres in the sentence, and that word meanings are derived based on sentential usage. He also provides four categories of words—nouns, verbs, pre-verbs, and particles/invariants—and a test for nouns both concrete and abstract: words which can be indicated by the pronoun *that*.

PâGini (c. 4th century BCE) opposes the Yâska view that sentences are primary, and proposes a grammar for composing semantics from morphemic roots. Transcending the ritual text to consider living language, PâGini specifies a comprehensive set of about 4,000 aphoristic rules (*sutras*) that:

1. Map the semantics of verb argument structures into thematic roles
2. Provide morphosyntactic rules for creating verb forms and nominal forms whose seven cases are called *karaka* (similar to case) that generate the morphology

3. Take these morphological structures and consider phonological processes (e.g., root or stem modification) by which the final phonological form is obtained

In addition, the PâGinian school also provides a list of 2000 verb roots which form the objects on which these rules are applied, a list of sounds (the so-called *Shiva-sutras*), and a list of 260 words not derivable by the rules.

The extremely succinct specification of these rules and their complex interactions led to considerable commentary and extrapolation over the following centuries. The phonological structure includes defining a notion of sound universals similar to the modern phoneme, the systematization of consonants based on oral cavity constriction, and vowels based on height and duration. However, it is the ambition of mapping these from morpheme to semantics that is truly remarkable in modern terms.

Grammarians following PâGini include Kâtyâyana (c. 3rd century BCE), who wrote aphorisms on PâGini (the *Varttika*) and advanced mathematics; Patañjali (2nd century BCE), known for his commentary on selected topics in PâGini's grammar (the *Mahabhasya*) and on Kâtyâyana's aphorisms, as well as, according to some, the author of the *Yoga Sutras*, and *Pingala*, with his mathematical approach to prosody. Several debates ranged over centuries, for example, on whether word-meaning mappings were conventional (*Vaisheshika-Nyaya*) or eternal (*Kâtyâyana-Patañjali-MîmâCsâ*).

The *Nyaya Sutras* specified three types of meaning: the individual (*this cow*), the type universal (*cowhood*), and the image (*draw the cow*). That the sound of a word also forms a class (sound-universal) was observed by Bhart[hari (c. 500 CE), who also posits that language-universals are the units of thought, close to the nominalist or even the linguistic determinism position. Bhart[hari also considers the sentence to be ontologically primary (word meanings are learned given their sentential use).

Of the six canonical texts or *Vedangas* that formed the core syllabus in Brahminic education from the 1st century CE until the 18th century, four dealt with language:

- *Shiksha* (*œikcâ*): phonetics and phonology (sandhi), Gârgeya and commentators
- *Chandas* (*chandas*): prosody or meter, Pingala and commentators
- *Vyakarana* (*vyâkaraGa*): grammar, PâGini and commentators
- *Nirukta* (*nirukta*): etymology, Yâska and commentators

Bhartrihari around 500 CE introduced a philosophy of meaning with his *sphoma* doctrine.

This body of work became known in 19th-century Europe, where it influenced modern linguistics initially through Franz Bopp, who mainly looked at PâGini. Subsequently, a wider body of work influenced Sanskrit scholars such as Ferdinand de Saussure, Leonard Bloomfield, and Roman Jakobson. Frits Staal discussed the possible European impact of Indian ideas on language. After outlining the various aspects of the contact, Staal posits the theory that the idea of formal rules in language, first proposed by de Saussure in 1894, and finally developed by Chomsky in 1957, based on which formal rules were also introduced in computational languages, may indeed lie in the European exposure to the formal rules of Paninian grammar. In particular, de Saussure, who lectured on Sanskrit for three decades, may have been influenced by PâGini and Bhartrihari; his idea of the unity of signifier-signified in the sign is somewhat similar to the notion of Sphoma. More importantly, the very idea that formal rules can be applied to areas outside of logic or mathematics, may itself have been catalyzed by Europe's contact with the work of Sanskrit grammarians.

The Pali Grammar of Kacchayana, dated to the early centuries CE, describes the language of the Buddhist canon.

The *Tolkâppiyam* (dated to 3rd century BCE) presents a grammar of Tamil, derivatives of which are still used today.

Greece

The Greeks developed an alphabet based on a system previously used by the Phoenicians, adding signs for vowels and for extra consonants appropriate to their idiom (see Robins,

1997). As a result of the introduction of writing, poetry such as the Homeric poems became written and several editions were created and commented on, forming the basis of philology and criticism.

Along with written speech, the Greeks commenced studying grammatical and philosophical issues. A philosophical discussion about the nature and origins of language can be found as early as the works of Plato. A subject of concern was whether language was man-made, a social artifact, or supernatural in origin. Plato in his *Cratylus* presents the naturalistic view, that word meanings emerge from a natural process, independent of the language user. His arguments are partly based on examples of compounding, where the meaning of the whole is usually related to the constituents, although by the end he admits a small role for convention. The sophists and Socrates introduced dialectics as a new text genre. The Platonic dialogs contain definitions of the meters of the poems and tragedy, the form and the structure of those texts (see the *Republic* and *Phaidros, Ion,* etc.).

Aristotle supports the conventional origins of meaning. He defined the logic of speech and of the argument. Furthermore, Aristotle's works on rhetoric and poetics became of the utmost importance for the understanding of tragedy, poetry, public discussions etc. as text genres. Aristotle's work on logic interrelates with his special interest in language, and his work on this area was fundamentally important for the development of the study of language (*logos* in Greek means both "language" and "logic reasoning"). In *Categories,* Aristotle defines what is meant by "synonymous" or univocal words, what is meant by "homonymous" or equivocal words, and what is meant by "paronymous" or denominative words. He divides forms of speech as being:

- Either simple, without composition or structure, such as "man," "horse," "fights," etc.
- Or having composition and structure, such as "a man fights," "the horse runs," etc.

Next, he distinguishes between a subject of predication, namely that of which anything is affirmed or denied, and a subject of inhesion. A thing is said to be inherent in a subject, when, though it is not a part of the subject, it cannot possibly exist without the subject, e.g., shape in a thing having a shape. The categories are not abstract platonic entities but are found in speech, these are substance, quantity, quality, relation, place, time, position, state, action and affection. In *de Interpretatione*, Aristotle analyzes categoric propositions, and draws a series of basic conclusions on the routine issues of classifying and defining basic linguistic forms, such as simple terms and propositions, nouns and verbs, negation, the quantity of simple propositions (primitive roots of the quantifiers in modern symbolic logic), investigations on the excluded middle (which to Aristotle isn't applicable to future tense propositions — the Problem of future contingents), and on modal propositions.

The Stoics made linguistics an important part of their system of the cosmos and the human. They played an important role in defining the linguistic sign-terms adopted later on by Ferdinand de Saussure like "significant" and "signifié". The Stoics studied phonetics, grammar and etymology as separate levels of study. In phonetics and phonology the articulators were defined. The syllable became an important structure for the understanding of speech organization. One of the most important contributions of the Stoics in language study was the gradual definition of the terminology and theory echoed in modern linguistics.

Alexandrian grammarians also studied speech sounds and prosody; they defined parts of speech with notions such as "noun", "verb", etc. There was also a discussion about the role of analogy in language, in this discussion the grammatici in Alexandria supported the view that language and especially morphology is based on analogy or paradigm, whereas the grammatic in schools in Asia Minor consider that language is not based on analogical bases but rather on exceptions.

Alexandrians, like their predecessors, were very interested in meter and its role in poetry. The metrical "feet" in the Greek was based on the length of time taken to pronounce each syllable, with syllables categorized according to their weight as either "long" syllables or "short" syllables (also known as "heavy" and "light" syllables, respectively, to distinguish them from long and short vowels). The foot is often compared to a musical measure and the long and short syllables to whole notes and half notes. The basic unit in Greek and Latin prosody is a mora, which is defined as a single short syllable.

A long syllable is equivalent to two moras. A long syllable contains either a long vowel, a diphthong, or a short vowel followed by two or more consonants. Various rules of elision sometimes prevent a grammatical syllable from making a full syllable, and certain other lengthening and shortening rules (such as correption) can create long or short syllables in contexts where one would expect the opposite. The most important Classical meter as defined by the Alexandrian grammarians was the dactylic hexameter, the meter of Homeric poetry. This form uses verses of six feet. The first four feet are normally dactyls, but can be spondees. The fifth foot is almost always a dactyl. The sixth foot is either a spondee or a trochee. The initial syllable of either foot is called the ictus, the basic "beat" of the verse. There is usually a caesura after the ictus of the third foot.

Subsequently, the text *Tékhnç grammatiké* (c. 100 BCE, Gk. *gramma* meant letter, and this title means "Art of letters"), possibly written by Dionysius Thrax (170 – 90 BCE), lists eight parts of speech and lays out the broad details of Greek morphology including the case structures. This text was intended as a pedagogic guide (as was Panini), and also covers punctuation and some aspects of prosody. Other grammars by Charisius (mainly a compilation of Thrax, as well as lost texts by Remmius Palaemon and others) and Diomedes (focusing more on prosody) were popular in Rome as pedagogic material for teaching Greek to native Latin-speakers.

One of the most prominent scholars of Alexandria and of the antiquity was Apollonius Dyscolus. Apollonius wrote more than thirty treatises on questions of syntax, semantics, morphology, prosody, orthography, dialectology, and more. Happily, four of these are preserved—we still have a *Syntax* in four books, and three one-book monographs on pronouns, adverbs, and connectives, respectively.

Lexicography become an important domain of study as many grammarians compiled dictionaries, thesauri and lists of special words "ëÝîåéò" that were old, or dialectical or special (such as medical words or botanic words) at that period. In the early medieval times we find more categories of dictionaries like the dictionary of Suida (considered the first encyclopedic dictionary), etymological dictionaries etc.

At that period, the Greek language functioned as a *lingua franca*, a language spoken throughout the known world (for the Greeks and Romans) of that time and, as a result, modern linguistics struggles to overcome this. With the Greeks a tradition commenced in the study of language. The Romans and the medieval world followed, and their laborious work is considered today as a part of our everyday language. Think, for example, of notions such as the word, the syllable, the verb, the subject etc.

Rome

In the 4th century, Aelius Donatus compiled the Latin grammar *Ars Grammatica* that was to be the defining school text through the Middle Ages. A smaller version, *Ars Minor*, covered only the eight parts of speech; eventually when books came to be printed in the 15th century, this was one of the first books to be printed. Schoolboys subjected to all this education gave us the current meaning of "grammar" (attested in English since 1176).

China

Similar to the Indian tradition, Chinese philology, *Xiaoxue* (\x["elementary studies"), began as an aid to understanding classics in the Han dynasty (c. 3rd century BCE). *Xiaoxue* came to be divided into three branches: *Xungu* (–ŠAŠ "exegesis"), *Wenzi* (‡eW["script [analysis]") and *Yinyun* (ó—û— "[study of] sounds") and reached its golden age in the 17th century CE (Qing Dynasty). The glossary *Erya* (c. 3rd century BCE), comparable to the Indian *Nighantu,* is regarded as the first linguistic work in China. *Shuowen Jiezi* (c. 2nd century BCE), the first Chinese dictionary, classifies Chinese characters by radicals, a practice that would be followed by most subsequent lexicographers. Two more pioneering works produced during the Han Dynasty are *Fangyan,* the first Chinese work concerning dialects, and *Shiming,* devoted to etymology.

As in ancient Greece, early Chinese thinkers were concerned with the relationship between names and reality. Confucius (6th century BCE) famously emphasized the moral commitment implicit in a name, (*zhengming*) stating that the moral collapse of the pre-Qin was a result of the failure to rectify behaviour to meet the moral commitment inherent in names: "Good government consists in the ruler being a ruler, the minister being a minister, the father being a father, and the son being a son... If names be not correct, language is not in accordance with the truth of things." (*Analects* 12.11,13.3).

However, what is the reality implied by a name? The later Mohists or the group known as School of Names (ming jia, 479-221 BCE), consider that *ming* (

T "name") may refer to three kinds of *shi* (æ["actuality"): type universals (horse), individual (John), and unrestricted (thing). They adopt a realist position on the name-reality connection - universals arise because "the world itself fixes the patterns of similarity and difference by which things should be divided into kinds". The philosophical tradition is well known for conundra resembling the sophists, e.g. when Gongsun Longzi (4th century BCE) questions if in copula statements (*X is Y*), are *X* and *Y* identical or is *X* a subclass of *Y*. This is the famous paradox "a white horse is not a horse".

Xun Zi (3rd century BCE) revisits the principle of *zhengming,* but instead of rectifying behaviour to suit the names, his emphasis is on rectifying language to correctly reflect reality. This is consistent with a more "conventional" view of word origins (*yueding sucheng* }š[×Ob). China began late, and was influenced by the Indian tradition, after Buddhism had become popular in China. The rime dictionary is a type of dictionary arranged by tone and rime, in which the pronunciations of characters are indicated by *fanqie* spellings. Rime tables were later produced to aid the understanding of *fanqie*.

Philological studies flourished during the Qing Dynasty, with Duan Yucai and Wang Niansun as the towering figures. The last great philologist of the era was Zhang Binglin, who also helped lay the foundation of modern Chinese linguistics. The Western comparative method was brought into China by Bernard Karlgren, the first scholar to reconstruct Middle Chinese and Old Chinese with Latin alphabet (not IPA). Important modern Chinese linguists include Y. R. Chao, Luo Changpei, Li Fanggui and Wang Li.

The ancient commentators on the classics paid much attention to syntax and the use of particles. But the first Chinese grammar, in the modern sense of the word, was produced by Ma Jianzhong (late 19th century). His grammar was based on the Latin (prescriptive) model.

Middle Ages

Arabic grammar

Due to the rapid expansion of Islam in the 8th century, many people learned Arabic as a lingua franca. For this reason, the earliest grammatical treatises on Arabic are often written by non-native speakers. The earliest grammarian who is known to us is ¿Abd Allâh ibn Abî Is%âq al-$a ramî (died 735-736 CE, 117 AH). The efforts of three generations of grammarians culminated in the book of the Persian linguist Sibâwayhi (c. 760-793). Sibawayh made a detailed and professional description of Arabic in 760 in his monumental work, *Al-kitab fi al-nahw* (ÇáßÊÇÈ Ýí ÇáäÍæ, *The Book on Grammar*). In his book he distinguished phonetics from phonology.

European vernaculars

The Irish *Sanas Cormaic* 'Cormac's Glossary' is Europe's first etymological and encyclopedic dictionary in any non-Classical language.

The Modistae or "speculative grammarians" in the 13th century introduced the notion of universal grammar.

In *De vulgari eloquentia* ("On the Eloquence of Vernacular"), Dante expanded the scope of linguistic enquiry from Latin/ Greek to include the languages of the day. Other linguistic works of the same period concerning the vernaculars include the First Grammatical Treatise (Icelandic) or the Auraicept na n-Éces (Irish).

The Renaissance and Baroque period saw an intensified interest in linguistics, notably for the purpose of Bible translations by the Jesuits, and also related to philosophical speculation on philosophical languages and the origin of language.

Modern linguistics

Modern linguistics does not begin until the late 18th century, and the romantic or animist theses of Johann Gottfried Herder and Johann Christoph Adelung remained influential well into the 19th century.

Historical linguistics

In the 18th century James Burnett, Lord Monboddo analyzed numerous languages and deduced logical elements of the evolution of human language. His thinking was interleaved with his precursive concepts of biological evolution. Some of his early concepts have been validated and are considered correct today. In his *The Sanscrit Language* (1786), Sir William Jones proposed that Sanskrit and Persian had resemblances to classical Greek, Latin, Gothic, and Celtic languages. From this idea sprung the field of comparative linguistics and historical linguistics. Through the 19th century, European linguistics centered on the comparative history of the Indo-European languages, with a concern for finding their common roots and tracing their development.

In the 1820s, Wilhelm von Humboldt observed that human language was a rule-governed system, anticipating a theme that was to become central in the formal work on syntax and semantics of language in the 20th century. Of this observation he said that it allowed language to make "infinite use of finite means" (*Über den Dualis* 1827).

It was only in the late 19th century that the Neogrammarian approach of Karl Brugmann and others introduced a rigid notion of sound law.

Descriptive linguistics

In Europe there was a parallel development of structural linguistics, influenced most strongly by Ferdinand de Saussure, a Swiss professor of Indo-European and general linguistics whose lectures on general linguistics, published posthumously by his students, set the direction of European linguistic analysis from the 1920s on; his approach has been widely adopted in other fields under the broad term "Structuralism".

During the second World War, Leonard Bloomfield and several of his students and colleagues developed teaching materials for a variety of languages whose knowledge was needed for the war effort. This work led to an increasing prominence of the field of linguistics, which became a recognized discipline in most American universities only after the war.

In 1965, William Stokoe, a linguist from Gallaudet University published an analysis which proved that American Sign Language fits the criteria for a natural language.

Generative linguistics

Other subfields

Frcm roughly 1980 onwards, pragmatic, functional, and cognitive approaches have steadily gained ground, both in the United States and in Europe.

8

Teaching Proficiency though Reading and Storytelling

TPR Storytelling (Teaching Proficiency through Reading and Storytelling or TPRS) is a method of teaching foreign languages. TPRS lessons use a mixture of reading and storytelling to help students learn a foreign language in a classroom setting. The method works in three steps: in step one the new vocabulary structures to be learned are taught using a combination of translation, gestures, and personalized questions; in step two those structures are used in a spoken class story; and finally, in step three, these same structures are used in a class reading. Throughout these three steps, the teacher will use a number of techniques to help make the target language comprehensible to the students, including careful limiting of vocabulary, constant asking of easy comprehension questions, frequent comprehension checks, and very short grammar explanations known as "pop-up grammar". Many teachers also assign additional reading activities such as free voluntary reading, and there have been several easy novels written by TPRS teachers for this purpose.

Proponents of TPR Storytelling, basing their argument on the second language acquisition theories of Stephen Krashen, hold that the best way to help students develop both fluency and accuracy in a language is to expose them to large amounts of comprehensible input. The steps and techniques in TPR Storytelling help teachers to provide this input by making the language spoken in class both comprehensible and engaging. In addition, TPR Storytelling uses many concepts from mastery learning. Each lesson is focused on just three vocabulary phrases or fewer, enabling teachers to concentrate on teaching each phrase thoroughly. Teachers also make sure that the students internalize each phrase before moving on to new material, giving additional story lessons with the same vocabulary when necessary.

TPR Storytelling is unusual in that it is a grassroots movement among language teachers. After being developed by Blaine Ray in the 1990s, the method has gained popular appeal with language teachers who claim that they can reach more students and get better results than they could with previous methods. However, so far it has seen little support from publishers or academic institutions. Teachers have instead published their own materials and teaching manuals, and training in TPR Storytelling is generally offered at workshops by existing TPRS teachers rather than at teacher training college.

HISTORY

TPR Storytelling was developed by Blaine Ray, a high school Spanish teacher in California, during the 1990s. Ray had found great initial success teaching using Total Physical Response (TPR), but was disappointed when his students stopped finding this technique to be interesting. Ray was familiar with Stephen Krashen's theories, and he was confident that his students would acquire Spanish naturally if he gave them enough comprehensible input. He set about finding a way to combine TPR with stories, with input from Krashen and from other foreign language teachers, and the result was Total Physical Response Storytelling.

This new method continued to evolve with the input of teachers, and by 2000 there was a much larger emphasis on reading and the spoken class story, with the time spent doing traditional TPR being greatly reduced. To reflect these changes, the TPRS acronym was changed to stand for Teaching Proficiency through Reading and Storytelling. TPRS is now trademarked by Blaine Ray.

Although TPR Storytelling is a growing movement among foreign language teachers, particularly in the United States, it has received little coverage in academia. While the movement originated in the United States, it is beginning to spread to other countries. In the United States the method has gained vocal support from an increasing core of language teachers, and some school districts use it exclusively in their foreign language programs. It has also been used in language revitalization programs.

Method

TPR Storytelling is broadly divided into three steps, with each being regarded as essential for a successful program.

Step one: establish meaning

In this step the students are introduced to the new vocabulary phrases for the lesson. There is no set number of new items to be introduced in a given session; however, three is generally considered the maximum number that can be effectively taught in a lesson. Limiting the phrases like this allows the teacher to focus on them and provide lots of repetitions for the students. This emphasis on thoroughly learning new material is designed to give the students a feeling of confidence and to provide sufficient repetitions to facilitate acquisition (unconscious control in recognition and output) of the new items.

The three phrases (structures) are written on the blackboard, or another place where the students can easily see them, and are translated into the students' native language if a shared native language is available. If students forget what a phrase means, they can glance at the board and check the meaning at any time.

The teacher may elect to practice the new phrases using gestures, in a style modeled after traditional TPR. This gives the students the chance to get used to how the phrases sound before hearing them in context. It is also intended to keep the atmosphere of the class relaxed and conducive to learning.

Then the teacher asks questions about the students using the target phrases. These questions are known as *Personalized Questions and Answers* (PQA). To ensure these questions are comprehensible to the students, the teacher uses a variety of techniques and comprehension checks. Depending on the responses from the students and the atmosphere of the class, these questions might lead into a scene or skit often referred to as *extended PQA*. The details discovered by the teacher from PQA are often used as the basis for the class story.

The goal of the teacher during step one is to provide as many spoken repetitions of the new structures in context as possible. This lays the foundation for student recognition of the structures during the storytelling time.

Step two: spoken class story

In step two, students hear the three structures many times in the context of a spoken class story. This story is usually short, simple, and interesting, and will contain multiple instances of the target structures used in context. The number of times the structures are heard is further increased by the *circling* questioning technique. TPRS teachers aim to say each new structure at least 50 times in the course of a story, and it is not unusual to hear those structures 100 times.

The teacher does not so much tell the story as ask the story. The teacher will usually use a skeleton script with very few details, and then flesh the story out using details provided by the students in the target language, making a personalized story for each class. Using the circling technique, teachers can ask for these new details while still keeping the target language completely comprehensible. Advanced TPRS teachers are able to improvise, creating stories solely based on student answers to questions about the day's vocabulary structures. The focus is always on the target structures, allowing the details to support those structures.

The actions in the story may be acted out by volunteers from the class. The teacher will usually try to select actors who won't be intimidated to keep the atmosphere as relaxed and fun as possible. When the teacher makes a statement that advances the story plot, the actors will act out that statement and then wait while the teacher continues with the circling questions. Ideally, the actors will act in a humorous, emotional, or otherwise memorable way. This helps students to make visual and emotional connections to the new language structures they are hearing.

The story will often take place in distinct locations. The main character in the story may start off in one location with a problem that they need to solve. They may move to a second location, where they try to solve the problem, but fail. Then they may move to a third location where they resolve the problem. This narrative device is used to maximize the repetitions of the target structures, to make the story easy to understand, and to make the target phrases easy to remember. "Keeping space", or having students or the teacher physically move to locations in the classroom that represent the various locations in the story, is an aid to students in understanding the action and language they are hearing. After the story has finished the teacher may retell it in briefer form, retell it with errors having students correct them, or ask the students to retell the story, allowing them to use the structures they just learned. This can be in pairs, in groups, or one student retelling in front of the class.

Step three: reading

Step three is where the students learn to read the language structures that they have heard in steps one and two. A number of reading activities are used in TPRS. The first, and most common, is a class reading, where the students read and discuss a story that uses the same language structures as the story in step two. The next most common activity is free voluntary reading, where students are free to read any book they choose in the language being learned. The other activities are shared reading and homework reading. For shared reading, as in first-language literacy activities, the teacher brings in a children's picture book, and reads it to the students in class, making it comprehensible through circling and other means. Homework reading, as the name implies, means assigning specific reading for students to do at home. All readings in TPRS are comprehensible to the students, which means a very low ratio of unknown words (if any).

CLASS READING

The class reading is the most common type of reading activity in TPR Storytelling. TPRS teachers will typically include a class reading as part of every TPRS lesson. This reading is based on the story that the students learned in step two - sometimes it can be the same story, and sometimes it uses the same language structures but with different content. Ideally, the story should be structured so that students will be able to understand most of the story on first view.

The teacher will often begin the class reading by reading aloud the story, or a portion of the story, then having the students translate it into their first language. This translation could be done with individual students, or chorally by the whole class. Translation is utilized selectively in this way as a direct method of ensuring an accurate understanding of the language meaning. As the students have already dealt with the language structures in steps one and two, they can often do this at a natural speed. If necessary, the teacher can help them translate any words they don't know. This process aims to ensure that all of the students understand all of the words in the reading, as well as the meaning of the reading as a whole.

Next, the class will discuss the reading in the target language. With the goal of making the discussion 100% comprehensible, the teacher will use the same TPRS techniques as in step two. Also, the teacher may make use of the pop-up grammar technique, where grammar points contained in the reading are explained very briefly - in 5 seconds or less. A limited number of grammar points are focused on in any particular reading and they are "popped up" frequently to enhance student retention. The discussion can touch on a wide range of topics related to the reading. Usually the teacher will ask questions about the reading itself, and about the students and their lives. Comparing and contrasting the material in the reading to the PQA and the story gives extra repetitions of the target structures. Discussions of culture and even history are possible, depending on the content of the reading and the level of the students.

Free voluntary reading

Many TPRS teachers include Free voluntary reading (FVR) in their foreign language programmes. The research for FVR is very strong, and has consistently shown that FVR is as good or better than taught language lessons. Free voluntary reading can be done in the classroom or at home, but many teachers prefer to focus on spoken stories in class, as it is hard for students to get listening input outside school. However, TPRS teachers often educate students about FVR in class, introducing books for them to read, and giving advice on good reading practices.

Shared reading

Shared reading, often called "Kindergarten Day", refers to the practice of the teacher reading a children's picture story book to the students. The name is intended to conjure up the image of being read to as a child, but the activity can be done with any age group. The teacher reads to the students, showing them the pictures, asking them questions, and generally making the story comprehensible.

Homework reading

As the name implies, this is a specific reading that is assigned to all students for homework. The teacher can give a quiz on the reading when the students get back to class. This can be used to prepare students for a class discussion, but it is usually only used with advanced students as at home the students may have no one to turn to if they get stuck.

Techniques

Many smaller teaching techniques are key to the success of TPR Storytelling. They range from the simple, such as speaking slowly or paying close attention to the students' eyes, to the complex, like the *circling* technique of asking questions. These techniques all have the same basic aim of keeping the class comprehensible, interesting, and as efficient as possible for language acquisition.

Circling

"Circling" is the practice of asking a series of simple questions about a statement, all in the target language. It is intended to provide repetition of the target vocabulary in context and enable students to learn the vocabulary, grammar and phonology of their new language in a holistic way. There are four basic types of circling questions: "yes" questions, "no" questions, either/or questions, and "wh" questions such as what, where, when, and how many. There are also more advanced circling techniques which teachers can optionally include, such as the "three for one" and false statements. The teacher expects a response from the students after each statement or question, to check whether they have understood. If the teacher says a statement, then the students show that they understand by responding with an expression of interest such as "Oooh!" or "Aaaaah". If the teacher asks a question, then the students answer the question.

The students can answer the questions with just one or two words. The point of asking these questions is not to force the students to speak; rather, the questions are a method of checking comprehension while simultaneously repeating the target vocabulary in context. Therefore students need not worry about speaking in full sentences, and indeed this would detract from the process of concentrating on the input provided by the teacher. By answering using single words or very short phrases the students can keep their attention focused on the words to be learned.

Circling questions are always about content that has already been established. If a question is about something not yet established, then it is not considered a *circling* question. Consider the example on the right, "Dave wants a Ferrari." The following questions all ask for details not already established in the statement "Dave wants a Ferrari", and so are not examples of circling questions:

- *Teacher:* Why does Dave want a Ferrari?
- *Teacher:* How many Ferraris does Dave want?
- *Teacher:* Where does Dave want to drive his Ferrari?

Staying in bounds

Staying in bounds means only using words that the students understand. Words that are in bounds are:

- Words that all the students have already learned
- Cognates
- Proper nouns that the students know

Any words not in the list above are considered "out-of-bounds". Teachers must be on constant alert to keep their language in bounds. If a teacher does say something out-of-bounds, then the solution is to make it comprehensible, by writing it on the board and translating it immediately. If a teacher can stay in bounds all the time, and can speak slowly enough for the students to understand, then their class will be 100% comprehensible. This helps the students become confident in their language abilities and motivates them to succeed.

Slow

Even if students know the words that the teacher says, they will not understand if the teacher speaks too quickly. By speaking slowly, teachers give students more time to process the language and therefore they have more chance of understanding. When students first hear vocabulary or grammar, the necessary gap between each word can be as long as two full seconds. As students get used to the language structures, the teacher can slowly increase the speed.

Comprehension checks

The most direct way of finding out if students understand the language is to ask them what it means. In TPR Storytelling, teachers check comprehension early and often. There are a few ways of doing this:

Time-out sign

The teacher agrees on a sign for the students to use if they don't understand something. This is intended to save them from being embarrassed about not knowing something they think everybody else understands.

Finger count

The students hold up their fingers to show how much they understand. Ten fingers means they understood 100%, seven fingers means they understood 70%, five fingers means 50%, etc.

"What does <INSERT WORD HERE> mean?"

The teacher asks the students what specific words mean. Teachers generally use this after they asked a circling question but didn't get a strong response. This question is usually asked in the students' first language, to ensure understanding.

"What did I just say?"

The teacher asks the students "What did I just say?" in the students' first language. This way the students can be sure of the full meaning of the sentence or question they just heard. This should not be used as an attempt to catch students out; rather it is just a check to remind students of something they cannot remember at that moment.

Pop-up grammar

"Pop-up grammar" is the practice of making very short grammar explanations about the specific vocabulary students are learning at that moment. This technique is most often used in the class reading of step three, but it can be used at any time. The teacher draws the students attention to a grammatical feature of one of the sentences they have been learning in the story, and explains it in five seconds or less. This brevity is intended to keep focus on the meaning of the language as much as possible.

Personalization

Personalizing the language class is a key way to make the target language interesting and meaningful for students, and personalization is used extensively in TPR Storytelling. A personalized message is much more likely to be comprehensible and interesting than one that is not personalized. Using this in classes can be as easy as asking students simple questions about their lives in the target language. Other good personalization techniques are the use of celebrities or of other characters the students know (such as the school principal).

Teach to the eyes

Teaching to the eyes is a way of connecting with students while talking to them in the foreign language. More importantly, looking the students directly in the eyes while speaking gives the teacher a good indication of whether or not they understand what is being said. As the name suggests, to do this teachers will look into the eyes of individual students while they teach. Teachers are encouraged to choose one student and talk to them directly. After they have finished talking to that student, they can pick another student in a different part of the room to talk to. Focusing attention on individual students like this helps teachers to assess student comprehension levels, and also keeps the teacher's intonation conversational and interesting. It is also helpful in preventing problems with discipline. Students' eyes will reveal if they understand or if there needs to be more clarification.

Teaching materials

A number of teaching materials have been developed for use with TPR Storytelling. There are books of suggested lesson plans, manuals explaining TPRS methodology, listening material, substitute DVDs, and a series of target language readers beginning with *Poor Ana*. These readers have been translated into multiple languages and include appropriate cultural references for each target language. These materials are generally written by TPRS teachers themselves; so far, the large publishing companies have been reluctant to publish materials that aren't based upon a fixed grammar syllabus. Small TPRS publishers like TPRS Publishing, Chalkboard Productions and Albany Language Learning/Squid For Brains are appearing to fill the need for materials to fit the TPRS community.

Training

Teaching using TPR Storytelling is a very different experience from most other ways of teaching language. It requires juggling of many techniques in the classroom, and also an ability to make meaningful connections with students in the target language. This is extremely hard to do without training and practice, so it is recommended that teachers attend at least one workshop or training session before they try TPR Storytelling in their classrooms.

Workshops

Many TPRS workshops are available in the United States, including those by Blaine Ray, Susan Gross, Ben Slavic, TPRS Publishing, Karen Rowan, Teach for June, Chalkboard Productions, and many more. It is more difficult to find workshops outside of the United States. In the Netherlands, TPR Storytelling workshops, training and coaching are provided by Taalleermethoden.nl and TPRS Nederland. Chalkboard Productions does online webinar training that is accessible from anywhere with an Internet connection. Albany Language Learning specializes in TPRS for Chinese programs.

Conferences

There are two main conferences for TPRS teachers: NTPRS and an international conference hosted by TPRS Publishers, Inc. NTPRS stands for National TPRS, and takes place every year in the United States. In recent years the international conferences have been hosted at Club Med Resorts in Mexico and the Dominican Republic. The 2012 conference will take place in Punta Cana, and lasts for one week.

Journals

Various researchers and TPRS teachers come together to create the International Journal of Foreign Language Teaching. It is a free online journal aimed at language teachers, and contains both research papers related to language acquisition and articles about language teaching.

Theory

TPR Storytelling is based on two key theoretical pillars: the input hypothesis, and mastery learning.

Input hypothesis

The Input Hypothesis, proposed by Dr. Stephen Krashen, suggests that language development is a function of the input received by the learner. Krashen asserts that there are two distinct ways of learning language: language "learning" and language "acquisition". Language "learning" is learning that takes conscious effort on the part of the learner. It is characterized by learning grammar rules, memorizing vocabulary lists, and performing speaking drills. Language "acquisition" is learning that is subconscious and takes little or no effort on the part of the learner. It is characterized by listening and understanding to messages, reading interesting books and articles, and other enjoyable activities that take place in the language being learned. According to Krashen's theory, the only thing that can lead to fluency in the language is language "acquisition". Language "learning" can only be used as a way to consciously edit speech or writing, and it is never the cause of spontaneous, unrehearsed speech or writing.

In light of this theory, TPRS teachers spend the vast majority of their class time on input-based activities. The table below shows the activities used in TPR Storytelling, and whether they encourage language learning, language acquisition, or both. The activities that include a language learning component all take up a relatively short amount of class time. On the other hand, the pure acquisition activities take up large amounts of time. For typical TPRS classes, the ratio works out at about 5% of time spent on learning and 95% of time spent on acquisition.

The affective filter

Another key component of Krashen's theory is the affective filter. The affective filter hypothesis states that language is more easily acquired when people are relaxed and open to learning. On the other hand, if people are experiencing negative emotions such as anxiety, self-doubt, and boredom, language is much less likely to be acquired.

For this reason TPRS teachers always try to make students look good in the stories and discussions. For example, an otherwise average student could be given the role of a star baseball pitcher in a class story. It is usually considered good form to make celebrities look bad in comparison to the students. The class story in question might see the pitcher winning a game against an all-star team of professional batters, ideally in a humorous way. This use of humor and making the students look good is built on the idea that students learn language better when they are enjoying themselves.

Mastery learning

Mastery learning is a method of instruction in which students thoroughly learn all material they are studying. Students do not progress on to learning new material until they have mastered current material. This gives students a feeling of control, and indeed, of mastery. In language learning this is particularly important, as this feeling of control is directly related to the ability to learn. This is demonstrated by Krashen's research on the "affective filter".

The mastery approach to learning manifests itself in TPR Storytelling in many ways. Firstly, the number of new vocabulary phrases to be learned in each lesson is usually no more than three. More words than this may be introduced during the lesson, but the three phrases are the only ones that the students will be *expected* to know. Secondly, these vocabulary phrases are repeated many, many times, in context, using the "circling" technique. This repetition helps the students to internalize the words thoroughly. In addition, the same words are used during the class reading, giving even more repetition. If after this the students still aren't comfortable with the target words, the teacher can simply tell a new story using the same vocabulary phrases in the next lesson. Thirdly, teachers will try as far as possible to review all previously covered vocabulary in every lesson, finding ways to work the old vocabulary structures into class stories and class discussions.

Research

In addition to the research backing up the general theoretical foundations of TPR Storytelling, there exists a growing number of studies dealing with TPRS specifically. The results of these studies indicate that TPR Storytelling is much more efficient than traditional methods. For example, Asher compared a class of 30 students taught with TPR Storytelling with another class of 30 students taught with the audio-lingual method (ALM). When they listened to a story they had never heard before, but that had familiar vocabulary, the TPRS students "had significantly higher comprehension" than the ALM students.

Garczynski followed two groups of students over a six-week period, one of which was taught with TPR Storytelling, and the other of which was taught with the audio-lingual method. Both groups of students learned the same vocabulary from the same textbook. The students who learned with TPR Storytelling scored slightly higher than the students who learned with the audio-lingual method, and the TPR Storytelling students showed a much greater rate of improvement than their ALM peers.

TPR Storytelling is a method for teaching foreign languages that was invented by Blaine Ray, a Spanish teacher in Bakersfield, California, in 1990. Concerned that his students were disinterested in the unexciting process of learning a language from a textbook, he began to use James Asher's Total Physical Response to teach Spanish. Asher says that students acquire their second languages as they acquired their first languages. Our students learn as babies learn. Therefore, we should not expect them to produce the language before they have had an ample amount of time to listen to it. Blaine experienced great success, and the students began to be excited about his class. Although TPR has been the most effective method for acquiring a second language since it was invented in the 1960s, Blaine found that after hitting the "TPR wall," he was unsure of what to do to move from the imperative to the narrative and descriptive modes of speech. He found that changing from commands to the third person singular allowed him to tell stories, a long-term memory technique. He found that asking the students to act out the parts of the characters in the stories preserved the highly effective physical element that had been so powerful in Classical TPR. As the technique was developed over the years, it became an all-encompassing method and methodology. The method combines Dr. James Asher's Total Physical Response (TPR) with Dr. Stephen Krashen's language acquisition strategies, allowing us to teach grammar, reading and writing along with vocabulary.

The TPRS Objective

As TPRS was originally developed, the objective was to create a method that would prepare students for the College

Board Advanced Placement Exam from level 1. In addition, teachers report higher AP scores, with some students passing the AP exam in as few as 3 years of language study. Although nationwide fewer than 10% of our high school students proceed to the highest levels of foreign language offered in our schools and even fewer proceed to college foreign language studies, we have seen enrollment in our programs increase by as much as 400% after TPRS programs were introduced.

TPR Storytelling begins with the introduction of vocabulary and complex structures. The teacher then

"asks" the story using a questioning technique called "circling." The first two steps are followed up with reading. Students rapidly acquire the second language just as Dr. Krashen imagined: effortlessly and involuntarily. The method relies heavily on the five hypotheses of The Natural Approach: the acquisition hypothesis, the input hypothesis, the natural order hypothesis, the affective filter hypothesis and the monitor hypothesis, which are explained in detail in Foreign Language Education the Easy Way, by Dr. Stephen Krashen.

A TPRS program is not complete without a very heavy emphasis on reading. Blaine Ray has written several easy readers for the first and second levels. We also recommend a Free Voluntary Reading program. Krashen's research supports the assertion that children need two things in order to learn to read in any language: access to books and a quiet, comfortable place to read. We also read to our students, just as we would if they were our own small children, learning their first languages for the first time.

Why TPRS Works

The most important element of a successful TPR Storytelling program is the awareness that our focus is our students, not our book or even our story. A good relationship with students is the foundation of a TPRS program. We establish this connection by personalizing our stories. Every story is bizarre, in order to maintain the interest of our students, and personalized, because the only thing our students are truly interested in is themselves. The instructional pace should be based entirely upon an assessment by the teacher of how thoroughly the students have internalized the language. The number one, most important element in any TPRS program is the quantity and quality of the unconditional love, positive feedback, pats on the back and hearty applause provided to the students by the teacher. Most teachers feel that they have begun to implement TPRS effectively after approximately 4 workshops. Although the techniques, the 7 steps and beginning and advanced strategies for creating a phenomenal TPRS classroom can be taught and learned in workshops, it is teachers who dedicate themselves to expressing love and approval towards their students that keep their students coming back year after year to acquire enough language to become bilingual —— and that can't be taught.

Bibliography

- *A Companion to English Renaissance Literature and Culture*, ed. Michael Hattaway (2000.)
- *A Glossary of Literary Terms*, M. H. Abrams. (Fort Worth, Texas: Harcourt Brace, 1999, pp. 165–6.
- A Handbook of the Cornish Language, by Henry Jenner A Project Gutenberg eBook; A brief history of the Cornish language.
- Ben Jonson." *Encyclopædia Britannica. Encyclopædia Britannica Online Academic Edition*.
- Bimal Krishna Matilal (1990). *The Word and the World: India's Contribution to the Study of Language*. Delhi; New York: Oxford University Press. ISBN 0-19-562515-3.
- Bradley 1991, 40, 48.
- Bradley 1991, 85; Muir 2005, 12–16.
- Burrow 2004.
- *Chapman's Homer: The Iliad*. Ed. Allardyce Nicoll. Bollingen Series 41. Princeton: Princeton UP, 1998; *Chapman's Homer: The Odyssey*. Ed. Allardyce Nicoll. Bollingen Series 41. Princeton: Princeton UP, 2000.
- Christopher Marlowe." Encyclopædia Britannica. Encyclopædia Britannica Online. Encyclopædia Britannica

Inc., 2013. Web. 6 April 2013. <http: / / www.britannica.com / EBchecked / topic / 365890 / Christopher-Marlowe>.

- David Crystal, *A Dictionary of Linguistics & Phonetics* (Blackwell Publishing, 2003). p. 431.
- *Dictionary of Literary Terms and Literary Theory* J. A. Cuddon. (London: Penguin Books,1999), p.523.
- *Dictionary of Literary Terms and Literary Theory*, p. 523.
- Dowden 1881, 57.
- Dowden 1881, 60; Frye 2005, 123; McDonald 2006, 15.
- Edmund Colledge, O.S.A. and James Walsh, S.J. (1978). "Julian of Norwich". *Showings* (Paulist Press). ISBN 978-0-8091-2091-8.
- Even in vocabulary. "A British reader of *Time* or *Newsweek* would note distinctly American expressions only a few times on any page, matching the few distinctly British expressions an American reader of *The Economist* would note." Edward Finegan in *Language in the USA: Themes for the Twenty-first Century*. Eds Charles Albert Ferguson, Edward Finegan, Shirley Brice Heath, John R. Rickford (Cambridge University Press, 2004). p. 29. See also: David Crystal, *the Cambridge Encyclopedia of the English Language*] (Cambridge University Press, 2003), p. 304.
- Frances A. Yates, *The life of an Italian in Shakespeare's England*.
- Frederick J. Newmeyer (2005). *The History of Linguistics*. Linguistic Society of America. ISBN 0-415-11553-1.
- Gassner, John; Quinn, Edward (1969). "England: middle ages". *The Reader's Encyclopedia of World Drama*. London: Methuen. pp. 203–204. OCLC 249158675.
- Goldstein, Brian; Fabiano, Leah; Washington, Patricia Swasey (2005), "Phonological Skills in Predominantly English-Speaking, Predominantly Spanish-Speaking, and Spanish–English Bilingual Children", *Language, Speech, and Hearing Services in Schools* 36 (3): 201–218, doi:10.1044/0161-1461(2005/021)
- *Gorboduc* and *Titus Andronicus*"; James D. Carroll, *Notes and Queries*, 2004, pp. 51, 267–269.

- Goto, Hiromu (1971), "Auditory perception by normal Japanese adults of the sounds "l" and "r"", *Neuropsychologia* 9 (3): 317–323, doi:10.1016/0028-3932(71)90027-3, PMID 5149302
- Gower, John". *Dictionary of National Biography*. London: Smith, Elder & Co. 1885–1900.
- Gut, Ulrike (2009), *Non-native speech. A corpus-based analysis of phonological and phonetic properties of L2 English and German.*, Frankfurt: Peter Lang
- Hallé, Pierre A.; Best, Catherine T.; Levitt, Andrea (1999), "Phonetic vs. phonological influences on French listeners' perception of American English approximants", *Journal of Phonetics* 27 (3): 281–306, doi:10.1006/jpho.1999.0097
- http://www.archive.org/details/spanishtragedya00kydgoog
- Hwa-Froelich, Deborah; Hodson, Barbara W; Edwards, Harold T (2003), "Characteristics of Vietnamese Phonology", *American Journal of Speech-Language Pathology* 11 (3): 264–273, doi:10.1044/1058-0360(2002/031)
- Jeffers, Robert J.; Lehiste, Ilse (1979), *Principles and Methods for Historical Linguistics*, MIT press, ISBN 0-262-60011-0
- John E. Joseph, Nigel Love, and Talbot J. Taylor (2001). *Landmarks in Linguistic Thought II: The Western Tradition in the Twentieth Century*. London: Routledge. ISBN 0-415-06396-5.
- Kees Versteegh (1997). *Landmarks in Linguistic Thought III: The Arabic Linguistic Tradition*. London; New York: Routledge. ISBN 0-415-14062-5.
- Keith Allan (2007). *The Western Classical Tradition in Linguistics*. London: Equinox.
- Khattab, Ghada (2002), "/r/ production in English and Arabic bilingual and monolingual speakers", in Nelson, Diane, *Leeds Working Papers in Linguistics and Phonetics* 9, pp. 91–129
- Kovács, János; Siptár, Péter (2006), *A-Z angol kiejtés*, Budapest: Corvina Kiadó, ISBN 963-13-5557-8

- LaCharité, Darlene; Prévost, Philippe (1999), Greenhill, Annabel; Tano, Cheryl; Littlefield, Heather, eds., *Proceedings of the 23rd Annual Boston University Conference on Language Development* 2, Somerville, Massachusetts: Cascadilla Press, pp. 373–385
- MacDonald, Marguerite (1989), "The influence of Spanish phonology on the English spoken by United States Hispanics", in Bjarkman, Peter; Hammond, Robert, *American Spanish pronunciation: Theoretical and applied perspectives*, Washington, D.C.: Georgetown University Press, pp. 215–236, ISBN 9780878404933
- Mario Pei (1965). *Invitation to Linguistics*. Doubleday & Company. ISBN 0-385-06584-1.
- Mikics, David (2007). *A New Handbook of Literary Terms*. New Haven, CT: Yale University Press. p. 194. ISBN 978-0-300-10636-7.
- Munro, Miles; Mann, Virginia (2005), "Age of immersion as a predictor of foreign accent", *Applied Psycholinguistics* 26 (3): 311–341, doi:10.1017/S0142716405050198
- mystery, n 9". *Oxford English Dictionary*. Oxford, England: Oxford University Press. December 2009.
- Nádasdy, Ádám (2006), *Background to English Pronunciation*, Budapest: Nemzeti Tankönyvkiadó, ISBN 963-19-5791-8
- NB: "standard English" as used to describe written *and* spoken international English is a more contentious usage.
- Oxenford, Lyn (1958). *Playing Period Plays*. Chicago, IL: Coach House Press. p. 3. ISBN 0-85343-549-9.
- *Oxford Companion*. p. 422.
- Paradis, Carole; LaCharité, Darlene (2001), "Guttural deletion in loanwords", *Phonology* 18 (2): 255–300, doi:10.1017/S0952675701004079
- Pieter A. M. Seuren (1998). *Western linguistics: An historical introduction*. Wiley-blackwell. ISBN 0-631-20891-7.
- Properly speaking, Mysteries deal with Gospel events only. Miracle plays, on the other hand, are concerned with incidents derived from the legends of the saints of the

Church.' Ward, Augustus William (1875). *History of English dramatic literature*. London, England: Macmillan.

- Randy Allen Harris (1995) *The Linguistics Wars*, Oxford University Press, ISBN 0-19-509834-X
- Ravid, Dorit (1995), *Language Change in Child and Adult Hebrew: A Psycholinguistic Perspective*, Oxford University Press, ISBN 978-0-19-508893-9
- Revenge Tragedy" in *A Dictionary of Literary Terms and Literary Theory*, ed. J. A. Cuddon. (London: Penguin Books, 1999), pp. 744–6.
- Richardson and Johnston (1991, 97–98).
- Robert Henry Robins (1997). *A Short History of Linguistics*. London: Longman. ISBN 0-582-24994-5.
- Roy Harris and Talbot J. Taylor (1989). *Landmarks in Linguistic Thought: The Western Tradition from Socrates to Saussure*. London: Routledge. ISBN 0-415-00290-7.
- Shapiro 2005, 150; Gibbons 1993, 1; Ackroyd 2006, 356.
- Shoebottom, Paul (2007), "The differences between English and Hebrew", *Frankfurt International School*
- Stanley Wells and Michael Dobson, eds., *The Oxford Companion to Shakespeare* Oxford University Press, 2001, p. 439.
- Swan, Michael (2001). *Learner English: A Teacher's Guide to Interference and Other Problems, Volume 1*. Cambridge University Press. ISBN 9780521779395.
- *The Norton Anthology of English Literature*, Vol.1 (2000), pp.445 and *The Oxford Companion to English Literature* (1996), p. 775.
- *The Norton Anthology of English Literature: Sixteenth/Early Seventeenth Century*, Volume B, 2012, p. 647
- *The Oxford Companion to English Literature* (1996), p. 182.
- *The Oxford Companion to English Literature* (1996), p.266–7.
- *The Oxford Companion to English Literature* (1996). p. 546.
- *The Oxford Companion to English Literature*, ed. Margaret Drabble. (Oxford: Oxford University Press,1996), pp. 832, 935.

- *The Oxford Companion to Shakespeare* (2001), p. 439.
- Thompson, Irene (1991), "Foreign Accents Revisited: The English Pronunciation of Russian Immigrants", *Language Learning* 41 (2): 177–204, doi:10.1111/j.1467-1770.1991.tb00683.x
- Tillyard 1929.
- W. P. Lehmann, (ed.) (1967). *A Reader in Nineteenth Century Historical Indo-European Linguistics*. Indiana University Press. ISBN 0-253-34840-4.
- www.lib.rochester.edu/camelot/MaloryBooklet/Malory.htm>.